THE ROUGH GUIDE

FRENCH

PHRASEBOOK

Compiled by

www.roughguides.com

Credits

Compiled by Lexus with Nadine Mongeard Morandi
Lexus Series Editor: Sally Davies
Rough Guides Reference Director: Andrew Lockett
Rough Guides Series Editor: Mark Ellingham

First edition published in 1995.
Reprinted in 1995, 1996 and 1998.
This updated edition published in 2006 by
Rough Guides Ltd,
80 Strand, London WC2R 0RL
345 Hudson St, 4th Floor, New York 10014, USA
Email: mail@roughguides.co.uk.

Distributed by the Penguin Group.

Penguin Books Ltd, 80 Strand, London WC2R 0RL
Penguin Putnam, Inc., 375 Hudson Street, NY 10014, USA
Penguin Group (Australia), 250 Camberwell Road, Camberwell,
Victoria 3124, Australia
Penguin Books Canada Ltd, 10 Alcorn Avenue, Toronto,
Ontario, Canada M4V 1E4
Penguin Group (New Zealand), Cnr Rosedale and Airborne Roads,
Albany, Auckland, New Zealand

Typeset in Bembo and Helvetica to an original design by Henry Iles.
Printed in Singapore by SNP Security Printing Pte Ltd

© Lexus Ltd 2006
272pp.

British Library Cataloguing in Publication Data
A catalogue for this book is available from the British Library.

ISBN 13: 13: 978-1-84353-625-3
ISBN 10: 1-84353-625-0
7   9   8

The publishers and authors have done their best to ensure the
accuracy and currency of all information in The Rough Guide
French Phrasebook however, they can accept no responsibility for
any loss or inconvenience sustained by any reader using the book.

Online information about Rough Guides can be found at our website
www.roughguides.com

CONTENTS

Introduction   5

Basic Phrases   8

Scenarios   13

English - French   31

French - English   129

Menu Reader

Food 207

Drink 229

How the Language Works

Pronunciation 235

Abbreviations 235

Nouns 237

Articles ....

Prepositions ....

Adjectives and

Pronouns ....

Verbs ....

Questions ....

Dates ....

Days 262

Months 263

Time 263

Numbers 264

Conversion Tables 267

Introduction

The Rough Guide French phrasebook is a highly practical introduction to the contemporary language. Laid out in clear A-Z style, it uses key-word referencing to lead you straight to the words and phrases you want – so if you need to book a room, just look up 'room'. The Rough Guide gets straight to the point in every situation, in bars and shops, on trains and buses, and in hotels and banks.

The main part of the Rough Guide is a double dictionary: English-French then French-English. Before that, there's a section called **Basic Phrases** and to get you involved in two-way communication, the Rough Guide includes, in this new edition, a set of **Scenario** dialogues illustrating questions and responses in key situations such as renting a car and asking directions. You can hear these and then download them free from **www.roughguides.com/phrasebooks** for use on your computer or MP3 player.

Forming the heart of the guide, the **English-French** section gives easy-to-use transliterations of the French words wherever pronunciation might be a problem. Throughout this section, cross-references enable you to pinpoint key facts and phrases, while asterisked words indicate where further information can be found in a section at the end of the book called **How the Language Works**. This section sets out the fundamental rules of the language, with plenty of practical examples. You'll also find here other essentials like numbers, dates, telling the time and basic phrases. In the **French-English** dictionary, we've given you not just the phrases you'll be likely to hear (starting with a selection of slang and colloquialisms) but also many of the signs, labels, instructions and other basic words you may come across in print or in public places.

Near the back of the book too the Rough Guide offers an extensive **Menu Reader**. Consisting of food and drink sections (each starting with a list of essential terms), it's indispensable whether you're eating out, stopping for a quick drink, or browsing through a local food market.

bon voyage!
have a good trip!

Basic
Phrases

BASIC PHRASES

yes
oui
[wee]

no
non
[nON]

OK
d'accord
[dakor]

hello
bonjour
[bONjoor]

good morning
bonjour
[bON-joor]

good evening
bonsoir
[bON-swa]

good night
bonne nuit
[bon nwee]

goodbye
au revoir
[o ruh-vwa]

please
s'il vous plaît
[seel voo play]
(if using 'tu' form) s'il te plaît
[seel tuh play]

yes please
oui, merci
[wee mairsee]

thanks, thank you
merci
[mairsee]

thank you very much
merci beaucoup
[mairsee bo-koo]

no thanks
non, merci
[nON mairsee]

don't mention it
je vous en prie
[juh voo zON pree]

how do you do?
(when being introduced)
enchanté!
[ONshONtay]

how are you?
comment vas-tu/allez-vous?
[komON va-too/alay-voo]

fine, thanks, and you?
bien, merci, et toi/vous?
[b-yAN mairsee ay twa/voo]

pleased to meet you
enchanté!
[ONshONtay]

excuse me
(to get past, to get attention)
pardon
[par-dON]
(to say sorry) excusez-moi,
pardon
[eskOOzay-mwa]

sorry: (I'm) sorry
je suis désolé, excusez-moi
[juh swee dayzolay, eskOOzay-mwa]

sorry?
(didn't understand) pardon?
[par-dON]

I understand
je comprends
[juh kONprON]

I don't understand
je ne comprends pas
[pa]

do you speak English?
parlez-vous l'anglais?
[parlay-voo ONglay]

I don't speak ...
je ne parle pas ...
[juh nuh parl pa]

could you say it slowly?
pourriez-vous parler plus
lentement?
[pooree-ay-voo parlay plOO lONtmON]

could you repeat that?
pourriez-vous répéter?
[pooree-ay-voo raypaytay]

could you write it down?
pouvez-vous me l'écrire?
[poovay-voo muh laykreer]

I'd like ...
je voudrais ...
[juh voodray]

can I have a ...?
j'aimerais ...
[jemray]

do you have ...?
as-tu/avez-vous ...?
[atOO/avay-voo]

how much is it?
c'est combien?
[say kONb-yAN]

cheers!
(toast)
santé!
[sONtay]
(thanks) merci!
[mairsee]

it is ...
c'est ...
[say]

where is ...?
où est ...?
[oo ay]

is it far from here?
c'est loin d'ici?
[say lwAN dee-see]

9

Scenarios

1. Accommodation

is there an inexpensive hotel you can recommend?
▶ pouvez-vous me recommander un hôtel bon marché?
[poovay-voo muh ruhkomONday AN otel bON marshay]

désolé, ils sont tous complets ◀
[dayzolay, eel sON tooss KONplay]
I'm sorry, they all seem to be fully booked

can you give me the name of a good middle-range hotel?
▶ pouvez-vous me donner le nom d'un bon hôtel à prix moyen
[poovay-voo muh donay luh nON dAN bonotel a pree mwa-yAN]

voyons; vous voulez être dans le centre? ◀
[vwa-yON; voo voolay zetr dON luh sONtr]
let me have a look, do you want to be in the centre?

if possible
▶ si possible
[see posseebl]

est-ce que ça vous dérange d'être un peu en dehors de la ville? ◀
[eskuh sa voo dayrONj detr AN puh ON duh-or duh la veel]
do you mind being a little way out of town?

not too far out
▶ pas trop en dehors
[pa tro ON duh-or]

where is it on the map?
▶ où est-ce sur le plan?
[oo ess sOOr luh plON]

can you write the name and address down?
▶ pouvez-vous me noter le nom et l'adresse?
[poovay-voo muh notay luh nON ay ladress]

I'm looking for a room in a private house
▶ je cherche une chambre chez l'habitant
[juh shairsh OOn shONbr shay labeetON]

2. Banks

bank account	le compte en banque	[kONt ON bONk]
to change money	changer de l'argent	[shONjay duh larjON]
cheque	le chèque	[shek]
to deposit	déposer	[daypozay]
euro	l'euro	[urro]
pin number	le code	[kod]
pound	la livre	[leevr]
to withdraw	retirer	[ruhteeray]

can you change this into euros?
▶ pouvez-vous changer ceci en euros?
[poovay-voo shONjay suhsee ON nurro]

comment désirez-vous votre argent? ◀
[komON dayzeeray-voo votr arjON]
how would you like the money?

small notes	big notes
▶ petites coupures	▶ grosses coupures
[puhteet koopOOr]	[gross koopOOr]

do you have information in English about opening an account?
▶ avez-vous des informations en anglais pour l'ouverture d'un compte?
[avay-voo dayzANformass-yON ON nONglay poor loovairtOOr dAN kONt]

oui, quelle sorte de compte désirez-vous ouvrir? ◀
[wee kel sort duh kONt dayzeeray-voo zoovreer]
yes what sort of account do you want?

I'd like a current account
je voudrais ouvrir un compte courant
[juh voodray zoovreer AN kONt koorON]

votre passeport, s'il vous plaît ◀
[votr pass-por seel voo play]
your passport, please

can I use this card to draw some cash?
▶ puis-je retirer de l'argent avec cette carte?
[pweej ruhteeray duh larjON avek set kart]

vous devez aller à la caisse ◀
[voo duhvay zalay ala kess]
you have to go to the cashier's desk

I want to transfer this to my account at the Banque de France
▶ je voudrais transférer ceci sur mon compte à la Banque de France
[juh voodray trONss-fayray suhsee sOOr mON kONt ala bONk duh frONss]

d'accord, mais vous devrez régler la communication ◀
[dakor, may voo duhvray rayglay la komOOneekass-yON]
OK, but we'll have to charge you for the phonecall

3. Booking a room

shower	la douche	[doosh]
telephone in the room	le téléphone dans la chambre	[taylayfon dON la shONbr]
payphone in the lobby	téléphone public dans le hall	[taylayfon pOObleek dON luh ol]

do you have any rooms?
▶ avez-vous des chambres libres?
[avay-voo day shONbr leebr]

pour combien de personnes? ◀
[poor kONb-yAN duh pairson]
for how many people?

for one/for two
▶ pour une personne/pour deux personnes
[poor OOn pairson/poor duh pairson]

oui, nous avons des chambres libres ◀
[wee noo zavON day shONbr leebr]
yes, we have rooms

pour combien de temps?
[poor kONb-yAN duh tON]
for how many nights?

just for one night
juste pour une nuit ◀
[jOOst poor OOn nwee]

how much is it?
▶ combien est-ce?
[kONb-yAN ess]

90 euros avec salle de bain et 70 euros sans ◀
[katr vAN dee zurro avek sal duh bAN ay swassONt deess SON]
90 euros with bathroom and 70 euros without bathroom

does that include breakfast?
▶ le petit-déjeuner est-il compris?
[luh puhtee dayjuhnay ayteel kONpree]

can I see a room with bathroom?
▶ puis-je voir une chambre avec salle de bain?
[pweej vwahr OOn shONbr avek sal duh bAN]

ok, I'll take it
▶ d'accord, je la prend
[dakor, juh la prON]

when do I have to check out?
▶ quand dois-je libérer la chambre?
[kON dwaj leebayray la shONbr]

is there anywhere I can leave luggage?
▶ puis-je laisser mes bagages quelque part?
[pweej lessay may bagahj kelkuh par]

4. Car hire

automatic	automatique	[otomateek]
full tank	le réservoir plein	[raysairvwahr plAN]
manual	manuelle	[manwel]
rented car	la voiture de location	[vwatoor duh lokass-yON]

I'd like to rent a car
▶ je voudrais louer une voiture
[juh voodray looay oon vwatoor]

pour combien de temps? ◀
[poor kONb-yAN duh tON]
for how long?

two days
▶ deux jours
[duh joor]

I'll take the ...
▶ je prend la ...
[juh prON la ...]

is that with unlimited mileage?
▶ est-ce que c'est avec kilométrage illimité?
[eskuh say tavek kilomaytrahj eeleemeetay]

oui ◀
[wee]
yes

puis-je voir votre permis de conduire, s'il vous plaît? ◀
[pweej vwahr votr pairmee duh kONdweer seel voo play]
can I see your driving licence, please?

et votre passeport ◀
[ay votr pass-por]
and your passport

is insurance included?
▶ l'assurance est-elle comprise?
[lassoorONss etel kONpreez]

oui, mais il y a une franchise de cent euros ◀
[wee mayzeel ya oon frONsheez duh sON urro]
yes, but you have to pay the first 100 euros

pouvez-vous laisser cent euros de caution? ◀
[poovay-voo lessay sON urro duh koss-yON]
can you leave a deposit of 100 euros?

and if this office is closed, where do I leave the keys?
▶ et si cette agence est fermée, où dois-je laisser les clés?
[ay see set ajONss ay fairmay oo dwaj lessay lay klay]

laissez-les dans cette boîte ◀
[lessay-lay dON set bwat]
you drop them in that box

16

5. Communications

ADSL modem	le modem ADSL	[modem aday-essel]
at	arobase	[arobaz]
dial-up modem	le modem par téléphone	[modem par taylayfon]
dot	point	[pwAN]
Internet	l'Internet	[ANtairnet]
mobile (phone)	le portable	[portahbl]
password	le code	[kod]
telephone socket adaptor	l'adaptateur pour prise téléphonique	[adaptaturr poor preez taylayfoneek]
wireless hotspot	la zone d'accès sans fil	[zon daxay sON feel]

is there an Internet café around here?
▶ y a-t-il un café internet par ici?
[yateel AN kafay ANtairnet par ee-see]

can I send email from here?
▶ puis-je envoyer des emails d'ici?
[pweej ONvvwa-yay day zeemail dee-see]

where's the at sign on the keyboard?
▶ où est le signe arobase sur le clavier?
[oo ay luh seeñ arobaz sOOr luh klav-yay]

can you switch this to a UK keyboard?
▶ pouvez-vous le mettre en clavier britannique?
[poovay-voo luh metr ON klav-yay breetaneek]

can you help me log on?
▶ pouvez-vous m'aider à me connecter?
[poovay-voo mayday a muh konektay]

can you put me through to ...?
▶ pouvez-vous me passer ...?
[poovay-voo muh passay]

I'm not getting a connection, can you help?
▶ je n'arrive pas à me connecter, pouvez-vous m'aider?
[juh nareev pa a muh konektay poovay-voo mayday]

where can I get a top-up card for my mobile?
▶ où puis-je acheter une recharge pour mon portable?
[oo pweej ashuhtay OOn ruhsharj poor mON portahbl]

zero zéro [zayro]	five cinq [sANK]
one un [AN]	six six [seess]
two deux [duh]	seven sept [set]
three trois [trwa]	eight huit [weet]
four quatre [katr]	nine neuf [nuhf]

6. Directions

hi, I'm looking for rue de la Paix
▶ bonjour, je cherche la rue de la Paix
[boNjoor juh shairsh la roo duh la pay]

hi, rue de la Paix, do you know where it is?
bonjour, la rue de la Paix, vous connaissez?
[boNjoor la roo duh la pay voo konessay]

désolé, je ne connais pas ◀
[dayzolay juh nuh konay pa]
sorry, never heard of it

hi, can you tell me where rue de la Paix is?
▶ bonjour, pouvez-vous me dire où se trouve la rue de la Paix?
[boNjoor poovay-voo muh deer oo suh troov la roo duh la pay]

je ne suis pas d'ici non plus ◀
[juh nuh swee pa dee-see noN ploo]
I'm a stranger here too

where?
où?
[oo]

which direction?
quelle direction?
[kel deereks-yoN]

▶ au deuxième feu à gauche
[o duhz-yeym fuh a gohsh]
left at the second traffic lights

▶ juste au coin
[joosto kwaN]
around the corner

▶ ensuite c'est la première à droite
[oNsweet say la pruhm-yair a drwat]
then it's the first street on the right

après le ... [apray luh] past the ...	en face de [oN fass duh] opposite	plus loin [ploo lwaN] further	rue [roo] street
devant [duhvoN] in front of	à gauche [a gohsh] on the left	près de [pray duh] near	tourner [toornay] turn off
à droite [a drwat] on the right	juste après [joost apray] just after	prochain, prochaine [proshAN, pro-shen] next	tout droit [too drwa] straight ahead
en arrière [oNnar-yair] back	là-bas [laba] over there		

18

7. Emergencies

accident	l'accident	[akseedON]
ambulance	l'ambulance	[ONbooloNss]
consul	le consul	[kONsool]
embassy	l'ambassade	[ONbassad]
fire brigade	les pompiers	[pONp-yay]
police	la police	[poleess]

help!
▶ à l'aide!
[a led]

can you help me?
▶ pouvez-vous m'aider?
[poovay-voo mayday]

please come with me! it's really very urgent
▶ suivez-moi s'il vous plait! c'est vraiment très urgent
[sweevay-mwa seel voo play say vraymON tray zoorjON]

I've lost (my keys)
▶ j'ai perdu (mes clés)
[jay pairdoo (may klay)]

(my mobile) is not working
▶ (mon portable) ne marche pas
[(mON portahbl) nuh marsh pa]

(my purse) has been stolen
▶ on m'a volé (mon sac à main)
[ON ma volay mON sakamAN]

I've been mugged
▶ on m'a agressée
[ON ma agressay]

comment vous-appelez vous? ◀
[komON voo zaplay-voo]
what's your name?

montrez-moi votre passeport ◀
[mONtray mwa votr pass-por]
I need to see your passport

I'm sorry, all my papers have been stolen
▶ désolé, on m'a volé tous mes papiers
[dayzolay ON ma volay too may pap-yay]

8. Friends

hi, how're you doing?
▶ bonjour, ça va?
[bONjoor sa va]

oui, et toi? ◀
[wee ay twa]
ok, and you?

---

yeah, fine
▶ oui, ça va
[wee sa va]

not bad
▶ pas mal
[pa mal]

---

d'you know Mark?
▶ tu connais Mark?
[tOO konay mark]

oui, nous nous connaissons ◀
[wee noo noo konessON]
yeah, we know each other

and this is Hannah
▶ et voici Hannah
[ay vwa-see hanna]

---

where do you know each other from?
▶ d'où vous connaissez-vous?
[doo voo konessay-voo]

nous nous sommes rencontrés chez Léo ◀
[noo noo som rONkONtray shay lay-o]
we met at Léo's place

---

that was some party, eh?
▶ c'était une fête super, hein?
[saytay OOn fet sOOpair AN]

géniale ◀
[jayñal]
the best

---

are you guys coming for a beer?
▶ vous venez prendre une bière?
[voo vuhnay prONdr OOn b-yair]

cool, on vient ◀
[kool ON v-yAN]
cool, let's go

non, j'ai rendez-vous avec Lola ◀
[nON jay rONday-voo avek lola]
no, I'm meeting Lola

---

see you at Luke's place tonight
▶ à ce soir chez Luke
[a suh swahr shay lOOk]

à plus ◀
[a plOOss]
see you

20

9. Health

I'm not feeling very well
▶ je ne me sens pas très bien
[juh nuh muh sON pa tray b-yAN]

can you get a doctor?
▶ pouvez-vous appelez un médecin?
[poovay-voo aplay AN maydsAN]

▶ où avez-vous mal?
[oo avay-voo mal]
where does it hurt?

it hurts here
j'ai mal ici ◀
[jay mal ee-see]

▶ avez-vous mal tout le temps?
[avay-voo mal too luh tON]
is the pain constant?

it's not a constant pain
je n'ai pas mal tout le temps ◀
[juh nay pa mal too luh tON]

can I make an appointment?
▶ est-ce que je peux prendre rendez-vous?
[eskuh juh puh proNdr rONday-voo]

can you give me something for ...?
▶ pouvez-vous me donner quelque
  chose contre ...?
[poovay-voo muh donay kelkuh shohz kONtr]

yes, I have insurance
▶ oui, je suis assuré
[wee juh swee zassOOray]

antibiotics	les antibiotiques	[ONteeb-yoteek]
antiseptic ointment	la pommade antiseptique	[pomad ONteesepteek]
cystitis	la cystite	[seesteet]
dentist	le dentiste	[dONteest]
diarrhoea	la diarrhée	[d-yaray]
doctor	le médecin	[maydsAN]
hospital	l'hôpital	[opee-tal]
ill	malade	[malad]
medicine	le médicament	[maydeekamON]
painkillers	les analgésiques	[analjayzeek]
pharmacy	la pharmacie	[farmassee]
to prescribe	prescrire	[preskreer]
thrush	le muguet	[mOOgay]

10. Language difficulties

a few words	quelques mots	[kelkuh mo]
interpreter	l'interprète	[ANtairpret]
to translate	traduire	[tradweer]

votre carte de crédit a été refusée ◀
[votr kart duh kraydee a aytay ruhfoozay]
your credit card has been refused

what, I don't understand; do you speak English?
▶ pardon, je ne comprend pas; parlez-vous anglais?
[pardON juh nuh kONprON pa; parlay-voo ONglay]

ce n'est pas valide ◀
[suh nay pa valeed]
this isn't valid

could you say that again? slowly
▶ pouvez-vous répéter? doucement ◀
[poovay-voo raypaytay] [dooss-mON]

I understand very little French
▶ je ne comprend pas beaucoup le français
[juh nuh kONprON pa bokoo luh frONsay]

I speak French very badly
▶ je parle très mal le français
[juh parl tray mal luh frONsay]

vous ne pouvez pas payer avec cette carte ◀
[voo nuh poovay pa pay-yay avek set kart]
you can't use this card to pay

▶ comprenez-vous? sorry, no
[kONpruhnay-voo] non, désolé ◀
do you understand? [nON dayzolay]

is there someone who speaks English?
▶ est-ce qu'il y a quelqu'un qui parle anglais?
[eskeel ya kelkAN kee parl ONglay]

oh, now I understand **is that ok now?**
▶ ah, je comprend maintenant ▶ est-ce que ça va maintenant?
[ah juh kONprON mANtnON] [eskuh sa va mANtnON]

11. Meeting people

hello
▶ bonjour
[bONjoor]

---

bonjour, je m'appelle Marie ◀
[bONjoor juh mapel maree]
hello, my name's Marie

Graham, from England, Thirsk
▶ Graham, de Thirsk en Angleterre
[graham duh thirsk ON nONgluhtair]

---

je ne connais pas, où est-ce? ◀
[juh nuh konay pa, oo ess]
don't know that, where is it?

---

not far from York, in the North; and you?
▶ pas très loin de York, dans le nord; et vous?
[pas tray lwaN duh york dON luh nor; ay voo]

---

je suis de Pau; vous êtes ici tout seul? ◀
[juh swee duh po; voo zet zee-see too surl]
I'm from Pau; here by yourself?

---

no, I'm with my wife and two kids
▶ non, avec ma femme et mes deux enfants
[nON avek ma fam ay may duh zONfON]

---

what do you do?   je suis dans l'informatique ◀
▶ qu'est-ce que vous faites?   [juh swee dON lANformateek]
[keskuh voo fet]   I'm in computers

---

me too
▶ moi aussi
[mwa o-see]

here's my wife now
▶ voici ma femme
[vwa-see ma fam]

---

enchanté de faire votre connaissance ◀
[ONshONtay duh fair votr konessONss]
nice to meet you

12. Post offices

airmail	par avion	[par av-yON]
post card	la carte postale	[kart postal]
post office	la poste	[posst]
stamp	le timbre	[tANbr]

what time does the post office close?
▶ à quelle heure ferme la poste?
[a kel urr fairm la posst]

▶ à dix-sept heures les jours de semaine
[a deesset urr lay joor duh suhmen]
five o'clock weekdays

is the post office open on Saturdays?   jusqu'à midi ◀
▶ la poste est-elle ouverte le samedi?   [jOOska meedee]
[la posst aytel oovairt luh sam-dee]   until twelve

I'd like to send this registered to England
▶ j'aimerais envoyer ceci en Angleterre en recommandé
[jemray zONvwy-yay suhsee ON nONgluhtair ON ruhkomONday]

très bien, ce sera dix euros ◀
[tray b-yAN suh suhra dee zurro]
certainly, that will cost 10 euros

and also two stamps for England, please
▶ et deux timbres pour l'Angleterre, s'il vous plaît
[ay duh tANbr poor lONgluhtair seelvooplay]

do you have some airmail stickers?
▶ avez-vous des étiquettes par avion?
[avay-voo day zayteeket par av-yON]

do you have any mail for me?
▶ avez-vous du courrier pour moi?
[avay-voo dOO koor-yay poor mwa]

colis	parcels
étranger	international
intérieur	domestic

24

13. Restaurants

bill	l'addition	[adeess-yON]
menu	le menu	[muhnOO]
table	la table	[tahbl]

can we have a non-smoking table?
▶ pouvons-nous avoir une table pour non-fumeurs?
[poovON-noo zavwahr OOn tahbl poor nON fOOmurr]

there are two of us
▶ nous sommes deux
[noo som duh]

there are four of us
▶ nous sommes quatre
[noo som katr]

what's this?
▶ qu'est-ce que c'est?
[keskuh say]

c'est une sorte de poisson ◀
[say tOOn sort duh pwassON]
it's a type of fish

c'est une spécialité locale ◀
[say tOOn spayss-yaleetay lokal]
it's a local speciality

entrez, je vais vous montrer ◀
[ONtray juh vay voo mONtray]
come inside and I'll show you

we would like two of these, one of these, and one of those
▶ nous en voudrions deux comme ceci, un comme ceci, et un comme cela
[noo zON voodree-yON duh kom suhsee AN kom suhsee ay AN kom suhla]

▶ et comme boisson?
[ay kom bwassON]
and to drink?

red wine
▶ du vin rouge
[dOO vAN rooj]

white wine
▶ du vin blanc
[dOO vAN blON]

a beer and two orange juices
▶ une bière et deux jus d'orange
[OOn bee-air ay duh jOO dorONj]

some more bread please
▶ encore un peu de pain, s'il vous plaît
[ONkor un puh duh pAN seel voo play]

▶ cela vous a plu?
[suhla voo za plOO]
how was your meal?

excellent, very nice!
▶ excellent!, très bon!
[exselON tray bON]

▶ autre chose?
[ohtr shohz]
anything else?

just the bill thanks
▶ non, l'addition, merci
[nON ladeess-yon mairsee]

14. Shopping

puis-je vous aider? ◀
[pweej voo zayday]
can I help you?

can I just have a look around?
▶ est-ce que je peux juste regarder?
[eskuh juh puh jOOst ruhgarday]

yes, I'm looking for ...
▶ oui, je cherche ...
[wee juh shairsh ...]

how much is this?
▶ combien ça coûte?
[kONb-yAN sa koot]

trente-deux euros ◀
[trONt duh zurro]
thirty-two euros

OK, I think I'll have to leave it; it's a little too expensive for me
▶ bon, je vais devoir laisser; c'est un peu trop cher pour moi
[bON juh vay duhvwar lessay say tAN puh tro shair poor mwa]

et ceci? ◀
[ay suhsee]
how about this?

can I pay by credit card?
▶ puis-je payer par carte de crédit?
[pweej pay-yay par kart duh kraydee]

it's too big
▶ c'est trop grand
[say tro grON]

it's too small
▶ c'est trop petit
[say tro puhtee]

it's for my son – he's about this high
▶ c'est pour mon fils – il est à peu près grand comme ça
[say poor mON feess - eelay ta puh pray grON kom sa]

▶ désirez-vous autre chose?
[dayzeeray voo ohtr shohz]
will there be anything else?

that's all thanks
▶ non, merci, c'est tout
[nON mairsee say too]

make it twenty euros and I'll take it
▶ pour vingt euros j'achète
[poor vAN turro jashet]

fine, I'll take it
▶ d'accord, j'achète
[dakor jashet]

caisse	échanger	fermé	ouvert	soldes
cash desk	to exchange	closed	open	sale

15. Sightseeing

art gallery	le musée d'art	[moozay dar]
bus tour	la visite en bus	[veezeet ON boos]
city centre	le centre ville	[sONtr veel]
closed	fermé	[fairmay]
guide	le guide	[geed]
museum	le musée	[moozay]
open	ouvert	[oovair]

I'm interested in seeing the old town
▶ j'aimerais voir la vieille ville
[jemray vwahr la v-yay veel]

are there guided tours?
▶ y a-t-il des visites guidées?
[yateel day veezeet geeday]

désolé, c'est complet ◀
[dayzolay say kONplay]
I'm sorry, it's fully booked

how much would you charge to drive us around for four hours?
▶ combien nous prendriez-vous pour nous faire visiter pendant quatre heures?
[kONb-yAN noo prONdr-yay-voo poor noo fair veezeetay pONdON katr urr]

can we book tickets for the concert here?
▶ pouvons-nous réserver des billets pour le concert ici?
[poovON-noo rayzairvay day bee-yay poor luh kONsair ee-see]

▶ oui, sous quel nom?
[wee soo kel nON]
yes, in what name?

quelle carte de crédit? ◀
[kel kart duh kraydee]
which credit card?

where do we get the tickets?
▶ ou devons-nous prendre les billets?
[oo duhvON noo prONdr lay bee-yay]

à l'entrée ◀
[a lONtray]
at the entrance

is it open on Sundays?
▶ est-ce ouvert le dimanche?
[ess oovair luh deemONsh]

how much is it to get in?
▶ combien coûte l'entrée?
[kONb-yAN koot lONtray]

are there reductions for groups of 6?
▶ y a-t-il des réductions pour les groupes de six personnes?
[yateel day raydooks-yON poor lay groop duh see pairson]

that was really impressive!
▶ c'était fantastique!
[saytay fONtasteek]

16. Trains

to change trains	changer de train	[shONjay duh trAN]
platform	le quai	[kay]
return	l'aller-retour	[alay-ruhtoor]
single	l'aller simple	[alay sANpl]
station	la gare	[gar]
stop	l'arrêt	[aray]
ticket	le billet	[bee-yay]

how much is ...?
▶ combien coûte ...?
[kONb-yAN koot]

a single, second class to ...
▶ un aller simple, deuxième classe, pour ...
[AN alay sANpl, duhz-yem klass, poor ...]

two returns, second class to ...
▶ deux allers-retours, deuxième classe, pour ...
[duh zalay-ruhtoor duhz-yem klass, poor ...]

for today	for tomorrow	for next Tuesday
▶ pour aujourd'hui	▶ pour demain	▶ pour mardi prochain
[poor ojoordwee]	[poor duhmAN]	[poor mardee proshAN]

il y a un supplément à payer pour le TGV ◀
[eel ya AN sooplaymON a pay-yay poor luh tayjayvay]
there's a supplement for the TGV

voulez-vous réserver une place? ◀
[voolay-voo rayzairvay OOn plass]
do you want to make a seat reservation?

vous devez changer à Bordeaux ◀
[voo duhvay shONjay a bordo]
you have to change at Bordeaux

is this seat free?
▶ cette place est-elle libre?
[set plass aytel leebr]

excuse me, which station are we at?
▶ excusez-moi, quel est cet arrêt?
[exkOOzay mwa kelay setaray]

is this where I change for Nice?
▶ est-ce ici que je dois changer de train pour Nice?
[es ee-see kuh juh dwa shONjay duh trAN poor neess]

English

→

French

A

a, an* un, une [AN, OOn]

about: about 20 environ vingt [ONveerON]

it's about 5 o'clock il est cinq heures environ

a film about France un film sur la France [sOOr]

above au-dessus de [o-duh-sOO duh]

abroad à l'étranger [a laytrONjay]

absolutely (I agree) absolument [absolOOmON]

accelerator l'accélérateur **m** [axaylayraturr]

accept accepter [axeptay]

accident l'accident **m** [axeedON]

there's been an accident il y a eu un accident [eelya OO]

accommodation le logement [lojmON]

accurate précis [praysee]

ache la douleur [doolurr]

my back aches j'ai mal au dos [jay]

across: across the road de l'autre côté de la route [duh lohtr kohtay duh]

adapter l'adaptateur **m** [adaptaturr]

(plug) la prise multiple [preez mOOlteepl]

address l'adresse **f** [adress]

what's your address? quelle est votre adresse? [kel ay votr]

address book le carnet d'adresses [karnay dadress]

admission charge le droit d'entrée [drwa dONtray]

adult l'adulte **mf** [adOOlt]

advance: in advance d'avance [davONss]

aeroplane l'avion **m** [av-yON]

after après [apray]

after you après toi/vous [twa/voo]

afternoon l'après-midi **m** [apray-meedee]

in the afternoon l'après-midi

this afternoon cet après-midi

aftershave l'après-rasage **m** [apray-razahj]

aftersun cream la crème après-soleil [krem apray-solay]

afterwards ensuite [ONsweet]

again de nouveau [duh noovo]

against contre [kONtr]

age l'âge **m** [ahj]

ago: a week ago il y a une semaine [eelya]

an hour ago il y a une heure

agree: I agree je suis d'accord [juh swee dakor]

AIDS le SIDA [seeda]

air l'air **m**

by air en avion [ON avyON]

air-conditioning la climatisation [kleemateezass-yON]

airmail: by airmail par avion [avyON]

airmail envelope l'enveloppe par avion **f** [ONvlop par avyON]

airport l'aéroport **m** [a-airopor]

to the airport, please à l'aéroport, s'il vous plaît

airport bus la navette de l'aéroport [navet]

aisle seat la place côté couloir [plass kohtay koolwahr]

alarm clock le réveil [rayvay]

alcohol l'alcool **m** [alkol]

alcoholic alcoolisé [alkoleezay]

Algeria l'Algérie **f** [aljayree]

Algerian (adj) algérien [aljayree-AN]

all: all the boys tous les garçons [too]

all the girls toutes les filles [toot]

all of it tout [too]

all of them tous [tooss]

that's all, thanks c'est tout, merci

allergic: I'm allergic to ... je suis allergique à ... [juh swee alairjeek]

allowed: is it allowed? est-ce que c'est permis? [eskuh say pairmee]

all right d'accord [dakor]

I'm all right ça va [sa]

are you all right? ça va?

almond l'amande **f** [amOnd]

almost presque [presk]

alone seul [surl]

alphabet l'alphabet **m** [alfabay]

a ah	h ash	o o	v vay		
b bay	i ee	p pay	w doobl-vay		
c say	j jee	q koo	x eeks		
d day	k ka	r air	y ee-grek		
e uh	l el	s ess	z zed		
f ef	m em	t tay			
g jay	n en	u oo			

Alps les Alpes **fpl** [alp]

already déjà [dayja]

also aussi [o-see]

although bien que [b-yAN kuh]

altogether en tout [ON too]

always toujours [toojoor]

am*: I am je suis [juh swee]

a.m.: at seven a.m. à sept heures du matin [urr doo matAN]

amazing (surprising) étonnant [aytonON]

(very good) remarquable [ruhmark-abl]

ambulance l'ambulance **f** [ONbOOlONss]

call an ambulance! appelez une ambulance! [aplay]

America l'Amérique **f** [amayreek]

American américain(e) [amayreekAN, -ken]

I'm American (man/woman) je suis américain/américaine

among parmi [parmee]

amount la quantité [kONteetay]

(money) la somme [som]

amp: a 13-amp fuse un fusible de 13 ampères [foozeebl ... ONpair]

amphitheatre l'amphithéâtre **m** [ONfeetay-ahtr]

and et [ay]

Andorra Andorre **f** [ONdor]

angry fâché [fashay]

animal l'animal **m** [aneemal]

ankle la cheville [shuhvee]

anniversary (wedding) l'anniversaire de mariage **m**

[aneevairsair duh maree-ahj]

annoy: this man's annoying
me cet homme m'importune
[ANportOOn]

annoying ennuyeux
[ONwee-uh]

another un autre [ohtr]
  can we have another room?
  est-ce que nous pouvons
  avoir une autre chambre?
  [eskuh noo poovON zavwa OOn
  ohtr]

another beer, please encore
une bière, s'il vous plaît
[ONkor]

antibiotics les antibiotiques
[ONteebeeooteek]

antifreeze l'antigel m
[ONteejel]

antihistamine
l'antihistaminique m [ONtee-
eestameeneek]

antique: is it an antique? est-
ce un objet d'époque? [ess AN
objay daypok]

antique shop l'antiquaire m
[ONteekair]

antiseptic le désinfectant
[dayZANfektON]

any: have you got any bread/
tomatoes? avez-vous du
pain/des tomates? [avay-voo
dOO .../day]

do you have any change?
avez-vous de la monnaie?
[duh]

sorry, I don't have any
désolé, je n'en ai pas [juh nON
ay pa]

anybody quelqu'un [kelkAN]
  does anybody here speak
  English? est-ce qu'il y a
  quelqu'un ici qui parle
  anglais? [eskeel-ya]
  there wasn't anybody there
  il n'y avait personne
  [pairson]

anything n'importe quoi

dialogues

anything else? désirez-
vous autre chose?
[dayzeeray-voo ohtr shohz]
nothing else, thanks c'est
tout, merci [say too
mairsee]

would you like anything to
drink? veux-tu/voulez-
vous boire quelque chose?
[vuh-tOO/voolay-voo bwahr
kelkuh-shohz]
I don't want anything,
thanks je ne veux rien,
merci [ree-AN]

apart from sauf [sohf]
apartment l'appartement m
[apartmON]
appendicitis l'appendicite f
[apONdeesseet]
aperitif l'apéritif m
[apayreeteef]
apology les excuses [exkOOz]
appetizer l'entrée f [ONtray]
apple la pomme [pom]
appointment le rendez-vous

dialogue

good afternoon, how can I help you? bonjour monsieur/madame, que puis-je faire pour vous? [kuh pweej fair poor voo]

I'd like to make an appointment j'aimerais prendre rendez-vous [jemray proNdr]

what time would you like? quelle heure vous conviendrait-elle? [kel urr voo koNvee-ANdrayt-el]

three o'clock trois heures

I'm afraid that's not possible, is four o'clock all right? cela ne va pas être possible, est-ce que quatre heures vous irait? [vooz eeray]

yes, that will be fine oui, cela ira parfaitement [eera parfetmoN]

the name was ...? c'est monsieur/madame ...? [say]

apricot l'abricot **m** [abreeko]
April avril [avreel]
are*: we are nous sommes [noo som]
you are tu es/vous êtes [too ay, voo zet]
they are ils sont [eel soN]
area la région [rayjee-oN]
area code l'indicatif **m** [ANdeekateef]

arm le bras [bra]
arrange: will you arrange it for us? pouvez-vous vous en occuper? [poovay-voo voo zoN okoopay]
arrival l'arrivée **f** [areevay]
arrive arriver [areevay]
when do we arrive? à quelle heure arrivons-nous? [areevoN-noo]
has my fax arrived yet? mon fax est-il arrivé? [areevay]
we arrived today nous sommes arrivés aujourd'hui
art l'art **m** [ar]
art gallery le musée d'art [moozay]
artist l'artiste **mf** [arteest]
as: as big as aussi gros que [ohsee gro kuh]
as soon as possible dès que possible [day]
ashtray le cendrier [soNdreeay]
ask demander [duhmoNday]
I didn't ask for this ce n'est pas ce que j'ai commandé [suh nay pa suh kuh jay komoNday]
could you ask him to ...? peux-tu/pouvez-vous lui demander de ...? [puh-too/poovay-voo lwee ...]
asleep: she's asleep elle dort [dor]
aspirin l'aspirine **f** [aspeereen]
asthma l'asthme **m** [as-muh]
astonishing étonnant [aytonoN]
at: at the hotel à l'hôtel [a]
at the station à la gare
at the café au café [o]

at six o'clock à six heures

at Paul's chez Paul [shay]

athletics l'athlétisme m
[atlayteess-muh]

Atlantic l'Atlantique m
[atlONteek]

attractive séduisant
[saydweezON]

aubergine l'aubergine f

August août [oo]

aunt la tante [tONt]

Australia l'Australie f [ostralee]

Australian australien(ne)
[ostralee-AN, -en]

I'm Australian (man/woman) je
suis australien/australienne

Austria l'Autriche f [otreesh]

automatic (car) la voiture
automatique [vwatoor
otomateek]

autumn l'automne m [oton]
in the autumn en automne
[ON]

avenue l'avenue f

average (not good) moyen
[mwy-AN]
on average en moyenne [ON
mwy-en]

awake: is he awake? est-il
réveillé? [rayvay-yay]

away: go away! allez-vous en!
[alay-voo zON]
is it far away? est-ce que c'est
loin? [eskuh say lwAN]

awful affreux [afruh]

axle l'essieu m [ess-yuh]

B

baby le bébé [baybay]

baby food les aliments pour
bébé [aleemON poor]

baby's bottle le biberon
[beeberON]

baby-sitter le/la baby-sitter

back (of body) le dos [doh]
(back part) l'arrière m [aree-air]
at the back à l'arrière
can I have my money back?
est-ce que vous pouvez me
rendre mon argent? [eskuh
voo poovay muh rONdr]
to come back revenir [ruh-
veneer]
to go back rentrer [rONtray]

backache le mal de reins [duh
rAN]

bad mauvais [movay]
a bad headache un violent
mal de tête [veeolON]

badly mal

bag le sac
(handbag) le sac à main [mAN]
(suitcase) la valise [valeez]

baggage les bagages mpl
[bagahj]

baggage check la consigne
[kONseeñ]

baggage claim le retrait des
bagages [ruhtray]

bakery la boulangerie
[boolONjree]

balcony le balcon [balkON]
a room with a balcony une
chambre avec balcon

bald chauve [shohv]
ball (large) le ballon [balON]
  (small) la balle [bal]
ballet le ballet
banana la banane [banan]
band (musical) l'orchestre **m** [orkestr]
  (pop, rock) le groupe
bandage le pansement [pONsmON]
Bandaids® les pansements **mpl** [pONsmON]
bank (money) la banque [bONk]
bank account le compte en banque [kONt ON bONk]
bar le bar
  a bar of chocolate une tablette de chocolat [tablet duh shokola]
barber's le coiffeur pour hommes [kwafurr poor om]
basket le panier [pan-yay]
bath le bain [bAN]
  can I have a bath? est-ce que je peux prendre un bain? [eskuh juh puh prONdr AN bAN]
bathroom la salle de bain [sal duh bAN]
  with a private bathroom avec salle de bain
bath towel la serviette de bain
battery la pile [peel]
  (for car) la batterie
bay la baie [bay]
be* être [etr]
beach la plage [plahj]
beach mat la natte [nat]
beach umbrella le parasol

beans les haricots [areeko]
  runner beans les haricots à rames [ram]
  broad beans les fèves [fev]
beard la barbe [barb]
beautiful beau, **f** belle [bo, bel]
because parce que [parss-kuh]
  because of ... à cause de ... [a kohz duh]
bed le lit [lee]
  I'm going to bed je vais me coucher [juh vay muh kooshay]
bed and breakfast la chambre avec petit déjeuner [shONbr avek puhtee dayjuhnay]
bedroom la chambre à coucher [shONbr a kooshay]
beef le bœuf [burf]
beer la bière [bee-air]
  two beers, please deux bières, s'il vous plaît [bee-air]
before avant [avON]
begin: when does it begin? à quelle heure est-ce que ça commence? [sa kom-mONss]
beginner le débutant, la débutante [dayboOtON, -tONt]
beginning: at the beginning au début [o dayboO]
behind derrière [dairyair]
  behind me derrière moi
beige beige [bej]
Belgian belge [belj]
  (man/woman) le/la Belge
Belgium la Belgique [beljeek]
believe croire [krwahr]
below sous [soo]
belt la ceinture [sANtoOr]
bend (in road) le virage [veerahj]

berth (on ship) la couchette [kooshet]

beside: beside the ... à côté du/de la ... [a kotay doo]

best le meilleur [may-yurr]

better mieux [m-yuh]

are you feeling better? est-ce que tu te sens/vous vous sentez mieux? [eskuh too tuh son/voo voo sontay]

between entre [ontr]

beyond au delà [o duhla]

bicycle le vélo [vaylo]

big grand [gron]

too big trop grand

it's not big enough ce n'est pas assez grand [pa zassay]

bike le vélo [vaylo]

(motorbike) la moto

bikini le bikini

bill l'addition f [adeess-yon]

(US) le billet (de banque) [bee-yay duh bonk]

could I have the bill, please? l'addition, s'il vous plaît

bin la poubelle [poo-bel]

bin liners les sacs poubelle mpl

binding (ski) la fixation [feexass-yon]

bird l'oiseau m [wazo]

biro® le stylo-bille [steelo-bee]

birthday l'anniversaire m [aneevairsair]

happy birthday! bon anniversaire!

biscuit le biscuit [beeskwee]

bit: a little bit un peu [an puh]

a big bit un gros morceau [gro morso]

a bit of ... un morceau de ...

a bit expensive un peu cher

bite (by insect) la piqûre [peekoor]

(by dog) la morsure [morsoor]

bitter (taste etc) amer [amair]

black noir [nwahr]

blanket la couverture [koovairtoor]

bleach (for toilet) l'eau de Javel f [ohd javel]

bless you! santé! [sontay]

blind aveugle [avurgl]

blind (on window) le store [stor]

blister l'ampoule f [onpool]

blocked (road, pipe, sink) bouché [booshay]

block of flats l'immeuble m [eemurbl]

blond(e) blond [blon]

blood le sang [son]

high blood pressure l'hypertension f [eepairtons-yon]

blouse le chemisier [shuhmeez-yay]

blow-dry le brushing

I'd like a cut and blow-dry je voudrais une coupe et un brushing

blue bleu [bluh]

blusher le rouge à joues [rooj a joo]

boarding house la pension [pons-yon]

boarding pass la carte d'embarquement [donbarkuh-mon]

boat le bateau [bato]

body le corps [kor]
boil (water) faire bouillir [fair booyeer]
(potatoes etc) faire cuire à l'eau [kweer a lo]
boiled egg l'œuf à la coque **m** [urf ala kok]
bone l'os **m** [oss]
bonnet (of car) le capot [kapo]
book le livre [leevr]
(verb) réserver [rayzairvay]
can I book a seat? est-ce que je peux réserver une place?

dialogue

I'd like to book a table for two j'aimerais réserver une table pour deux [jemray rayzairvay]
what time would you like it booked for? pour quelle heure voudriez-vous réserver? [poor kel urr voodree-ay-voo]
half past seven sept heures et demi
that's fine très bien
and your name? votre nom?

bookshop/bookstore la librairie [leebrairee]
boot (footwear) la botte [bot]
(of car) le coffre [kofr]
border (of country) la frontière [front-yair]
bored: I'm bored je m'ennuie [juh mON-nwee]

boring ennuyeux [ON-nwee-yuh]
born: I was born in Manchester je suis né à Manchester [juh swee nay]
I was born in 1960 je suis né en mille neuf cent soixante [ON meel nuhf sON swassONt]
borrow emprunter [ONprANtay]
may I borrow ...? puis-je emprunter ...?
both les deux [lay duh]
bother: sorry to bother you je suis désolé de vous déranger [juh swee dayzolay duh voo dayrON-jay]
bottle la bouteille [bootay]
a bottle of house red une bouteille de rouge maison [mezzON]
bottle-opener l'ouvre-bouteille **m** [oovr-bootay]
bottom (of person) le derrière [dairyair]
at the bottom of ... (hill etc) en bas de ... [ON ba duh]
box la boîte [bwat]
box office le guichet [geeshay]
boy le garçon [garsON]
boyfriend le petit ami [puhtee tami]
bra le soutien-gorge [soot-yAN-gorj]
bracelet le bracelet [braslay]
brake le frein [frAN]
brandy le cognac
bread le pain [pAN]
white bread du pain blanc [blON]
brown bread du pain noir

[nwar]

wholemeal bread du pain complet [kONplay]

break casser [kassay]

I've broken the ... j'ai cassé le ... [jay kassay]

I think I've broken my wrist je crois que je me suis cassé le poignet [juh muh swee]

breakdown la panne [pan]

I've had a breakdown je suis tombé en panne [juh swee tONbay ON]

breakdown service le service de dépannage [sairveess duh daypanahj]

breakfast le petit déjeuner [ptee day-juhnay]

English/full breakfast le petit déjeuner anglais [ONglay]

break-in: I've had a break-in il y a eu un cambriolage [eel ya OO AN kONbreeolahj]

breast le sein [SAN]

breathe respirer [respeeray]

breeze la brise [breez]

bridge (over river) le pont [pON]

brief court [koor]

briefcase la serviette

bright (light etc) clair

bright red rouge vif [veef]

brilliant (idea, person) génial [jayn-yal]

bring apporter [aportay]

I'll bring it back later je le rapporterai plus tard [raportuhray]

Britain la Grande-Bretagne [grONd-bruhtañ]

British britannique [breetaneek]

Brittany la Bretagne [bruhtañ]

brochure le prospectus [prospektOOss]

broken cassé [kassay]

bronchitis la bronchite [brONsheet]

brooch la broche [brosh]

broom le balai [balay]

brother le frère [frair]

brother-in-law le beau-frère [bo-frair]

brown marron [marON]

(hair) brun [brAN]

bruise le bleu [bluh]

brush (for hair) la brosse [bross]

(artist's) le pinceau [pAN-so]

(for cleaning) le balai [balay]

Brussels Bruxelles [brOOssel]

bucket le seau [so]

buffet car le wagon-restaurant [vagON-restorON]

buggy (for child) le landau [lONdo]

building le bâtiment [bateemON]

bulb l'ampoule f [ONpool]

I need a new bulb j'ai besoin d'une nouvelle ampoule

bumper le pare-chocs [par-shok]

bunk la couchette [kooshet]

bureau de change le bureau de change

burglary le cambriolage [kONbreeolahj]

burn la brûlure [brOOlOOr]

(verb) brûler [brOOlay]

burnt: this is burnt c'est brûlé [brOOlay]

burst: a burst pipe un tuyau
crevé [twee-o kruhvay]
bus le bus [bOOss]
  what number bus is it to ...?
  quel bus va à ...? [kel]
  when is the next bus to ...? à
  quelle heure part le prochain
  bus pour ...? [a kel urr par luh
  proshAN]
  what time is the last bus? à
  quelle heure passe le dernier
  bus? [dairn-yay]
  **could you let me know when
  we get there?** est-ce que
  vous pourrez me dire quand
  on y sera? [eskuh voo pooray muh
  deer kON tON ee suhra]

dialogue

  does this bus go to ...? est-
  ce que ce bus va à ...?
  no, you need a number ...
  non, vous devez prendre
  le ... [prONdr]
  where does it leave from?
  où est-ce que je le prends?
  [weskuh juh luh prON]

business les affaires **fpl** [lay
zafair]
bus station la gare routière
[gar root-yair]
bus stop l'arrêt d'autobus **m**
[aray dotobOOss]
bust la poitrine [pwatreen]
busy (person) occupé [okOOpay]
  the restaurant is very busy il
  y a beaucoup de monde dans

le restaurant [eel ya bohkoo duh
mONd]
I'm busy tomorrow demain,
je suis pris(e) [duhmAN juh swee
pree/preez]
but mais [may]
butcher's la boucherie
[booshree]
butter le beurre [burr]
button le bouton [bootON]
buy acheter [ashtay]
  where can I buy ...? où puis-
  je acheter ...? [oo pweej]
by: by bus/car en bus/voiture
[ON]
  written by ... écrit par ...
  by the window près de la
  fenêtre [pray duh]
  by the sea au bord de la mer
  [o bor]
  by Thursday pour jeudi [poor]
bye au revoir [o ruh-vwa]

C

cabbage le chou [shOO]
cabin (on ship) la cabine
[kabeen]
cable car le téléférique
[taylayfayreek]
café le café
cagoule le K-way® [ka-way]
cake le gâteau [gato]
cake shop la pâtisserie
call appeler [aplay]
  (to phone) téléphoner
  [taylayfonay]
  what's it called? comment ça

s'appelle? [komON sa sa-pel]
he/she is called ... il/elle
s'appelle ...
please call the doctor
appelez le docteur, s'il vous
plaît [aplay]
**please give me a call at 7.30
a.m. tomorrow** pouvez-vous
me réveiller à sept heures
trente demain matin?
[poovay-voo muh rayvayay]
please ask him to call me
pouvez-vous lui demander
de m'appeler?
call back: I'll call back later
je reviendrai plus tard
[ruhveeANdray]
(phone back) je rappelerai plus
tard [rapelray]
**call round: I'll call round
tomorrow** je passerai demain
[passuhray]
camcorder le caméscope
[kamayskop]
camera (for stills) l'appareil-
photo **m** [aparay-]
camera shop le photographe
[fotograf]
camp camper [kONpay]
can we camp here? est-ce
qu'on peut camper ici? [eskON
puh]
camping gas le butagaz
campsite le terrain de
camping [terrAN duh kONpeeng]
can (tin) la boîte [bwat]
a can of beer une bière en
boîte [bee-air ON]
can*: can you ...? peux-tu/

pouvez-vous ...? [puh-too/
poovay-voo]
can I have ...? est-ce que je
peux avoir ...? [eskuh juh puh
avwahr]
I can't ... je ne peux pas ...
[juh nuh puh pa]
Canada le Canada
Canadian canadien(ne)
[kanadee-AN, -ee-en]
I'm Canadian (man/woman) je
suis canadien/canadienne
canal le canal
cancel annuler [anOOlay]
candies les bonbons
[bONbON]
candle la bougie [boo-jee]
canoe le canoë [kano-ay]
canoeing le canoë
can-opener l'ouvre-boîte **m**
[oovr-bwat]
cap (hat) la casquette [kasket]
(of bottle) la capsule
car la voiture [vwatOOr]
by car en voiture
carafe une carafe
**a carafe of house white,
please** une carafe de blanc
maison, s'il vous plaît
[mezzON]
caravan la caravane
caravan site le terrain de
camping pour caravanes
[terrAN duh kONpeeng poor]
carburettor le carburateur
[karbOOraturr]
card (birthday etc) la carte [kart]
here's my (business) card
voici ma carte [vwa-see]

cardigan le gilet [jeelay]

cardphone le téléphone à carte [taylayfon a kart]

careful prudent [prOOdON]
be careful! faites attention! [fet zatONs-yON]

caretaker le/la concierge

car ferry le ferry

car hire la location de voitures [lokass-yON duh vwatOOr]

car park le parking [parkeeng]

carpet la moquette [moket]

carriage (of train) le wagon [vagON]

carrier bag le sac en plastique [ON plasteek]

carrot la carotte [karrot]

carry porter [portay]

carry-cot le porte-bébé [port-baybay]

carton (of orange juice etc) le carton [kartON]

carwash le lave-auto [lav-oto]

case (suitcase) la valise [valeez]

cash l'argent liquide **m** [arjON leekeed]
(verb) encaisser
will you cash this for me? est-ce que vous pouvez encaisser cela pour moi? [eskuh voo poovay]

cash desk la caisse [kess]

cash dispenser le distributeur automatique de billets de banque [deestreebOOturr otomateek duh bee-yay duh bONk]

cashier (cash desk) la caisse [kess]

cassette la cassette

cassette recorder le magnétophone à cassettes [man-yetofon]

castle le château [shato]

casualty department le service des urgences [sairveess day zOOrjONss]

cat le chat [sha]

catch attraper [atrapay]
where do we catch the bus to ...? où est-ce qu'on peut prendre le bus pour ...? [weskON puh prONdr luh bOOss]

cathedral la cathédrale [kataydral]

Catholic (adj) catholique [katoleek]

cauliflower le chou-fleur [shoo-flurr]

cave la grotte [grot]

CD le CD [say-day]

ceiling le plafond [plafON]

celery le céleri en branche [saylree ON brONsh]

cellar (for wine) la cave [kahv]

cemetery le cimetière [seemtee-air]

Centigrade* centigrade [sONteegrad]

centimetre* le centimètre [sONteemetr]

central central [sON-tral]

central heating le chauffage central [shofahj sON-tral]

centre le centre [sONtr]
how do we get to the city centre? comment va-t-on au centre-ville? [komON vatON o sONtr-veel]

it's in the city centre c'est dans le centre-ville

cereal les céréales [sayray-al]

certainly certainement [sairten-mON]

certainly not certainement pas [pa]

chair la chaise [shez]

champagne le champagne [shONpañ]

change (money) la monnaie [monay]

(verb) changer [shONjay]

can I change this for ...? j'aimerais échanger ceci contre ... [jemray ayshONjay suhsee]

I don't have any change je n'ai pas de monnaie [juh nay pa duh]

can you give me change for a 50-euro note? pouvez-vous me faire la monnaie sur un billet de cinquante euros? [muh fair]

dialogue

do we have to change (trains)? est-ce qu'il faut changer? [eskeel fo]

yes, change at Bordeaux oui, il faut changer à Bordeaux

no, it's direct non, c'est direct [deerekt]

changed: to get changed se changer [shONjay]

Channel la Manche [mONsh]

Channel Islands les îles Anglo-Normandes [eel ONglo-normONd]

Channel Tunnel le tunnel sous la Manche [tOOnel soo la mONsh]

chapel la chapelle [shapel]

charge (verb) faire payer

cheap bon marché [bON marshay]

do you have anything cheaper? avez-vous quelque chose de meilleur marché? [avay-voo kelkuh shohz duh may-yurr marshay]

check (US) le chèque [shek]
(US: bill) l'addition f [adeess-yON]
(verb) vérifier [vayreef-yay]

could you check the ..., please? pouvez-vous vérifier ..., s'il vous plaît?

checkbook le chéquier [shaykee-ay]

check-in l'enregistrement des bagages m [ONrejeestruh-mON day bagahj]

check in (at airport) se faire enregistrer [suh fair ONrejeestray]

where do we have to check in? où est l'enregistrement?

checkout (in shop) la caisse [kess]

cheek (on face) la joue [joo]

cheerio! (bye-bye) au revoir! [o ruh-vwa]

cheers! (toast) santé! [sONtay]

(thanks) merci! [mairsee]
cheese le fromage [fromahj]
chemist's (shop) la pharmacie [farmassee]
cheque le chèque [shek]
  do you take cheques? est-ce que vous acceptez les chèques? [eskuh voo zaxeptay]
cheque book le chéquier [shaykee-ay]
cheque card la carte d'identité bancaire [kart deedONteetay bONkair]
cherry la cerise [suhreez]
chess les échecs [lay zayshek]
chest (body) la poitrine [pwatreen]
chewing gum le chewing-gum [shween-gom]
chicken la poule [pool]
  (meat) le poulet [poolay]
chickenpox la varicelle [vareessel]
child l'enfant mf [ON-fON]
  children les enfants
child minder le/la gardien(ne) d'enfants [gardee-AN, -ee-en]
children's pool la piscine pour enfants [peesseen]
children's portion la portion pour enfants [pors-yON]
chin le menton [mONtON]
china la porcelaine
Chinese chinois [sheenwa]
chips les frites [freet]
chocolate le chocolat [shokola]
  milk chocolate le chocolat au lait [o lay]
  plain chocolate le chocolat à

croquer [a krokay]
  a hot chocolate un chocolat chaud [sho]
choose choisir [shwazeer]
Christian name le prénom [praynON]
Christmas Noël [no-el]
  Christmas Eve la veille de Noël [vay duh]
  merry Christmas! joyeux Noël! [jwy-uh]
church l'église f [aygleez]
cider le cidre [seedr]
cigar le cigare [see-gar]
cigarette la cigarette [see-]
cigarette lighter le briquet [breekay]
cinema le cinéma [seenayma]
circle le cercle [sairkl]
  (in theatre) le balcon [balkON]
city la ville [veel]
city centre le centre-ville [sONtr-veel]
clean (adj) propre [propr]
  can you clean these for me? pouvez-vous me nettoyer ça? [poovay-voo muh net-wy-ay sa]
cleaning solution (for contact lenses) la solution de nettoyage [solOOss-yON duh net-wy-ahj]
cleansing lotion (cosmetic) la crème démaquillante [krem daymakeeyONt]
clear clair [klair]
clever intelligent [ANtayleejON]
cliff la falaise [falez]
climbing l'escalade f
cling film le cellophane

[selofan]

clinic la clinique [kleeneek]

cloakroom (for coats) le vestiaire [vestee-air]

clock l'horloge f [orloj]

close fermer [fairmay]

dialogue

what time do you close?
à quelle heure est-ce que vous fermez? [a kel urr eskuh voo fairmay]
we close at 8 pm on weekdays and 6 pm on Saturdays nous fermons à huit heures pendant la semaine et à six heures le samedi [noo fairmON]
do you close for lunch?
est-ce que vous fermez pour déjeuner?
yes, between 1 and 3.30 pm oui, entre une heure et trois heures et demi

closed fermé [fairmay]

cloth (fabric) le tissu [teessOO]
(for cleaning etc) le chiffon [sheefON]

clothes les vêtements [vetmON]

clothes line la corde à linge [kord a lANj]

clothes peg la pince à linge [pANSS]

cloud le nuage [nOO-ahj]

cloudy nuageux [nOO-ahjuh]

clutch l'embrayage m [ONbray-ahj]

coach (bus) le car
(on train) le wagon [vagON]

coach station la gare routière [gar rootee-air]

coach trip l'excursion en autocar f [exkOOrss-yON ON otokar]

coast la côte [koht]
on the coast sur la côte

coat (long coat) le manteau [mONto]
(jacket) la veste [vest]

coathanger le cintre [sANtr]

cockroach le cafard [kafar]

cocoa le cacao [kakow]

coconut la noix de coco [nwa duh]

code (when dialling) l'indicatif m [ANdeekateef]
what's the (dialling) code for outside Paris? quel est l'indicatif pour la province? [kel ay lANdeekateef poor]

coffee le café
two coffees, please deux cafés, s'il vous plaît [kafay]

coin la pièce [p-yess]

Coke® le coca-cola

cold (weather, food etc) froid [frwa]
I'm cold j'ai froid [jay]
I have a cold je me suis enrhumé [juh muh swee zONrOOmay]

collapse: he's collapsed il s'est effondré [eel set ayfONdray]

collar le col

collect: I've come to collect ... je suis venu chercher ... [juh swee vuhnoo shairshay]

collect call une communication en PCV [-kass-yon ON pay-say-vay]

college l'université f [ooneevairseetay]

colour la couleur [koolurr]

do you have this in other colours? l'avez-vous en d'autres teintes? [lavay voo ON dohtr tANt]

colour film la pellicule couleur [pelikool]

comb le peigne [peñ]

come venir [vuhneer]

dialogue

> where do you come from? d'où es-tu/êtes-vous? [doo ay-too/et-voo]
> I come from Edinburgh je suis d'Édimbourg [juh swee]

come back revenir

I'll come back tomorrow je reviens demain [juh ruhv-yAN]

come in entrer [ONtray]

comfortable confortable [kONfort-abl]

compact disc le disque compact

company (business) la société [sos-yay-tay]

compartment (on train) le compartiment [kONparteemON]

compass la boussole [boossol]

complain se plaindre [suh plANdr]

complaint la réclamation [rayklamass-yON]

I have a complaint j'ai une réclamation à faire

completely complètement [kONpletmON]

computer l'ordinateur m [ordeenaturr]

concert le concert [kONsair]

concussion la commotion cérébrale [komoss-yON sayray-bral]

conditioner (for hair) l'après-shampoing m [apray-shONpwAN]

condom le préservatif [prayzairvateef]

conference la conférence [kONfay-rONss]

confirm confirmer [kONfeermay]

congratulations! félicitations! [fayleesseetass-yON]

connecting flight le vol qui assure la correspondance [kee assoor la korespONdONss]

connection (in travelling) la correspondance

conscious conscient [kONs-yON]

constipation la constipation [kONsteepass-yON]

consulate le consulat [kONsoo-la]

contact contacter [kONtaktay]

contact lenses les lentilles de contact fpl [lONtee]

contraceptive le contraceptif [kONtrasepteef]

convenient (location) pratique [prateek]

(time) qui convient [kee kONvee-AN]

that's not convenient cela ne me convient pas

cook le cuisinier, la cuisinière [kweezeenee-ay, -yair]

not cooked (is underdone) pas cuit [pa kwee]

cooker la cuisinière [kweezeenyair]

cookie le biscuit [beeskwee]

cooking utensils les ustensiles de cuisine [OOstONseel duh kweezeen]

cool (day, weather) frais, f fraîche [fray, fresh]

cork (in bottle) le bouchon [booshON]

corkscrew le tire-bouchon [teer-booshON]

corner: on the corner (of street) au coin de la rue [kwAN duh la rOO]

in the corner dans le coin

cornflakes les cornflakes

correct (adj) correct, exact

corridor le couloir [koolwahr]

Corsica la Corse [korss]

Corsican (adj) corse

cosmetics les produits de beauté [prodwee duh bohtay]

cost coûter [kootay]

how much does it cost? combien ça coûte? [kONb-yAN sa koot]

cot (for baby) le lit d'enfant [lee dONfON]

cotton le coton [kotON]

cotton wool le coton hydrophile [kotON eedrofeel]

couch (sofa) le canapé [kanapay]

couchette la couchette

cough la toux [too]

cough medicine le sirop contre la toux [seero kONtr]

could: could you ...? pourriez-vous ...? [pooree-ay-voo]

could I have ...? j'aimerais ... [jemray]

I couldn't ... je ne pouvais pas ... [juh nuh poovay pa]

country (nation) le pays [payee] (countryside) la campagne [kONpañ]

countryside la campagne

couple (man and woman) le couple [koopl]

a couple of ... quelques ... [kelkuh]

courier le/la guide [geed]

course (of meal) le plat [pla]

of course bien sûr [b-yAN sOOr]

of course not bien sûr que non [kuh nON]

cousin le cousin, la cousine [koozAN, koozeen]

cow la vache [vash]

crab le crabe [krab]

cracker (biscuit) le biscuit salé [beeskwee salay]

craft shop la boutique d'artisanat [arteezana]

crash la collision [koleez-yON]

I've had a crash j'ai eu un

accident [jay ∞ AN axeedON]
crazy fou, **f** folle [foo, fol]
cream (on milk, in cake, lotion) la
crème [krem]
(colour) crème
creche (for babies) la crèche
credit card la carte de crédit
[kart duh kraydee]

dialogue

can I pay by credit card?
est-ce que je peux payer
par carte de crédit? [eskuh
juh puh pay-ay]
which card do you want
to use? avec quelle carte
désirez-vous payer?
yes, sir oui monsieur
what's the number? quel
est le numéro? [nOOmayro]
and the expiry date? et la
date d'expiration?

crisps les chips **fpl** [cheeps]
crockery la vaisselle
[vess-el]
crossing (by sea) la traversée
[travairsay]
crossroads le carrefour
[karfoor]
crowd la foule [fool]
crowded (streets, bars) bondé
[bONday]
crown (on tooth) la couronne
[kooron]
cruise (by ship) la croisière
[krwaz-yair]
crutches les béquilles **fpl**

[baykee]
cry pleurer [plurray]
cucumber le concombre
[kONkONbr]
cup la tasse [tass]
a cup of ..., please une tasse
de ..., s'il vous plaît
cupboard l'armoire **f** [armwahr]
curly (hair) frisé
current le courant [koorON]
curtains les rideaux **mpl** [reedo]
cushion le coussin
[koossAN]
custom la coutume
[kootOOm]
Customs la douane [dwan]
cut la coupure [koopOOr]
(hair) la coupe [koop]
(verb) couper [koopay]
I've cut myself je me suis
coupé [juh muh swee koopay]
cutlery les couverts
[kouvair]
cycling le cyclisme [seekleess-
muh]
cyclist le/la cycliste
[seekleest]

D

dad le papa
daily: they run daily il y en
a tous les jours [eel yON a too
lay joor]
a daily paper un (journal)
quotidien [joornal koteedee-AN]
damage endommager
[ONdoma-jay]

damaged abîmé [abeemay]

I'm sorry, I've damaged this je suis désolé, j'ai abimé ça [jay abeemay]

damn! zut! [zoot]

damp (adj) humide [oo-meed]

dance la danse [dONss]

(verb) danser [dONsay]

would you like to dance? veux-tu/voulez-vous danser avec moi? [vuh-too/voolay-voo – avek mwa]

dangerous dangereux [dONj-ruh]

Danish danois [danwa]

dark (adj: colour) foncé [fONsay]

(hair) brun [brAN]

it's getting dark il commence à faire sombre [eel komONss a fair sONbr]

date*: what's the date today? quel jour sommes-nous? [kel joor som-noo]

let's make a date for next Monday prenons rendez-vous pour lundi prochain [pruhnON]

dates (fruit) les dattes **fpl** [dat]

daughter la fille [fee]

daughter-in-law la belle-fille [bel-fee]

dawn l'aurore **f** [oror]

at dawn au lever du jour [o luhvay doo joor]

day le jour [joor]

the day after le lendemain [lONdmAN]

the day after tomorrow après-demain [apray-duhmAN]

the day before la veille [vay]

the day before yesterday avant-hier [avON-tee-air]

every day chaque jour

are you open all day? est-ce que vous êtes ouverts toute la journée? [toot la joornay]

in two days' time dans deux jours

have a nice day bonne journée [bon joornay]

day trip l'excursion d'une journée **f** [exkoors-yON doon joornay]

dead mort [mor]

deaf sourd [soor]

deal (business) l'affaire **f**

it's a deal d'accord! [dakor]

death la mort [mor]

decaffeinated coffee le café décaféiné [daykafay-eenay]

December décembre [daysONbr]

decide décider [dayseeday]

we haven't decided yet nous n'avons pas encore décidé [noo navON pa zONkor dayseeday]

decision la décision [dayseez-yON]

deck (on ship) le pont [pON]

deckchair la chaise longue [shez lON-g]

deduct déduire [daydweer]

deep profond [profON]

definitely certainement [sairten-mON]

definitely not certainement pas [pa]

degree (qualification) le diplôme

[deeplohm]
delay le retard [ruhtar]
deliberately exprès [expray]
delicatessen l'épicerie fine f
[aypeesree feen]
delicious délicieux [dayleess-
yuh]
deliver livrer [leevray]
delivery (of mail) la distribution
[deestreeb00ss-yON]
Denmark le Danemark
[danmark]
dental floss le fil dentaire [feel
dONtair]
dentist le/la dentiste [dON-
teest]

dialogue

it's this one here c'est
celle-là [say sel-la]
this one? celle-ci? [sel-see]
no, that one non, celle-là
here? ici? [ee-see]
yes oui [wee]

dentures le dentier [dONt-yay]
deodorant le déodorant
[dayodorON]
department le service
[sairveess]
department store le grand
magasin [grON magazAN]
departure le départ [daypar]
departure lounge le hall de
départ [al duh]
depend: it depends ça dépend
[sa daypON]
it depends on ... ça dépend

de ...
deposit (as security) la caution
[kohs-yON]
(as part payment) l'acompte m
[akONt]
description la description
[deskreeps-yON]
dessert le dessert [desair]
destination la destination
[desteenass-yON]
develop développer [dayv-
lopay]

dialogue

could you develop these
films? pouvez-vous
développer ces pellicules?
[poovay-voo ... say peleek00l]
when will they be ready?
quand est-ce que ça sera
prêt? [kON teskuh sa suhra
pray]
tomorrow afternoon
demain après-midi
how much is the four-hour
service? combien coûte le
service de développement
en quatre heures?

diabetic le/la diabétique [dee-
abayteek]
diabetic foods les aliments
pour diabétiques [aleemON]
dial composer [kONpohzay]
dialling code l'indicatif m
[ANdeekateef]
diamond le diamant [dee-
amON]

diaper la couche [koosh]

diarrhoea la diarrhée [dee-aray]

diary (business etc) l'agenda m [ajANda]

(for personal experiences) le journal [joornal]

dictionary le dictionnaire [deex-yonair]

didn't* see not

die mourir [mooreer]

diesel (fuel) le gas-oil

diet le régime [ray-jeem]

I'm on a diet je suis au régime [juh swee zo]

I have to follow a special diet je dois suivre un régime spécial [dwa sweevr]

difference la différence [deefayrONss]

what's the difference? quelle est la différence? [kel ay]

different différent [deefayrON]

this one is different celui-ci est différent [suhlwee-see]

a different table une autre table [ohtr]

difficult difficile [deefeesseel]

difficulty la difficulté [deefeekOOltay]

dinghy (rubber) le canot pneumatique [kano p-nuhmateek]

(sailing) le dériveur [dayreevurr]

dining room la salle à manger [sal a mONjay]

dinner (evening meal) le dîner [deenay]

to have dinner dîner

direct (adj) direct [deerekt]

is there a direct train? est-ce qu'il y a un train direct? [eskeel ya]

direction le sens [sONss]

which direction is it? dans quelle direction est-ce? [dON kel deereex-yON ess]

is it in this direction? est-ce par là?

directory enquiries les renseignements [rONsen-yuhmON]

dirt la saleté [sal-tay]

dirty sale [sal]

disabled handicapé [ONdeekapay]

is there access for the disabled? est-ce que c'est aménagé pour les handicapés? [eskuh say amaynah-jay]

disappear disparaître [deesparetr]

it's disappeared (I've lost it) il/elle a disparu [deesparOO]

disappointed déçu [daysOO]

disappointing décevant [day-svON]

disaster le désastre [day-zastr]

disco la discothèque

discount le rabais [rabay]

disease la maladie [maladee]

disgusting dégoûtant [daygootON]

dish (meal, bowl) le plat [pla]

dishcloth le torchon à vaisselle [torshON a vess-el]

disinfectant le désinfectant

[dayzANfek-tON]

disk (for computer) la disquette

disposable diapers les couches jetables **fpl** [koosh juhtahbl]

disposable nappies les couches jetables **fpl**

distance la distance [deestONss]

in the distance au loin [o lwAN]

distilled water l'eau distillée f [o deesteelay]

district le quartier [kart-yay]

disturb déranger [dayrONjay]

diversion (detour) la déviation [dayvee-ass-yON]

diving board le plongeoir [plON-jwahr]

divorced divorcé [deevorsay]

dizzy: I feel dizzy j'ai la tête qui tourne [jay la tet kee toorn]

do faire [fair]

what shall we do? qu'est-ce qu'on fait? [keskON fay]

how do you do it? comment est-ce qu'on fait? [komON eskON fay]

will you do it for me? est-ce que tu peux/vous pouvez le faire pour moi? [eskuh too puh/voo poovay]

dialogues

how do you do? comment vas-tu/allez-vous? [va-too/ alay-voo]

nice to meet you enchanté

52

[ONshONtay]

what do you do? (work) qu'est-ce que tu fais/vous faites dans la vie? [kes kuh too fay/voo fet dON la vee]

I'm a teacher, and you? je suis enseignant(e), et toi/ vous? [twa]

I'm a student je suis étudiant(e)

what are you doing this evening? qu'est-ce que tu fais/vous faites ce soir? [suh swahr]

we're going out for a drink, do you want to join us? nous allons prendre un verre, veux-tu te/voulez-vous vous joindre à nous? [vuh-too tuh/voolay-voo voo jwANdr]

do you want cream? voulez-vous de la crème?

I do, but she doesn't moi oui, mais pas elle [mwa]

doctor le médecin [maydsAN]

we need a doctor nous avons besoin d'un médecin

please call a doctor appelez un médecin, s'il vous plaît [aplay]

dialogue

where does it hurt? où est-ce que ça fait mal? [weskuh

sa fay]
right here ici [ee-see]
does that hurt now? est-ce
que ça fait mal là?
yes oui [wee]
take this to the chemist
emmenez ça chez le
pharmacien [ONmuhnay sa
shay luh farmass-yAN]

document le document
[dokOOmON]
dog le chien [shee-AN]
doll la poupée [poopay]
domestic flight le vol
intérieur [ANtayree-urr]
don't!* non! [nON] see **not**
don't do that! ne faites pas ça!
[nuh fet pa sa]
door (of room) la porte [port]
(of train, car) la portière [port-
yair]
doorman le portier [port-yay]
double double [doobl]
double bed le grand lit [grON
lee]
double room la chambre pour
deux personnes [shONbr poor
duh pairson]
doughnut le beignet [benyay]
down en bas [ON ba]
put it down over there posez-
le là [pohzay-luh]
it's down there on the right
c'est par là sur la droite
it's further down the road
c'est plus loin sur cette route
[plOO lwAN sOOr set root]
downhill skiing le ski de

descente [duh duhsONt]
downmarket (restaurant etc)
simple [sANpl]
downstairs en bas [ON ba]
dozen la douzaine [doozen]
half a dozen une demi-
douzaine [duhmee-]
drain le tuyau d'écoulement
[twee-yo day-koolmON]
draught beer la bière pression
[bee-air press-yON]
draughty: it's draughty il y
a un courant d'air [eelya AN
koorON dair]
drawer le tiroir [teer-wa]
drawing le dessin [duh-sAN]
dreadful épouvantable
[aypoovONtabl]
dream le rêve [rev]
dress la robe [rob]
dressed: to get dressed
s'habiller [sabeeyay]
dressing (for cut) le pansement
[pONsmON]
(for salad) la vinaigrette
dressing gown la robe de
chambre [rob duh shONbr]
drink la boisson [bwassON]
(verb) boire [bwahr]
a cold drink une boisson
fraîche [fresh]
can I get you a drink? tu
prends/vous prenez un
verre? [tOO prON/voo pruhnay zAN
vair]
**what would you like (to
drink)?** qu'est-ce que tu
veux/vous voulez boire?
[keskuh]

no thanks, I don't drink non merci, je ne bois pas [juh nuh bwa pa]

I'll just have a drink of water un verre d'eau, c'est tout [vair do say too]

drinking water l'eau potable f [o pot-abl]

is this drinking water? est-ce que cette eau est potable? [eskuh]

drive conduire [kONdweer]

we drove here nous sommes venus en voiture [noo som vuhnoo en vwatOOr]

I'll drive you home je vais te/vous reconduire [juh vay tuh/voo ruhkONdweer]

driver (of car) le conducteur [kONdOOkturr]

(of bus) le chauffeur

driving licence le permis de conduire [pairmee duh kONdweer]

drop: just a drop, please (of drink) une petite goutte, s'il vous plaît [OOn puhteet goot]

drug (medical) le médicament [maydeekamON]

drugs (narcotics) la drogue [drog]

drunk (adj) ivre [eevr]

drunken driving la conduite en état d'ivresse [kONdweet ON ayta deevress]

drunkenness l'ivresse f [eevress]

dry (adj) sec, f sèche [sek, sesh]

dry-cleaner le teinturier [tANtOOree-ay]

duck le canard [kanar]

due: he was due to arrive yesterday il devait arriver hier [eel duhvay]

when is the train due? quand est-ce que le train doit arriver? [dwa]

dull (pain) sourd [soor]
(weather) sombre [sONbr]

dummy (baby's) la tétine [tayteen]

during pendant [pONdON]

dust la poussière [pooss-yair]

dusty poussiéreux [pooss-yayruh]

dustbin la poubelle [poo-bel]

Dutch hollandais [olONday]

duty-free hors taxes [or tax]

duty-free shop la boutique hors taxes

duvet la couette [kwet]

E

each (every) chaque [shak]

how much are they each? combien est-ce qu'ils sont la pièce? [kONb-yAN eskeel sON la p-yess]

ear l'oreille f [oray]

earache: I have earache j'ai mal à l'oreille [jay mal a loray]

early tôt [toh]

early in the morning tôt le matin

I called by earlier je suis passé
tout à l'heure [toot a lurr]
earring la boucle d'oreille
[bookl doray]
east l'est **m** [est]
 in the east à l'est
Easter Pâques [pak]
easy facile [fasseel]
eat manger [moNjay]
 we've already eaten, thanks
 nous avons déjà mangé,
 merci [noo zavoN dayja moNjay]
economy class la classe
 économique [klass
 aykonomeek]
egg l'œuf **m** [urf]
eggplant l'aubergine **f**
 [obairjeen]
either: either ... or ... soit ...
 soit ... [swa]
 either of them soit l'un soit
 l'autre
elastic l'élastique **m** [aylasteek]
elastic band l'élastique **m**
elbow le coude [kood]
electric électrique [aylektreek]
electrical appliances les
 appareils électriques **mpl**
 [aparay]
electric fire le radiateur
 électrique [rad-yaturr]
electrician l'électricien **m**
 [aylektreess-yAN]
electricity l'électricité **f**
 [aylektreesseetay]
elevator l'ascenseur **m** [asoNsurr]
else: something else autre
 chose [ohtr shohz]

somewhere else ailleurs
[i-yurr]

dialogue

would you like anything
else? désirez-vous autre
chose?
no, nothing else, thanks
non, c'est tout, merci
[say too]

e-mail l'e-mail **m**
e-mail address l'adresse
 e-mail **f**
embassy l'ambassade **f**
 [oNbasad]
emergency l'urgence **f**
 [oorjoNss]
 this is an emergency! c'est
 une urgence! [sayt oon]
emergency exit la sortie de
 secours [sortee duh suhkoor]
empty vide [veed]
end la fin [faN]
 (verb) finir [feeneer]
 at the end of the street au
 bout de la rue [o boo duh la roo]
 when does it end? quand
 ce que ça finit? [koNteskuh sa
 feenee]
engaged (toilet, telephone)
 occupé [okoopay]
 (to be married) fiancé [f-yoNsay]
engine (car) le moteur [moturr]
England l'Angleterre **f**
 [oNgluhtair]
English anglais [oNglay]
 I'm English (man/woman) je suis

anglais/anglaise [-ez]
do you speak English?
parlez-vous l'anglais? [parlay
voo]
enjoy: to enjoy oneself
s'amuser [samoozay]

dialogue

> **how did you like the film?**
> comment as-tu trouvé le
> film? [komON atoo troovay]
> **I enjoyed it very much** j'ai
> beaucoup aimé [jay bo-koo
> paymay]

enjoyable très agréable [tray
zagrayabl]
enlargement (of photo)
l'agrandissement **m**
[agroNdeesmON]
enormous énorme [aynorm]
enough assez [assay]
 there's not enough il n'y a
 pas assez [eel nya pa]
 it's not big enough ce n'est
 pas assez grand
 that's enough ça suffit [sa
 soofee]
entrance l'entrée **f** [ONtray]
envelope l'enveloppe **f** [ONvlop]
epileptic épileptique
[aypeelepteek]
equipment (for climbing etc)
l'équipement **m** [aykeepmON]
error l'erreur **f** [air-rurr]
especially spécialement [spays-
yalmON]
essential essentiel [aysONs-yel]

it is essential that ... il est
essentiel que ...
EU (European Union) l'Union
Européenne **f** [oon-yON urropay-
en]
euro l'euro **m** [urro]
Eurocheque l'Eurochèque **m**
[urroshek]
Eurocheque card la carte
Eurochèque [kart]
Europe l'Europe **f** [urrop]
European européen(ne)
[urropay-AN, -en]
even même [mem]
evening le soir [swahr]
 this evening ce soir
 in the evening le soir
evening meal le repas du soir
[ruhpa]
eventually finalement
[feenalmON]
ever jamais [jamay]

dialogue

> **have you ever been to
> Cannes?** est-ce que vous
> êtes déjà allé à Cannes?
> [eskuh voo zet dayja alay a]
> **yes, I was there two years
> ago** oui, j'y suis allé il y a
> deux ans

every chaque [shak]
 every day chaque jour
everyone tout le monde [too
luh mONd]
everything tout [too]
everywhere partout [partoo]

exactly! exactement! [exaktuhmON]

exam l'examen m [examAN]

example l'exemple m [exONpl]
  for example par exemple

excellent excellent [exsaylON]
  excellent! parfait! [parfay]

except sauf [sohf]

excess baggage l'excédent de bagages m [exsaydON duh bagahj]

exchange rate le cours du change [koor dOO shONj]

exciting passionnant [pass-yonON]

excuse me (to get past, to get attention) pardon [par-dON]
  (to say sorry) excusez-moi, pardon

exhaust (pipe) le tuyau d'échappement [twee-o dayshapmON]

exhausted (tired) épuisé [aypweezay]

exhibition l'exposition f [expozeess-yON]

exit la sortie [sortee]
  where's the nearest exit? où se trouve la sortie la plus proche?

expect attendre [atONdr]

expensive cher [shair]

experienced expérimenté [expayreemONtay]

explain expliquer [expleekay]
  can you explain that? pouvez-vous expliquer cela? [poovay-voo]

express (mail) par exprès [express]
  (train) express

extension le poste [posst]
  extension 21, please poste vingt-et-un, s'il vous plaît

extension lead la rallonge [ralONj]

extra: can we have an extra one? pouvons-nous en avoir un/une supplémentaire? [poovON-noo zON avvwahr AN/OOn sOOplaymONtair]
  do you charge extra for that? est-ce qu'il faut payer un supplément pour ça? [eskeel fo pay-ay AN sOOplaymON poor sa]

extraordinary (strange) extraordinaire

extremely extrêmement [extrem-mON]

eye l'œil m [uh-ee]
  will you keep an eye on my suitcase for me? est-ce que vous pouvez surveiller ma valise? [eskuh voo poovay sOOrvay-ay]

eyebrow pencil le crayon à sourcils [soorsee]

eye drops les gouttes pour les yeux [goot poor lay z-juh]

eyeglasses les lunettes [lOOnet]

eyeliner l'eye-liner m

eye make-up remover le démaquillant pour les yeux [daymalee-yON]

eye shadow l'ombre à paupière f [ONbr a pohp-yair]

F

face le visage [veezahj]

factory l'usine **f** [oozeen]

Fahrenheit* fahrenheit [faren-ī-t]

faint s'évanouir [sayvanweer]
she's fainted elle s'est évanouie [el set ayvanwee]
I feel faint je me sens mal [juh muh son]

fair la foire [fwahr]
(adj) juste [joost]

fairly (quite) assez [assay]

fake le faux [fo]

fall l'automne **m** [oton]
see autumn

fall (verb) tomber [tonbay]
she's had a fall elle est tombée [eel ay tonbay]

false faux, **f** fausse [fo, fohss]

family la famille [famee]

famous célèbre [saylebr]

fan (electrical) le ventilateur [vonteelaturr]
(hand held) l'éventail **m** [ayvont-ī]
(sports) le/la fan [fan]

fan belt la courroie du ventilateur [koorwa doo vonteelaturr]

fantastic fantastique [fontasteek]

far loin [lwan]

dialogue

is it far from here? c'est loin d'ici? [say lwan dee-see]

no, not very far non, pas très loin
it's about 20 kilometres c'est à vingt kilomètres environ [onveeron]

fare le prix (du billet) [pree (doo beeyay)]

farm la ferme [fairm]

fashionable à la mode [mod]

fast rapide [rapeed]

fat (person) gros, **f** grosse [gro, gross]
(on meat) le gras [gra]

father le père [pair]

father-in-law le beau-père [bo-pair]

faucet le robinet [robeenay]

fault le défaut [dayfo]
sorry, it was my fault désolé, c'est de ma faute [say duh ma foht]
it's not my fault ce n'est pas de ma faute

faulty (equipment) défectueux [dayfektoo-uh]

favourite préféré [prayfay-ray]

fax le fax
(verb) (person) envoyer un fax à [onvwy-ay]
(document) faxer [faxay]

February février [fayvree-ay]

feel sentir [sonteer]
I feel hot j'ai chaud [jay sho]
I feel unwell je ne me sens pas bien [juh nuh muh son pa b-yan]
I feel like going for a walk j'ai envie d'aller me promener

[jay ONvee]

how are you feeling?
comment te sens-tu/vous
sentez-vous? [komON tuh sON-
too/voo sONtay-voo]

I'm feeling better je me sens
mieux [juh muh sON m-yuh]

felt-tip pen le stylo-feutre
[steelo-furtr]

fence la barrière [baree-air]

fender le pare-chocs [par-shok]

ferry le ferry

festival le festival [festeeval]

fetch aller chercher [alay
shairshay]

I'll fetch him j'irai le chercher
[jeeray]

**will you come and fetch
me later?** est-ce que tu
peux/vous pouvez venir me
chercher plus tard? [eskuh too
puh/voo poovay vuh-neer muh]

feverish fiévreux [fee-evruh]

few: a few quelques-uns,
quelques-unes [kelkuh-zAN,
kelkuh-zoon]

a few days quelques jours

fiancé le fiancé [fee-ONsay]

fiancée la fiancée [fee-ONsay]

field le champ [shON]

fight la bagarre [bagar]

fill remplir [rONpleer]

fill in remplir [rONpleer]

do I have to fill this in? est-
ce que je dois remplir ceci?
[eskuh juh dwa]

fill up remplir [rONpleer]

fill it up, please le plein, s'il
vous plaît [luh plAN]

filling (in cake, sandwich) la
garniture
(in tooth) le plombage [plONbahj]

film (movie) le film [feelm]
(for camera) la pellicule
[peleekool]

dialogue

**do you have this kind of
film?** avez-vous ce genre
de pellicule? [avay-voo]
yes, how many exposures?
oui, avec combien de
poses? [kONb-yAN duh pohz]
36 trente-six

film processing le
développement de la
pellicule [dayv-lopmON]

filter coffee le café filtre [feeltr]

filter papers les filtres **mpl**

filthy crasseux [krassuh]

find trouver [troovay]

I can't find it je n'arrive pas à
le retrouver [juh nareev pa a luh
ruh-]

I've found it je l'ai trouvé [lay
troovay]

find out découvrir [daykoovreer]

**could you find out for
me?** pourriez-vous vous
renseigner pour moi? [pooree-
ay-voo voo rONsen-yay poor mwa]

fine (weather) beau [bo]
(punishment) l'amende **f** [amONd]

dialogues

how are you? comment vas-tu/allez-vous? [komON vatoo/alay-voo]
I'm fine thanks bien, merci [b-yAN]
and you? et toi/vous? [twa]

is that OK? est-ce que ça ira? [eskuh sa eera]
that's fine thanks ça ira très bien comme cela, merci [tray b-yAN kom suhla]

finger le doigt [dwa]
finish terminer [tairmeenay]
  I haven't finished yet je n'ai pas encore terminé [juh nay pa zoNkor tairmeenay]
  when does it finish? à quelle heure est-ce que ça finit? [a kel urr eskuh sa feenee]
fire le feu [fuh]
  can we light a fire here? pouvons-nous faire du feu ici? [poovON-noo fair doo]
  it's on fire il a pris feu [eel a pree]
fire alarm l'avertisseur d'incendie **m** [avairteessurr dANsONdee]
fire brigade les pompiers [pONp-yay]
fire escape la sortie de secours [sortee duh suhkoor]
fire extinguisher l'extincteur **m** [extANkturr]

first premier [pruhm-yay]
  I was first je suis arrivé avant vous [juh sweez areevay avON voo]
  at first tout d'abord [too dabor]
  the first time la première fois [pruhm-yair fwa]
  first on the left la première à gauche
first aid les premiers secours [pruhm-yay suhkoor]
first aid kit la trousse de premiers secours [trooss duh]
first class (compartment etc) de première (classe) [duh pruhm-yair klass]
first floor le premier [pruhm-yay]
  (US) le rez-de-chaussée [rayd-shoh-say]
first name le prénom [praynON]
fish le poisson [pwassON]
fishing village le village de pêcheurs [veelahj duh peshurr]
fishmonger's la poissonnerie [pwassonnuh-ree]
fit (attack) l'attaque **f** [atak]
  (verb) **it doesn't fit me** ce n'est pas la bonne taille [suh nay pa la bon tī]
fitting room la cabine d'essayage [kabeen dessay-ahj]
fix réparer [rayparay]
  can you fix this? pouvez-vous réparer ceci? [poovay-voo]
fizzy gazeux [gazuh]
flag le drapeau [drapo]
flannel le gant de toilette [gON duh twalet]
flash (for camera) le flash

flat (apartment) l'appartement **m**
[apartmON]
  (adj) plat [pla]
  I've got a flat tyre j'ai un
  pneu à plat [jay un pnuh]
flavour l'arôme **m** [arohm]
flea la puce [pOOss]
flight le vol
flight number le numéro de
  vol [nOOmay-ro]
flippers les palmes **fpl** [pal-m]
flood l'inondation **f** [eenONdass-
  yON]
floor (of room) le plancher
  [plONshay]
  (storey) l'étage **m** [aytahj]
  on the floor par terre [tair]
florist le/la fleuriste [flurreest]
flour la farine [fareen]
flower la fleur [flurr]
flu la grippe [greep]
fluent: he speaks fluent French
  il parle couramment le
  français [kooramON]
fly la mouche [moosh]
  (verb) voler [volay]
fly in arriver en avion [arrevay
  en av-yON]
fly out partir en avion [parteer]
fog le brouillard [broo-yar]
foggy: it's foggy il y a du
  brouillard [eelya dOO broo-yar]
folk dancing les danses
  folkloriques [dONss]
folk music la musique
  folklorique [mOOzeek]
follow suivre [sweevr]
  follow me suivez-moi
  [sweevay-mwa]

food la nourriture [nooreetOOr]
food poisoning l'intoxication
  alimentaire **f** [ANtoxeekass-yON
  aleemONtair]
food shop/store le magasin
  d'alimentation [magazAN
  daleemONtass-yON]
foot* le pied [p-yay]
  on foot à pied
football (game) le football
  (ball) le ballon de football
  [balON]
football match le match de
  football
for pour [poor]
  do you have something for
  ...? (headache/diarrhoea etc)
  avez-vous quelque chose
  contre ...? [avay-voo kelkuh-
  shohz kONtr]

dialogues

who's the chocolate
mousse for? la mousse au
chocolat, c'est pour qui?
that's for me c'est pour
moi [mwa]
and this one? et l'autre?
that's for her c'est pour
elle

where do I get the bus for
Gare de l'Est? où dois-je
prendre le bus pour aller
à la gare de l'Est? [oo dwaj
prONdr luh bOOss poor alay]
the bus for Gare de l'Est
leaves from rue de Rivoli

le bus qui va à la gare de l'Est part de la rue de Rivoli

how long have you been here? ça fait combien de temps que vous êtes ici? [sa fay kONb-yAN duh tON kuh voo zet ee-see]

I've been here for two days, how about you? je suis ici depuis deux jours, et vous? [juh swee zee-see duhpwee]

I've been here for a week je suis ici depuis une semaine

forehead le front [frON]

foreign étranger [aytrONjay]

foreigner l'étranger **m**, l'étrangère **f** [aytrONjay, -jair]

forest la forêt [foray]

forget oublier [ooblee-ay]
I forget, I've forgotten j'ai oublié [jay ooblee-ay]

fork (for eating) la fourchette [foorshet]
(in road) l'embranchement **m** [ONbrONshmON]

form (document) le formulaire

formal dress la tenue de soirée [tuhnoo duh swahray]

fortnight la quinzaine [kANzen]

fortunately heureusement [urrurzmON]

forward: could you forward my mail? est-ce que vous pouvez faire suivre mon courrier? [eskuh voo poovay fair sweevr mON koor-yay]

forwarding address l'adresse pour faire suivre le courrier **f**

foundation cream le fond de teint [fON duh tAN]

fountain la fontaine [fONten]

foyer (of hotel) le hall [awl]
(of theatre) le foyer

fracture la fracture [fraktOOr]

France la France [frONss]

free libre [leebr]
(no charge) gratuit [gratwee]
is it free (of charge)? est-ce que c'est gratuit? [eskuh say]

freeway l'autoroute **f** [otoroot]

freezer le congélateur [kONjaylaturr]

French français, **f** française [frONsay, -ez]

French fries les frites **fpl** [freet]

Frenchman le Français [frONsay]

Frenchwoman la Française [frONsez]

frequent fréquent [fraykON]
how frequent is the bus to Marseilles? à quels intervalles y a-t-il un bus pour Marseille? [a kel ANtairval yateel]

fresh frais, **f** fraîche [fray, fresh]

fresh orange l'orange pressée **f**

[oronj pressay]
Friday vendredi [vondruhdee]
fridge le frigo [freego]
fried frit [free]
fried egg l'œuf sur le plat m [urf soor luh pla]
friend l'ami m, l'amie f [amee]
friendly amical [ameekal]
from de [duh]
   when does the next train from Lyons arrive? à quelle heure arrive le prochain train en provenance de Lyon? [on provuhnonss]
   from Monday to Friday du lundi au vendredi [doo ... o]
   from next Thursday à partir de jeudi prochain [a parteer]

dialogue

   where are you from? d'où es-tu/êtes-vous? [doo ay-too/et-voo]
   I'm from Slough je suis de Slough [juh swee]

front l'avant m [avon]
   in front devant [duhvon]
   in front of the hotel devant l'hôtel
   at the front à l'avant
frost le gel [jel]
frozen gelé [juhlay]
frozen food les aliments surgelés [aleemon soorjuhlay]

fruit les fruits mpl [frwee]
fruit juice le jus de fruit [joo duh frwee]
fry frire [freer]
frying pan la poêle [pwal]
full plein [plan]
   it's full of ... c'est plein de ...
   I'm full j'ai trop mangé [jay tro monjay]
full board la pension complète [pons-yon konplet]
fun: it was fun on s'est bien amusé [on say b-yan amoozay]
funny (strange, amusing) drôle
furniture les meubles mpl [murbl]
further plus loin [ploo lwan]
   it's further down the road c'est plus loin sur cette route [root]

dialogue

   how much further is it to Figeac? il y a encore combien de kilomètres pour arriver à Figeac? [eelya onkor konb-yan duh keelometr]
   about 5 kilometres environ cinq kilomètres [onveeron]

fuse le fusible [foozeebl]
   the lights have fused les plombs ont sauté [lay plon on sohtay]
fuse box la boîte à fusibles [bwat]
fuse wire le fusible

future le futur [footoor]
in future à l'avenir [a lavneer]

G

gallon* le gallon [galON]
game (cards etc) le jeu [juh]
(match) la partie [partee]
(meat) le gibier [jeeb-yay]
garage (for fuel) la station
d'essence [stass-yON
dessONss]
(for repairs, parking) le garage
[garahj]
garden le jardin [jardAN]
garlic l'ail **m** [ī]
gas le gaz [ga]
(US) l'essence **f** [essONss]
gas cylinder (camping gas) la
bouteille de gaz [bootay]
gasoline (US) l'essence **f**
[essONss]
gas permeable lenses les
lentilles semi-rigides **fpl**
[lontee suhmee-reejeed]
gas station la station-service
[stass-yON-sairveess]
gate le portail [port-ī]
(at airport) la porte [port]
gay homosexuel
gay bar le bar d'homosexuels
gears les vitesses **fpl** [veetess]
gearbox la boîte de vitesses
[bwat]
gear lever le levier de vitesses
[luhv-yay]
general (adj) général [jaynay-ral]
Geneva Genève [juhnev]

gents (toilet) les toilettes pour
hommes [twalet poor om]
genuine (antique etc)
authentique [otONteek]
German allemand [almON]
German measles la rubéole
[roobay-ol]
Germany l'Allemagne **f** [almañ]
get (fetch) obtenir [obtuhneer]
**will you get me another one,
please?** est-ce que vous
pouvez m'en apporter un
autre, s'il vous plaît? [eskuh
voo poovay mON aportay AN ohtr]
how do I get to ...? pouvez-
vous m'indiquer comment
aller à ...? [poovay-voo
mANdeekay komON talay]
**do you know where I can get
them?** est-ce que vous savez
où je peux en trouver? [eskuh
voo savay oo juh puh zON troovay]

dialogue

can I get you a drink?
puis-je t'offrir/vous offrir
un verre? [pweej tofreer ...]
**no, I'll get this one,
what would you like?**
non, celui-là c'est pour
moi, que voudrais-tu/
voudriez-vous? [suhlwee-la
say poor mwa]
a glass of red wine un
verre de vin rouge

get back (return) rentrer
[rONtray]

get in (arrive) arriver [areevay]
get off descendre [duhsONdr]
  where do I get off? où dois-je descendre? [oo dwaj]
get on (to train etc) monter [mONtay]
get out (of car etc) descendre [duhsONdr]
get up (in the morning, stand up) se lever [suh luhvay]
gift le cadeau [kado]
gift shop la boutique de cadeaux
gin le gin [djeen]
  a gin and tonic, please un gin-tonic, s'il vous plaît
girl la fille [fee]
girlfriend la petite amie [puhteet amee]
give donner [donay]
  can you give me some change? pouvez-vous me donner de la monnaie? [poovay-voo]
  I gave it to him je le lui ai donné [juh luh lwee ay donay]
  will you give this to ...? pouvez-vous donner ceci à ...?

dialogue

how much do you want for this? combien en voulez-vous? [kONb-yAN ON voolay-voo]
100 euros cent euros
I'll give you 90 euros je vous en donne 90 euros [juh voo zON don]

give back rendre [rONdr]
glad content [kONtON]
glass le verre [vair]
  a glass of wine un verre de vin
glasses (spectacles) les lunettes [lOOnet]
gloves les gants **mpl** [gON]
glue la colle [kol]
go aller [alay]
  we'd like to go to the cathedral nous aimerions aller à la cathédrale [noo zemree-ON alay a]
  where are you going? où vas-tu/allez-vous? [oo vatoo/alay voo]
  where does this bus go? où va ce bus?
  let's go! allons-y! [alONzee]
  she's gone (left) elle est partie [partee]
  where has he gone? où est-il allé? [alay]
  I went there last week j'y suis allé la semaine dernière
  hamburger to go hamburger à emporter [ONportay]
go away partir [parteer]
  go away! va t'en!/allez-vous-en! [vatON/alay-voo-zON]
go back (return) retourner [ruhtoornay]
go down descendre [duhsONdr]
  (price) baisser [bessay]
go in entrer [ONtray]
go out (in the evening) sortir [sorteer]
  do you want to go out

tonight? veux-tu/voulez-vous sortir ce soir? [vuh-too/voolay-voo]

go through traverser [travairsay]

go up monter [mONtay]

goat la chèvre [shevr]

goat's cheese le fromage de chèvre [fromahj]

God Dieu [d-yuh]

goggles (ski) les lunettes de ski [lOOnet]

gold l'or m

golf le golf

golf course le terrain de golf [terrAN]

good bon, f bonne [bON, bon]

good! bien! [b-yAN]

it's no good ça ne va pas [sa nuh va pa]

goodbye au revoir [o ruh-vwa]

good evening bonsoir [bON-swa]

Good Friday le Vendredi Saint [vONdruhdee SAN]

good morning bonjour [bON-joor]

good night bonne nuit [bon nwee]

goose l'oie f [wa]

got: we've got to leave il faut que nous partions [eel fo kuh]

I've got to ... il faut que je ...

have you got any ...? est-ce que tu as/vous avez des/du ...? [eskuh too a/voo zavay ...]

government le gouvernement [goovairnuhmON]

gradually peu à peu [puh a puh]

grammar la grammaire

gram(me) le gramme

granddaughter la petite-fille [puhteet-fee]

grandfather le grand-père [grON-pair]

grandmother la grand-mère [grON-mair]

grandson le petit-fils [puhtee-feess]

grapefruit le pamplemousse [pONpluh-mooss]

grapefruit juice le jus de pamplemousse [joo]

grapes le raisin [rez-AN]

grass l'herbe f [airb]

grateful reconnaissant [ruhkonessON]

gravy la sauce au jus de viande [sohss o joo duh vee-ONd]

great (excellent) fantastique [fONtasteek]

that's great! c'est formidable! [say formee-dabl]

a great success un grand succès [grON sook-say]

Great Britain la Grande-Bretagne [grOnd-bruhtañ]

Greece la Grèce [gress]

greedy gourmand [goormON]

Greek grec

green vert [vair]

green card (car insurance) la carte verte [kart vairt]

greengrocer's le marchand de légumes [marshON duh laygOOm]

grey gris [gree]

grill le grill

grilled grillé [gree-yay]

grocer's l'épicerie f [aypeesree]

ground le sol
  on the ground par terre [tair]
ground floor le rez-de-chaussée [rayd-shoh-say]
group le groupe [groop]
guarantee la garantie [garONtee]
  is it guaranteed? y a-t-il une garantie? [yateel]
guest l'invité(e) [ANveetay]
guesthouse la pension [pONs-yON]
guide le guide [geed]
guidebook le guide
guided tour la visite guidée [veezeet geeday]
guitar la guitare [geetar]
gum (in mouth) la gencive [jONseev]
gun le fusil [fOOzee]
gym le gymnase [jeemnaz]

H

hair les cheveux **mpl** [shuhvuh]
hairbrush la brosse à cheveux [bross]
haircut la coupe de cheveux [koop]
hairdresser le coiffeur [kwafurr]
hairdryer le sèche-cheveux [sesh-shuhvuh]
hair gel le gel (pour les cheveux) [jel]
hairgrips les pinces à cheveux **fpl** [pANss]
hair spray la laque [lak]

half* la moitié [mwatee-ay]
half an hour une demi-heure [duhmee-urr]
half a litre un demi-litre
  about half that la moitié
half board la demi-pension [duhmee-pONs-yON]
half-bottle la demi bouteille [bootay]
half fare le demi-tarif [tareef]
half price moitié prix [mwatee-ay pree]
ham le jambon [jONbON]
hamburger le hamburger [ONboorgair]
hammer le marteau [marto]
hand la main [mAN]
handbag le sac à main
handbrake le frein à main [frAN]
handkerchief le mouchoir [mooshwahr]
handle la poignée [pwAN-yay]
hand luggage les bagages à main **mpl** [bagahj]
hang-gliding le deltaplane [-plahn]
hangover la gueule de bois [gurl duh bwa]
  I've got a hangover j'ai la gueule de bois
happen arriver [areevay]
  what's happening? qu'est-ce qui se passe? [kes-kee suh pass]
  what has happened? qu'est-ce qui s'est passé? [say passay]
happy heureux [ur-ruh]
  I'm not happy about this ça

ne me plaît pas [sa nuh muh play pa]
harbour le port [por]
hard dur [door]
(difficult) difficile [deefeesseel]
hard-boiled egg l'œuf dur m [urf]
hard lenses les lentilles dures fpl [lONtee door]
hardly à peine [a pen]
hardly ever presque jamais [presk jamay]
hardware shop la quincaillerie [kAN-ky-ree]
hat le chapeau [shapo]
hate détester [daytestay]
have* avoir [avwahr]
can I have a ...? j'aimerais ... [jemray]
do you have ...? as-tu/avez-vous ...? [atoo/avay-voo]
what'll you have? qu'est-ce que tu prends/vous prenez? [keskuh too prON/voo pruhnay]
I have to leave now je dois partir maintenant [juh dwa]
do I have to ...? est-ce que je dois ...? [eskuh]
can we have some ...? est-ce que nous pouvons avoir du ...?
we don't have any left nous n'en avons plus [noo nON avON ploo]
hayfever le rhume des foins [room day fwAN]
hazelnuts les noisettes fpl [nwazet]
he* il [eel]

head la tête [tet]
headache le mal de tête
headlights les phares mpl [far]
headphones les écouteurs mpl [aykooturr]
health food shop le magasin de produits diététiques m [magazAN duh prodwee dee-aytayteek]
healthy (food, climate) bon pour la santé [sONtay]
(person) bien portant [b-yAN portON]
hear entendre [ONtONdr]

dialogue

can you hear me? m'entendez-vous? [mONtONday-voo]
I can't hear you, could you repeat that? je ne vous entends pas, pouvez-vous répéter? [juh nuh voo zONtON pa poovay-voo raypaytay]

hearing aid l'audiophone m [odeeo-fon]
heart le cœur [kurr]
heart attack la crise cardiaque [kreez kard-yak]
heat la chaleur [shalurr]
heater (in room) le radiateur [rad-yaturr]
(in car) le chauffage [shohfahj]
heating le chauffage
heavy lourd [loor]
heel le talon [talON]
could you heel these?

pouvez-vous refaire les talons? [poovay-voo ruhfair]

heelbar le talon-minute [talON-meenoot]

height (of person) la taille [tï]
(of mountain) l'altitude **f**

helicopter l'hélicoptère **m** [ayleekoptair]

hello bonjour [bONjoor]
(in the evening) bonsoir [bONswahr]
(answer on phone) allô

helmet (for motorcycle) le casque [kask]

help l'aide **f** [ed]
(verb) aider [ayday]
help! au secours! [o suhkoor]
can you help me? est-ce que vous pouvez m'aider? [eskuh voo poovay]
thank you very much for your help merci de votre aide

helpful (person) serviable [sairvee-abl]
(objects) utile [ooteel]

hepatitis l'hépatite **f** [aypateet]

her*: I haven't seen her je ne l'ai pas vue
to her à elle [el]
for/with her pour/avec elle
that's her c'est elle
her towel sa serviette

herbal tea la tisane [teezahn]

herbs les fines herbes **fpl** [feen zairb]

here ici [ee-see]
here is/are ... voici ... [vwa-see]
here you are (offering) voilà [vwala]

hers*: that's hers c'est à elle [set a el]

hey! hé! [hay]

hi! (hello) salut! [saloo]

hide cacher [kashay]

high haut [o]

highchair la chaise haute [shez oht]

highway l'autoroute **f** [otoroot]

hill la colline [koleen]

him*: I haven't seen him je ne l'ai pas vu
to him à lui [lwee]
with him avec lui
for him pour lui
that's him c'est lui

hip la hanche [ONsh]

hire: for hire à louer [loo-ay]
(verb) louer
where can I hire a bike? où y a-t-il des vélos à louer? [oo yateel]

his*: it's his car c'est sa voiture
it's his bike c'est son vélo [sON]
that's his c'est à lui [set a lwee]

hit frapper [frapay]

hitch-hike faire de l'autostop [fair duh lotostop]

hobby le hobby [obbee]

hockey le hockey [ockee]

hold tenir [tuhneer]

hole le trou [troo]

holiday les vacances **fpl** [vakONss]
on holiday en vacances [ON]

Holland la Hollande [ollONd]

home la maison [mezzON]

at home (in my house etc) chez moi [shay mwa]
(in my country) dans mon pays [dON mON payee]
we go home tomorrow nous rentrons demain [rONtrON duhmAN]
honest honnête [onnet]
honey le miel [mee-el]
honeymoon la lune de miel [lOOn]
hood (US) le capot [kapo]
hope espérer [espayray]
I hope so j'espère que oui [jespair kuh wee]
I hope not j'espère que non
hopefully: hopefully he'll arrive soon espérons qu'il arrive bientôt [espairON]
horn (of car) le klaxon
horrible horrible [oreebl]
horse le cheval [shuhval]
horse riding l'équitation f [aykeetass-yON]
hospital l'hôpital m [opee-tal]
hospitality l'hospitalité f [-eetay]
thank you for your hospitality merci de votre hospitalité
hot chaud [sho]
(spicy) épicé [aypeessay]
I'm hot j'ai chaud [jay]
it's hot today il fait chaud aujourd'hui [eel fay]
hotel l'hôtel m [otel]
hotel room: in my hotel room dans ma chambre d'hôtel [shONbr]
hour l'heure f [urr]

house la maison [mezzON]
house wine la cuvée du patron [kOOvay dOO]
hovercraft l'aéroglisseur m [a-ayro-gleessurr]
how comment [komON]
how many? combien? [kONb-yAN]
how do you do? enchanté! [ONshONtay]

dialogues

how are you? comment vas-tu/allez-vous? [komON va-tOO/alay-voo]
fine, thanks, and you? bien, merci, et toi/vous? [twa]

how much is it? c'est combien?
... euros ... euros
I'll take it je le prends [juh luh prON]

humid humide [OOmeed]
humour l'humour m [OOmoor]
hungry: I'm hungry j'ai faim [jay fAN]
are you hungry? est-ce que tu as/vous avez faim? [eskuh too a/voo zavay]
hurry se dépêcher [suh daypeshay]
I'm in a hurry je suis pressé [juh swee pressay]
there's no hurry ce n'est pas pressé [suh nay pa]

English → French

hurry up! dépêche-toi!/
dépêchez-vous! [daypesh-twa/
daypeshay-voo]
hurt faire mal
it really hurts ça fait vraiment
mal [sa fay vraymON]
husband le mari [maree]
hydrofoil l'hydrofoil m
[eedro-]
hypermarket l'hypermarché m
[eepairmarshay]

I

I je [juh]
ice la glace [glass]
with ice avec des glaçons
[glassON]
no ice, thanks pas de glaçons,
merci
ice cream la glace [glass]
ice-cream cone le cornet de
glace [kornay]
iced coffee le café glacé
[glassay]
ice lolly l'esquimau m [eskeemo]
ice rink la patinoire
[pateenwahr]
ice skates les patins à glace
mpl [patAN a glass]
idea l'idée f [eeday]
idiot l'idiot m [eedee-o]
if si [see]
ignition l'allumage m [alOOmahj]
ill malade [malad]
I feel ill je ne me sens pas bien
[juh nuh muh sON pa b-yAN]
illness la maladie [maladee]

imitation (leather etc) l'imitation
f [eemeetass-yON]
immediately immédiatement
[eemaydee-atmON], tout de
suite [toot sweet]
important important [ANportON]
it's very important c'est très
important [say trayz]
it's not important ça ne fait
rien [sa nuh fay ree-AN]
impossible impossible [ANposs-
eebl]
impressive impressionnant
[ANpress-yonON]
improve améliorer
[amayleeoray]
I want to improve my French
je veux améliorer mon
français [juh vuh]
in: it's in the centre c'est au
centre [o sONtr]
in my car dans ma voiture
[dON]
in Dijon à Dijon
in two days from now d'ici
deux jours
in May en mai [ON]
in English en anglais
in French en français
is he in? il est là? [eel ay la]
in five minutes dans cinq
minutes
inch* le pouce [pooss]
include inclure [ANkloor]
does that include meals?
est-ce que les repas sont
compris? [eskuh lay ruhpa sON
kONpree]
is that included? est-ce que

71

c'est compris?

inconvenient inopportun [eenoportAN]

incredible (very good, amazing) incroyable [ANkrwy-abl]

Indian indien, f indienne [ANdee-AN, -en]

indicator (on car) le clignotant [kleen-yotON]

indigestion l'indigestion f [ANdeejest-yON]

indoor pool la piscine couverte [peesseen koovairt]

indoors à l'intérieur [lANtay-ree-urr]

inexpensive bon marché [bON marshay]

infection l'infection f [ANfex-yON]

infectious contagieux [kONtahj-yuh]

inflammation l'inflammation f [ANflamass-yON]

informal simple [sAN-pl]

information les renseignements mpl [rONsen-yuhmON]

do you have any information about ...? est-ce que vous avez des renseignements sur ...? [eskuh voo zavay]

information desk les renseignements [rONsen-yuhmON]

injection la piqûre [pee-kOOr]

injured blessé [blessay]

she's been injured elle est blessée

in-laws les beaux-parents [bo-parON]

inner tube la chambre à air [shONbr]

innocent innocent [eenosON]

insect l'insecte m [ANsekt]

insect bite la piqûre d'insecte [peekOOr]

do you have anything for insect bites? est-ce que vous avez quelque chose contre les piqûres d'insecte? [eskuh voo zavay kelkuh shohz]

insect repellent la crème anti-insecte [krem ONtee-ANsekt]

inside à l'intérieur [lANtayree-urr]

inside the hotel dans l'hôtel [dON]

let's sit inside allons nous asseoir à l'intérieur

insist insister [ANseestay]

I insist j'insiste [jANseest]

insomnia l'insomnie f [ANsomnee]

instant coffee le café soluble [solOObl]

instead à la place [plass]

give me that one instead donnez-moi celui-ci à la place [donay-mwa suhlwee-see]

instead of ... au lieu de ... [o l-yuh duh]

insulin l'insuline f [ANsOOleen]

insurance l'assurance f [assOOrONss]

intelligent intelligent [ANtayleejON]

interested: I'm interested in ... je m'intéresse à ... [mANtayress]

interesting intéressant [ANtayressON]

  that's very interesting c'est très intéressant

international international [ANtairnass-yonal]

interpret faire l'interprète [fair lANtairpret]

interpreter l'interprète **mf** [ANtairpret]

intersection le carrefour [karfoor]

interval (at theatre) l'entracte **m** [ONtrakt]

into dans [dON]

  I'm not into ... je n'aime pas ... [juh nem pa]

introduce présenter [prayzONtay]

  may I introduce ...? puis-je vous présenter ...? [pweej voo]

invitation l'invitation **f** [ANveetass-yON]

invite inviter [ANveetay]

Ireland l'Irlande **f** [eerlONd]

Irish irlandais [eerlONday]

  I'm Irish (man/woman) je suis irlandais/irlandaise [-ez]

iron (for ironing) le fer à repasser [fair a ruh-passay]

  can you iron these for me? pouvez-vous me repasser ces vêtements? [vetmON]

is* est [ay]

island l'île **f** [eel]

it* ça [sa]; il [eel]; elle [el]

  it is ... c'est ... [say]

  is it ...? est-ce ...? [ess]

  where is it? où est-ce que

c'est? [weskuh say]

  it's him c'est lui

  it was ... c'était ... [saytay]

Italian italien [eetalyAN]

Italy l'Italie **f** [eetalee]

itch: it itches ça me démange [sa muh daymONj]

J

jack (for car) le cric [kreek]

jacket la veste [vest]

jar le pot [po]

jam la confiture [kONfeetOOr]

jammed: it's jammed c'est coincé [say kwANsay]

January janvier [jONvee-ay]

jaw la mâchoire [mashwahr]

jazz le jazz

jealous jaloux [jaloo]

jeans le jean

jellyfish la méduse [maydOOz]

jersey le tricot [treeko]

jetty la jetée [juhtay]

Jewish juif, **f** juive [jweef, jweev]

jeweller's la bijouterie [beejootuhree]

jewellery les bijoux [beejoo]

job le travail [trav-ī]

jogging le jogging

  to go jogging faire du jogging [fair]

joke la plaisanterie [plezzONtree]

journey le voyage [vwy-ahj]

  have a good journey! bon voyage!

jug le pot [po]

a jug of water une carafe d'eau [do]
juice le jus [joo]
July juillet [jwee-yay]
jump sauter [sohtay]
jumper le pull [pool]
jump leads les câbles de démarrage [kahbl duh daymarahj]
junction le croisement [krwazmON]
June juin [jwAN]
just (only) seul [surl]
   just two seulement deux [surlmON]
   just for me seulement pour moi [poor mwa]
   just here juste ici [joost ee-see]
   not just now pas maintenant [pa]
   we've just arrived nous venons d'arriver [noo vuhnON dareevay]

K

keep garder [garday]
   keep the change gardez la monnaie [garday la monay]
   can I keep it? est-ce que je peux le garder? [eskuh juh puh]
   please keep it gardez-le
ketchup le ketchup
kettle la bouilloire [boo-ee-wahr]
key la clé [klay]
   the key for room 201, please la clé de la chambre deux

cent un, s'il vous plaît
key ring le porte-clé [port-klay]
kidneys (in body) les reins mpl [rAN]
   (food) les rognons mpl [roN-yON]
kill tuer [too-ay]
kilo* le kilo
kilometre* le kilomètre [keelo-metr]
   how many kilometres is it to ...? combien y a-t-il de kilomètres pour aller à ...? [kONb-yAN yateel]
kind aimable [em-abl]
   that's very kind c'est très aimable

dialogue

which kind do you want? de quel type voulez-vous?
I want this/that kind c'est de ce type que je veux

king le roi [rwa]
kiosk le kiosque
kiss le baiser [bezzay]
   (verb) embrasser [ONbrassay]
kitchen la cuisine [kweezeen]
kitchenette le coin-cuisine [kwAN-kweezeen]
Kleenex® les kleenex mpl
knee le genou [juh-noo]
knickers le slip [sleep]
knife le couteau [kooto]
knitwear les tricots [treeko]
knock frapper [frapay]
knock down renverser

[r0Nvairsay]

he's been knocked down il s'est fait renverser [eel say fay r0Nvairsay]

knock over renverser [r0Nvairsay]

know (somebody, a place) connaître [konetr]
(something) savoir [savwahr]

I don't know je ne sais pas [juh nuh say pa]

I didn't know that je ne savais pas [savay]

do you know where I can find ...? savez-vous où je peux trouver ...? [savay-voo]

L

label l'étiquette **f** [ayteeket]

ladies' (room) les toilettes (pour dames) [twalet poor dam]

ladies' wear les vêtements pour femmes [vetmON poor fam]

lady la dame [dam]

lager la bière [bee-air]

lake le lac

lamb l'agneau **m** [an-yo]

lamp la lampe [lONp]

lane (on motorway) la voie [vwa]
(small road) le chemin [shuhmAN]

language la langue [lONg]

language course le cours de langue [koor duh lONg]

large grand [grON]

last dernier [dairn-yay]

last week la semaine dernière

[suhmen dairn-yair]

last Friday vendredi dernier

last night hier soir [yair swahr]

what time is the last train to Nancy? à quelle heure part le dernier train pour Nancy? [kel urr par]

late tard [tar]

sorry I'm late je suis désolé d'être en retard [juh swee dayzolay detr ON ruhtar]

the train was very late le train avait beaucoup de retard [avay bo-koo duh]

we'll be late nous allons arriver en retard [noo zalON areevay]

it's getting late il se fait tard [eel suh fay]

later plus tard [plOO tar]

I'll come back later je reviendrai plus tard [juh ruhvee-ANdray]

see you later à tout à l'heure [a toota lurr]

later on plus tard

latest dernier [dairn-yay]

by Wednesday at the latest d'ici mercredi au plus tard [o plOO tar]

laugh rire [reer]

launderette/ laundromat la laverie automatique [lavree otomateek]

laundry (clothes) le linge sale [lANj sal]
(place) la blanchisserie [blONsheesree]

lavatory les toilettes [twalet]

law la loi [lwa]
lawn la pelouse [puhlooz]
lawyer l'avocat **m** [avoka]
laxative le laxatif [laxateef]
lazy paresseux [paressuh]
lead (electrical) le fil
(électrique) [feel aylektreek]
(verb) mener à [muhnay]
where does this lead to? où
cette route mène-t-elle? [oo
set root mentel]
leaf la feuille [fuh-ee]
leaflet le dépliant [daypleeON]
leak la fuite [fweet]
(verb) fuir [fweer]
the roof leaks il y a une fuite
dans le toit [eelya]
learn apprendre [aproNdr]
least: **not in the least** pas du
tout [pa doo too]
at least au moins [o mwAN]
leather le cuir [kweer]
leave (go away) partir [parteer]
I am leaving tomorrow je pars
demain [juh par]
he left yesterday il est parti
hier [eel ay partee]
**when does the bus for
Avignon leave?** à quelle
heure part le bus pour
Avignon? [par]
may I leave this here? puis-je
laisser ceci ici? [pweej lessay
suhsee ee-see]
I left my coat in the bar j'ai
oublié ma veste au bar [jay
ooblee-ay]
leeks les poireaux **mpl** [pwahro]
left la gauche [gohsh]

on the left à gauche
to the left sur la gauche [soor]
turn left tournez à gauche
there's none left il n'y en a
plus [eel n-yON a ploo]
left-handed gaucher [gohshay]
left luggage (office) la
consigne [kONseeñ]
leg la jambe [jONb]
lemon le citron [seetrON]
lemonade la limonade
[leemonad]
lemon tea le thé citron [tay
seetrON]
lend prêter [pretay]
will you lend me your ...?
pourrais-tu/pourriez-vous
me prêter ton/votre ...?
[pooray-too/pooree-ay-voo muh]
lens (of camera) l'objectif **m**
[objekteef]
lesbian la lesbienne
less moins [mwAN]
less than moins que
less expensive moins cher
lesson la leçon [luhsON]
let laisser [lessay]
will you let me know?
pouvez-vous me le faire
savoir? [poovay-voo muh luh fair
savwahr]
I'll let you know je te/vous
préviendrai [juh tuh/voo prayvee-
ANdray]
let's go for something to eat
allons manger un morceau
[alON mONjay]
let off laisser descendre [lessay
duhsONdr]

will you let me off at ...?
pouvez-vous me laisser
descendre à ..., s'il vous
plaît? [poovay-voo]

letter la lettre [letr]

**do you have any letters
for me?** est-ce qu'il y a du
courrier pour moi? [eskeel ya
doo kooree-ay poor mwa]

letterbox la boite à lettres
[bwat a letr]

lettuce la laitue [letoo]

lever le levier [luhv-yay]

library la bibliothèque

licence le permis [pairmee]

lid le couvercle [koovairkl]

lie (tell untruth) mentir [moNteer]

lie down s'étendre [saytoNdr]

life la vie [vee]

lifebelt la bouée de sauvetage
[boo-ay duh sohvtahj]

lifeguard le maître nageur
[metr nahjurr]

life jacket le gilet de sauvetage
[jeelay duh sohvtahj]

lift (in building) l'ascenseur **m**
[asoNsurr]

could you give me a lift?
pouvez-vous m'emmener?
[poovay-voo moNmuhnay]

would you like a lift? est-ce
que je peux vous déposer
quelque part? [eskuh juh puh
voo daypohzay kelkuh par]

lift pass le forfait de remonte-
pente [forfay duh ruhmoNt-poNt]

a daily/weekly lift pass un
forfait de remonte-pente
d'une journée/d'une

semaine

light la lumière [loom-yair]
(not heavy) léger [lay-jay]

do you have a light? avez-
vous du feu? [avay-voo doo fuh]

light green vert clair

light bulb l'ampoule **f** [oNpool]

lighter (cigarette) le briquet
[breekay]

lightning les éclairs [ayklair]

like aimer [aymay]

I like it ça me plaît [sah muh
play]

I like going for walks j'aime
bien aller me promener [jem
b-yAN]

I like you tu me plais [too muh
play]

I don't like it ça ne me plaît
pas

do you like ...? est-ce que tu
aimes/vous aimez ...? [too
em/voo zaymay]

I'd like a beer je voudrais une
bière [juh voodray]

I'd like to go swimming
j'aimerais nager [jemray]

would you like a drink?
veux-tu/voulez-vous boire
quelque chose? [vuh-too/voolay-
voo]

**would you like to go for a
walk?** veux-tu/voulez-vous
aller faire une promenade?

what's it like? comment est-
ce? [komoN ess]

one like this un comme ça
[kom]

lime le citron vert [seetroN vair]

Li

77

lime cordial le jus de citron vert [jOO]

line la ligne [leeñ]

could you give me an outside line? pouvez-vous me donner une ligne extérieure? [poovay-voo]

lip la lèvre [levr]

lip salve la pommade pour les lèvres [pomahd]

lipstick le rouge à lèvres [rooj]

liqueur la liqueur [leekurr]

listen écouter [aykootay]

litre* le litre [leetr]

a litre of white wine un litre de vin blanc

little petit [puhtee]

just a little, thanks un tout petit peu, s'il vous plaît [AN too puhtee puh]

a little milk un peu de lait

a little bit more un petit peu plus [plOOss]

live vivre [veevr]

we live together nous vivons ensemble [noo veevON zONsONbl]

dialogue

where do you live? où est-ce que tu habites/vous habitez? [weskuh tOO abeet/voo zabeetay]
I live in London je vis à Londres [vee]

lively vivant [veevON]

liver le foie [fwa]

loaf le pain [pAN]

lobby (in hotel) le hall [al]

lobster la langouste [lONgoost]

local local

a local wine/restaurant un vin de la région/un restaurant dans le quartier [duh la rayjON/... dON luh kart-yay]

lock la serrure [sair-rOOr] (verb) fermer à clé [fairmay a klay]

it's locked c'est fermé à clé [fairmay]

lock in enfermer à clé [ONfairmay]

lock out enfermer dehors [duh-or]

I've locked myself out je me suis enfermé dehors [juh muh swee zONfairmay]

locker (for luggage etc) le casier [kaz-yay]

lollipop la sucette [sOOsset]

London Londres [lONdr]

long long, f longue [lON, lON-g]

how long will it take to fix it? combien de temps est-ce que ça prendra pour le réparer? [kONb-yAN duh tON]

how long does it take? combien de temps est-ce que ça prend? [eskuh sa prON]

a long time longtemps [lONtON]

one day/two days longer un jour/deux jours en plus [ON plOOss]

long-distance call l'appel longue-distance **m**

loo les toilettes [twalet]

look regarder [ruhgarday]

I'm just looking, thanks je ne fais que regarder, merci [juh nuh fay kuh]

you don't look well tu n'as pas l'air dans ton assiette [too na pa lair dON tON ass-yet]

look out! attention! [atONs-yON]

can I have a look? puis-je regarder? [pweej]

look after garder [garday]

look at regarder [ruhgarday]

look for chercher [shairshay]

I'm looking for ... je cherche ... [juh shairsh]

look forward to: I'm looking forward to it je m'en réjouis à l'avance [juh mON rayjwee a lavONss]

loose (handle etc) lâche [lahsh]

lorry le camion [kam-yON]

lose perdre [pairdr]

I've lost my way je suis perdu [juh swee pairdoo]

I'm lost, I want to get to ... je suis perdu, je voudrais aller à ...

I've lost my (hand)bag j'ai perdu mon sac à main [jay]

lost property (office) les objets trouvés [objay troovay]

lot: a lot, lots beaucoup [bo-koo]

not a lot pas beaucoup [pa]

a lot of people beaucoup de monde

a lot bigger beaucoup plus gros

I like it a lot ça me plaît beaucoup

lotion la lotion [lohss-yON]

loud fort [for]

lounge le salon (in airport) la salle d'embarquement [sal dONbarkmON]

love l'amour **m** [amoor] (verb) aimer [aymay]

I love Corsica j'aime la Corse [jem]

lovely (view, present etc) ravissant [ravee-sON] (meal) délicieux [dayleess-yuh] (weather) magnifique [mAN-yeefeek]

low bas [ba]

luck la chance [shONss]

good luck! bonne chance! [bon]

luggage les bagages **mpl** [bagahj]

luggage trolley le chariot à bagages [sharee-o]

lump (on body) la grosseur [grossurr]

lunch le déjeuner [dayjuhnay]

lungs les poumons **mpl** [poomON]

Luxembourg le Luxembourg [lOOxONboor]

luxurious luxueux [lOOxOO-uh]

luxury le luxe [lOOx]

M

machine la machine
mad (insane) fou, f folle [foo, fol]
(angry) furieux [fooree-uh]
magazine le magazine
maid (in hotel) la femme de
chambre [fam duh shoNbr]
maiden name le nom de jeune
fille [noN duh jurn fee]
mail le courrier [kooree-ay]
(verb) poster [posstay]
is there any mail for me? est-
ce qu'il y a du courrier pour
moi? [eskeel ya doo]
mailbox la boite à lettres [bwat
a letr]
main principal [praNseepal]
main course le plat principal
[pla]
main post office la poste
principale [posst]
main road (in town) la rue
principale [roo]
(in country) la grande route
[groNd root]
mains switch le disjoncteur
[deesjoNkturr]
make (brand name) la marque
[mark]
(verb) faire [fair]
I make it 500 francs d'après
mes calculs, ça fait cinq cents
francs [dapray may kalkool sa fay]
what is it made of? en quoi
est-ce? [oN kwa ess]
make-up le maquillage
[makee-ahj]

man l'homme m [om]
manager le patron [pa-troN]
can I see the manager? puis-
je parler au patron? [pweej
parlay o]
manageress la directrice
[deerektreess]
manual (car) la voiture à
embrayage manuel [vwatoor a
oNbrī-ahj monooel]
many beaucoup [bo-koo]
not many pas beaucoup [pa]
map (of city) le plan [ploN]
(road map, geographical) la carte
[kart]
March mars [marss]
margarine la margarine
[marghareen]
market le marché [marshay]
marmalade la confiture
d'oranges [koNfeetoor doroNj]
married: I'm married je suis
marié [juh swee maree-ay]
are you married? êtes-vous
marié? [et-voo]
mascara le mascara
match (football etc) le match
matches les allumettes fpl
[aloomet]
material (fabric) le tissu [teessoo]
matter: it doesn't matter ça ne
fait rien [sa nuh fay ree-aN]
what's the matter? qu'est-ce
qu'il y a? [keskeel ya]
mattress le matelas [matla]
May mai [may]
may: may I have another one?
puis-je en avoir un autre?
[pweej]

may I come in? puis-je entrer?

may I see it? puis-je le/la voir?

may I sit here? est-ce que je peux m'asseoir ici? [eskuh juh puh masswahr]

maybe peut-être [puht-etr]

mayonnaise la mayonnaise

me* moi [mwa]

that's for me c'est pour moi

send it to me envoyez-le moi

me too moi aussi [o-see]

meal le repas [ruhpa]

dialogue

did you enjoy your meal? est-ce que vous avez fait un bon repas? [eskuh voo zavay fay tAN bON]

it was excellent, thank you c'était excellent, merci [saytay]

mean signifier [seen-yeefee-ay]

what do you mean? qu'est-ce que vous voulez dire? [keskuh-voo voolay deer]

dialogue

what does this word mean? que signifie ce mot? [kuh seen-yeefee suh mo]

it means ... in English ça veut dire ... en anglais [sa vuh deer]

measles la rougeole [roojol]

meat la viande [vee0Nd]

mechanic le mécanicien [maykaneess-yAN]

medicine le médicament [maydeekamoN]

Mediterranean la Méditerranée [maydeetairanay]

medium (size) moyen [mwy-AN]

medium-dry (wine) demi-sec [duhmee-sek]

medium-rare (steak) à point [pwAN]

medium-sized moyen [mwy-AN]

meet rencontrer [rONkONtray]

nice to meet you enchanté [ONshONtay]

where shall I meet you? où nous retrouverons-nous? [oo noo ruhtroovuhrON-noo]

meeting la réunion [rayoon-yON]

meeting place le point de rendez-vous [pwAN duh]

melon le melon [muhlON]

men les hommes [om]

mend réparer [rayparay]

could you mend this for me? pouvez-vous me réparer ça? [poovay-voo]

menswear les vêtements pour hommes [vetmON poor om]

mention mentionner [mONs-yONay]

don't mention it je vous en prie [juh voo zON pree]

menu la carte [kart]

may I see the menu, please? puis-je voir la carte, s'il vous plaît? [pweej vwahr] see **Menu Reader** page 206

message le message [messahj]

are there any messages for me? est-ce que quelqu'un a laissé un message pour moi? [eskuh kelkAN a lessay]

I want to leave a message for ... je voudrais laisser un message pour ... [juh voodray]

metal le métal [may-tal]

metre* le mètre [metr]

microwave le micro-ondes [meekro-ONd]

midday midi [meedee]

at midday à midi

middle: in the middle au milieu [o meel-yuh]

in the middle of the night au milieu de la nuit

the middle one celui du milieu

midnight minuit [meenwee]

at midnight à minuit

might: I might want to stay another day il est possible que je reste encore un jour [eel ay posseebl kuh]

I might not leave tomorrow il est possible que je ne parte pas demain

migraine la migraine [meegren]

mild (taste, weather) doux, f douce [doo, dooss]

mile* le mille [meel]

milk le lait [lay]

milkshake le milk-shake

millimetre* le millimètre [meelee-metr]

minced meat la viande hachée [veeONd ashay]

mind: never mind tant pis [tON pee]

I've changed my mind j'ai changé d'avis [jay shONjay davee]

dialogue

do you mind if I open the window? ça vous dérange si j'ouvre la fenêtre? [sa voo dayrONj see]

no, I don't mind non, ça ne me dérange pas [sa nuh muh]

mine*: it's mine c'est à moi [set a mwa]

mineral water l'eau minérale f [o meenayral]

mint-flavoured à la menthe [mONt]

mint cordial la menthe à l'eau [a lo]

mints (sweets) les bonbons à la menthe **mpl**

minute la minute [meenoot]

in a minute dans un instant [dON zan ANstON]

just a minute un instant

mirror le mirroir [meer-wahr]

Miss Mademoiselle [mad-mwazel]

miss rater [ratay]

I missed the bus j'ai raté le bus [jay ratay]

missing: to be missing manquer [mONkay]

one of my ... is missing il me manque un de mes ... [eel muh mOnk]

there's a suitcase missing il manque une valise

mist la brume [brOOm]

mistake l'erreur **f** [air-rurr]

I think there's a mistake je crois qu'il y a une erreur [juh krwa keelya]

sorry, I've made a mistake désolé, j'ai fait une erreur

misunderstanding le malentendu [malONtONdOO]

mix-up: sorry, there's been a mix-up désolé, il y a une erreur [dayzolay eelya OOn air-rurr]

mobile le (téléphone) portable [portahbl]

modern moderne [modairn]

modern art gallery la galerie d'art moderne [dar]

moisturizer la crème hydratante [krem eedratONt]

moment: I'll be back in a moment je reviens dans un instant [juh ruhv-yAN dON zAN ANstON]

Monday lundi [lANdee]

money l'argent **m** [arjON]

month le mois [mwa]

monument le monument [monOOmON]

moon la lune [lOOn]

moped la mobylette [mobeelet]

more* plus [plOOss]

can I have some more water, please? est-ce que je peux avoir encore un peu d'eau, s'il vous plaît? [eksuh juh puh avwahr ONkor]

more expensive/interesting plus cher/intéressant [plOO]

more than 50 plus de cinquante

more than that plus que ça [plOOss kuh sa]

a lot more beaucoup plus [bo-kOO]

dialogue

would you like some more? est-ce que vous en voulez encore? [eskuh voo zON voolay]

no, no more for me, thanks non, pas pour moi, merci

how about you? et vous?

I don't want any more, thanks je n'en veux plus, merci

morning le matin [matAN]

this morning ce matin

in the morning le matin

Moroccan marocain [marokAN]

Morocco le Maroc

mosquito le moustique [moosteek]

mosquito repellent le produit anti-moustiques [prodwee ONtee-]

most: I like that most of all c'est ce que je préfère [say suh kuh juh prayfair]

most of the time la plupart

du temps [ploopar]

most tourists la plupart des touristes

mostly principalement [prANseepal-mON]

mother la mère [mair]

motorbike la moto

motorboat le bateau à moteur [bato a moturr]

motorway l'autoroute **f** [otoroot]

mountain la montagne [mONtañ]

in the mountains à la montagne

mountaineering l'alpinisme **m** [alpeeneess-muh]

mouse la souris [sooree]

moustache la moustache [mooss-tash]

mouth la bouche [boosh]

mouth ulcer l'aphte **m** [afft]

move bouger [boojay]

he's moved to another room il a changé de chambre [eel a shONjay duh shONbr]

could you move your car? est-ce que vous pouvez déplacer votre voiture? [eskuh voo poovay dayplassay votr vwatoor]

could you move up a little? est-ce que vous pouvez vous pousser un peu? [poossay]

where has it moved to? où se trouve-t-il maintenant? [oo suh troovteel mANtuhnON]

movie le film [feelm]

movie theater le cinéma

[seenayma]

Mr Monsieur [muhss-yuh]

Mrs Madame [ma-dam]

Ms Madame; Mademoiselle [ma-dam, mad-mwazel]

much beaucoup [bo-koo]

much better/much worse beaucoup mieux/bien pire

much hotter beaucoup plus chaud

not much pas beaucoup [pa]

not very much pas tellement [telmON]

I don't want very much je n'en veux pas beaucoup [juh nON vuh pa]

mud la boue [boo]

mug (for drinking) la tasse [tass]

I've been mugged j'ai été dévalisé [jay aytay dayvaleezay]

mum la maman [ma-mON]

mumps les oreillons [oray-ON]

museum le musée [moozay]

mushrooms les champignons **mpl** [shONpeen-yON]

music la musique [moozeek]

musician le musicien, la musicienne [moozeess-yAN, -yen]

Muslim musulman [moozoolmON]

mussels les moules **fpl** [mool]

must*: I must je dois [juh dwa]

I mustn't drink alcohol il ne faut pas que je boive d'alcool [eel nuh fo pa juh]

mustard la moutarde [mootard]

my*: my room ma chambre

my passport mon passeport [mON]

my parents mes parents [may]
myself: I'll do it myself je le ferai moi-même [mwa-mem]
by myself tout seul [too surl]

N

nail (finger) l'ongle **m** [ONgl]
(metal) le clou [kloo]
nail varnish le vernis à ongles [vairnee]
name le nom [nON]
my name's John je m'appelle John [juh ma-pel]
what's your name? comment tu t'appelles/vous appelez-vous? [komON too ta-pel/voo zaplay-voo]
what is the name of this street? comment s'appelle cette rue? [sa-pel]
napkin la serviette [sairv-yet]
nappy la couche [koosh]
narrow (street) étroit [aytrwa]
nasty (person, taste) désagréable [dayzagray-abl]
(weather, accident) mauvais [mo-vay]
national national [nass-yonal]
nationality la nationalité [nass-yonaleetay]
natural naturel [natoo-rel]
nausea la nausée [no-zay]
navy (blue) (bleu) marine [bluh mareen]
near près [pray]
is it near the city centre? est-ce que c'est près du centre?
[eskuh say]
do you go near the harbour? est-ce que vous allez vers le port? [vair]
where is the nearest ...? où est le/la ... le/la plus proche? [pl00 prosh]
nearby tout près [too pray]
nearly presque [presk]
necessary nécessaire [naysessair]
neck le cou [koo]
necklace le collier [kol-yay]
necktie la cravate
need: I need ... j'ai besoin de ... [jay buhzwAN duh]
do I need to pay? est-ce que je dois payer? [eskuh juh dwa]
needle l'aiguille **f** [aygwee]
negative (film) le négatif [naygateef]
neither: neither (one) of them ni l'un ni l'autre [nee lAN nee lohtr]
neither ... nor ... ni ... ni ...
nephew le neveu [nuhvuh]
net (in sport) le filet [feelay]
Netherlands les Pays-Bas [payee-ba]
network map le plan du réseau [plON d00 rayzo]
never jamais [jamay]

dialogue

have you ever been to Monaco? êtes-vous déjà allé à Monaco? [et-voo dayja alay]

no, never, I've never been there non, jamais, je n'y suis jamais allé [juh nee swee]

new nouveau, **f** nouvelle [noovo, noovel]

news (radio, TV etc) les informations [ANformass-yON]

newsagent's le marchand de journaux [marshON duh joorno]

newspaper le journal [joor-nal]

newspaper kiosk le kiosque à journaux [keeosk]

New Year le Nouvel An [noovel ON]

Happy New Year! bonne année! [bon anay]

New Year's Eve la Saint-Sylvestre [SAN seelvestr]

New Zealand la Nouvelle-Zélande [noovel zaylOND]

New Zealander: I'm a New Zealander je suis Néo-Zélandais [nayozaylONday]

next prochain [proshAN]

the next on the left la prochaine à gauche [proshen a gohsh]

at the next stop au prochain arrêt

next week la semaine prochaine

next to à côté de [a kotay duh]

nice (food) bon [bON]

(looks, view etc) joli [jolee]

(person) sympathique, gentil [SANpateek, jONtee]

niece la nièce [nee-ess]

night la nuit [nwee]

at night la nuit

good night bonne nuit [bon]

nightclub la boîte de nuit [bwat duh nwee]

nightdress la chemise de nuit [shuhmeez]

night porter le gardien de nuit [gardee-AN]

no non [nON]

I've no change je n'ai pas de monnaie [juh nay pa duh]

there's no ... left il n'y a plus de ... [eel nya plOO]

no way! pas question! [pa kest-yON]

oh no! (upset) ce n'est pas possible! [suh nay pa posseebl]

nobody personne [pairson]

there's nobody there il n'y a personne [eel nya]

noise le bruit [brwee]

noisy: it's too noisy c'est trop bruyant [say tro brwee-yON]

non-alcoholic sans alcool [sON zalkol]

none aucun [o-kAN]

nonsmoking compartment le compartiment non-fumeurs [kONparteemON nON-fOOmurr]

noon midi [meedee]

no-one personne [pairson]

nor: nor do I moi non plus [mwa nON plOO]

normal normal [nor-mal]

north le nord [nor]

in the north dans le nord

north of Paris au nord de Paris [o]

northeast le nord-est [nor-est]

northern du nord [d∞]

northwest le nord-ouest [nor-west]

Northern Ireland l'Irlande du Nord **f** [eerlOND]

Norway la Norvège [norvej]

Norwegian (adj) norvégien [nor-vayj-yAN]

nose le nez [nay]

nosebleed le saignement de nez [sen-yuh-mON]

not** pas [pa]

no, I'm not hungry non, je n'ai pas faim [juh nay pa]

I don't want any, thank you je n'en veux pas, merci [nON vuh]

it's not necessary ce n'est pas nécessaire

I didn't know that je ne savais pas

not that one – this one pas celui-là – celui-ci [suhlwee-la suhlwee-see]

note (banknote) le billet (de banque) [bee-yay (duh bONk)]

notebook le cahier [ky-yay]

notepaper (for letters) le papier à lettres [pap-yay a letr]

nothing rien [ree-AN]

nothing for me, thanks pour moi rien, merci [poor mwa]

nothing else rien d'autre [dohtr]

novel le roman [romON]

November novembre [no-vONbr]

now maintenant [mANtnON]

number le numéro [n∞mayro]

I've got the wrong number j'ai fait un mauvais numéro [jay fay AN]

what is your phone number? quel est votre numéro de téléphone? [kel ay votr]

number plate la plaque d'immatriculation [plak deematreek∞lass-yON]

nurse (female) l'infirmière **f** [ANfeerm-yair]

(male) l'infirmier **m** [ANfeerm-yay]

nursery slope la piste pour débutants [peest poor dayb∞toN]

nut (for bolt) l'écrou **m** [aykroo]

nuts les noisettes **fpl** [nwazet]

O

o'clock*: it's 10 o'clock il est dix heures [urr]

occupied (toilet) occupé [ok∞pay]

October octobre [oktobr]

odd (strange) étrange [aytrONj]

of* de [duh]

off (lights) éteint [aytAN]

it's just off the Champs Elysées c'est tout près des Champs Elysées [too pray day]

we're off tomorrow (leaving) nous partons demain [noo partON]

offensive (language, behaviour) choquant [shokON]

office le bureau [b∞ro]

officer (said to policeman) monsieur l'agent [muhss-yuh lajON]

often souvent [soovON]
  not often pas souvent [pa]
  how often are the buses? à quel intervalle les bus passent-ils? [kel ANtairval]

oil l'huile f [weel]

ointment la pommade [pomahd]

OK d'accord [dakor]
  are you OK? ça va? [sa va]
  is that OK with you? est-ce que ça te/vous va? [eskuh sa tuh/voo]
  is it OK to ...? est-ce qu'on peut ...? [puh]
  that's OK thanks (it doesn't matter) merci, ça va [mairsee]
  I'm OK (nothing for me, I've got enough) ça va comme ça (I feel OK) ça va
  is this train OK for ...? ce train va bien à ...? [b-yAN]
  I said I'm sorry, OK? j'ai dit pardon, ça ne suffit pas? [sa nuh soofee pa]

old vieux, f vieille [v-yuh, v-yay]

dialogue

how old are you? quel âge as-tu/avez-vous? [kel ahj atoo/avay-voo]
I'm twenty-five j'ai vingt-cinq ans [jay]
and you? et vous?

old-fashioned démodé [daymoday]

old town (old part of town) la vieille ville [v-yay veel]
  in the old town dans la vieille ville

olive oil l'huile d'olive f [weel doleev]

olives les olives fpl [oleev]
  black/green olives les olives noires/vertes

omelette l'omelette f

on* sur [soor]
  on the street/beach dans la rue/à la plage [dON]
  is it on this road? est-ce que c'est sur cette route?
  on the plane dans l'avion
  on Saturday samedi
  on television à la télévision
  I haven't got it on me je ne l'ai pas sur moi [juh nuh lay pa soor mwa]
  this one's on me (drink) c'est ma tournée [say ma toornay]
  the light wasn't on la lumière n'était pas allumée [aloomay]
  what's on tonight? qu'est-ce qu'il y a ce soir? [keskeel-ya suh swahr]

once une fois [oon fwa]
  at once (immediately) tout de suite [toot sweet]

one* un, une [AN, oon]
  the white one le blanc, la blanche

one-way ticket: a one-way ticket to ... un aller simple pour ... [alay sANpl poor]

onion l'oignon **m** [on-yON]
only seulement [surlmON]
  only one seulement un(e)
  only just à peine [pen]
  it's only 6 o'clock il n'est que
  six heures [eel nay kuh]
  I've only just got here je viens
  d'arriver [juh v-yAN dareevay]
on/off switch l'interrupteur
  de marche/arrêt **m**
  [ANtairOOpturr duh marsh/aray]
open (adj) ouvert [oovair]
  (verb) ouvrir [oovreer]
  when do you open? à quelle
  heure est-ce que vous
  ouvrez? [a kel urr eskuh voo
  zoovray]
  I can't get it open je n'arrive
  pas à l'ouvrir [juh nareev pa]
  in the open air en plein air
  [ON plAN air]
opening times les heures
  d'ouverture [urr doovairtOOr]
open ticket le billet open
  [bee-yay]
opera l'opéra **m** [opayra]
operation l'opération **f**
  [opayrass-yON]
operator (telephone) le/la
  standardiste [stONdardeest]
opposite: the opposite
  direction le sens inverse
  [anvairss]
  opposite my hotel en face de
  mon hôtel [ON fass duh]
  the bar opposite le bar d'en
  face
optician l'opticien **m** [opteess-
  yAN]

or ou [oo]
orange (fruit) l'orange **f** [orONj]
  (colour) orange
orange juice le jus d'orange
  [jOO]
orchestra l'orchestre **m** [orkestr]
order: can we order now?
  est-ce que nous pouvons
  commander? [eskuh noo poovON
  komONday]
  I've already ordered, thanks
  j'ai déjà commandé, merci
  [jay dayja komONday]
  I didn't order this ce n'est pas
  ce que j'ai commandé [suh nay
  pa suh kuh]
  out of order hors service [or
  sairveess]
ordinary ordinaire [ordeenair]
other autre [ohtr]
  the other one l'autre
  the other day (recently) l'autre
  jour
  I'm waiting for the others
  j'attends les autres [lay zohtr]
  do you have any others? est-
  ce que vous en avez d'autres?
  [eskuh voo zON avay dohtr]
otherwise sinon [seenON]
our* notre, pl nos
ours* le/la nôtre [nohtr]
out: he's out il est sorti [eel ay
  sortee]
  three kilometres out of town à
  trois kilomètres de la ville
outdoors en plein air [ON plAN
  air]
outside (preposition) à
  l'extérieur de [extayree-urr duh]

can we sit outside? est-ce que nous pouvons nous mettre dehors? [eskuh noo poovON noo metr duh-or]

oven le four [foor]

over: over here par ici [ee-see]
over there là-bas [laba]
over 500 plus de cinq cents [plOO duh]
it's over (finished) c'est fini [say feenee]

overcharge: you've overcharged me il y a une erreur dans la note [eelya OOn air-rurr dON la not]

overcoat le pardessus [parduhsOO]

overnight (travel) de nuit [duh nwee]

overtake doubler [dooblay]

owe: how much do I owe you? qu'est-ce que je vous dois? [keskuh juh voo dwa]

own: my own ... mon propre ... [propr]
are you on your own? êtes-vous seul? [et-voo surl]
I'm on my own je suis seul [juh swee surl]

owner le/la propriétaire [propree-aytair]

P

pack: a pack of ... un paquet de ... [pakay duh]
(verb) faire ses bagages [fair say bagahj]

package (at post office) le colis [kolee]

package holiday les vacances organisées [vakONss organeezay]

packed lunch le casse-croûte [kass-kroot]

packet: a packet of cigarettes un paquet de cigarettes [pakay]

padlock le cadenas [kadna]

page (of book) la page [pahj]
could you page Mr ...? pouvez-vous faire appeler M. ...? [poovay-voo fair aplay]

pain la douleur [doolurr]
I have a pain here j'ai mal ici [jay mal ee-see]

painful douloureux [doolooruh]

painkillers les analgésiques **mpl** [an-aljayzeek]

paint la peinture [pANtoor]

painting (picture) le tableau [tablo]

pair: a pair of ... une paire de ... [pair duh]

Pakistani pakistanais [-ay]

palace le palais [palay]

pale pâle [pahl]
pale blue bleu clair [bluh klair]

pan la poêle [pwal]

panties le slip [sleep]

pants (underwear) le slip
(US) le pantalon [pONtalON]

pantyhose le collant [kolION]

paper le papier [papyay]
(newspaper) le journal [joor-nal]
a piece of paper un bout de papier [boo]

paper handkerchiefs les kleenex® **mpl**

parcel le colis [kolee]

pardon? (didn't understand) pardon? [par-dON]

parents: my parents mes parents [parON]

parents-in-law les beaux-parents [bo-]

park le parc
(verb) se garer [suh garay]
can I park here? est-ce que je peux me garer ici?

parking lot le parking [parkeeng]

part une partie [partee]

partner (boyfriend, girlfriend) le/la partenaire [partuhnair]

party (group) le groupe
(celebration) la fête [fet]

pass (in mountains) le col

passenger le passager, la passagère [passahjay, -jair]

passport le passeport [pass-por]

past*: in the past autrefois [ohtruh-fwa]
just past the information office tout de suite après le centre d'information [toot sweet apray]

path le sentier [sONt-yay]

pattern le motif [moteef]

pavement le trottoir [trotwahr]
on the pavement sur le trottoir

pavement café le café en terrasse [ON tairass]

pay (verb) payer [pay-ay]
can I pay, please? l'addition, s'il vous plaît [ladeess-yON]

it's already paid for ça a déjà été réglé [sa a day-ja aytay rayglay]

dialogue

who's paying? qui est-ce qui paie? [kee eskee pay]
I'll pay c'est moi qui paie [say mwa]
no, you paid last time, I'll pay non, tu as payé la dernière fois, cette fois c'est mon tour [tOO a pay-ay la dairn-yair fwa set fwa say mON toor]

pay phone la cabine téléphonique [kabeen taylayfoneek]

peaceful paisible [pezzeebl]

peach la pêche [pesh]

peanuts les cacahuètes fpl [kaka-wet]

pear la poire [pwahr]

peas les petits pois mpl [puhtee pwa]

peculiar (taste, custom) bizarre

pedestrian crossing le passage pour piétons [passahj poor p-yaytON]

pedestrian precinct la zone piétonne [zohn p-yaytON]

peg (for washing) la pince à linge [pANss a lANj]
(for tent) le piquet [peekay]

pen le stylo [steelo]

pencil le crayon [kray-ON]

penfriend le correspondant

[-dON], la correspondante
[-dONt]

penicillin la pénicilline
[payneesseeleen]

penknife le canif [kaneef]

pensioner le retraité, la
retraitée [ruhtraytay]

people les gens [jON]

the other people les autres
[lay zohtr]

too many people trop de
monde [tro duh mONd]

pepper (spice) le poivre
[pwahvr]

(vegetable) le poivron
[pwahvrON]

peppermint (sweet) le bonbon
à la menthe [bONbON ala mONt]

per: per night par nuit

how much per day? quel est
le prix par jour? [kel ay
pree par joor]

per cent pour cent [poor sON]

perfect parfait [parfay]

perfume le parfum [parfAN]

perhaps peut-être [puht-etr]

perhaps not peut-être que
non [kuh nON]

period (of time) la période
[payree-od]

(menstruation) les règles [regl]

perm la permanente
[pairmanONt]

permit l'autorisation f
[otoreezass-yON]

person la personne [pairson]

personal stereo le baladeur
[baladurr]

petrol l'essence f [essONss]

petrol can le bidon d'essence

[beedON dessONss]

petrol station la station-
service [stass-yON-sairveess]

pharmacy la pharmacie
[farmasee]

phone le téléphone [taylay-]
(verb) téléphoner

could you phone the police?
pourriez-vous téléphoner à
la police? [pooree-ay-voo]

phone book l'annuaire du
téléphone m [an00air d00
taylayfon]

phone box la cabine
téléphonique [kabeen
taylayfoneek]

phonecard la télécarte [taylay-
kart]

phone number le numéro de
téléphone [n00mayro]

photo la photographie [foto-
grafee]

excuse me, could you take a
photo of us? pourriez-vous
nous prendre en photo?
[pooree-ay-voo noo prONdr ON]

phrasebook le manuel de
conversation [man00el duh
kONvairsass-yON]

piano le piano

pickpocket le/la pickpocket

pick up: will you be there to
pick me up? est-ce que vous
viendrez me chercher? [eskuh
voo vee-ANdray muh shairshay]

picnic le pique-nique [peek-
neek]

picture l'image f [eemahj]

pie (meat) le pâté en croûte

[patay ON kroot]
(fruit) la tarte
piece le morceau [morso]
  a piece of ... un morceau
  de ...
pig le cochon [koshON]
pill la pilule [peelOOl]
  I'm on the pill je prends la
  pilule [juh prON]
pillow l'oreiller **m** [oray-yay]
pillow case la taie d'oreiller
  [tay]
pin l'épingle **f** [aypANgl]
pineapple l'ananas **m**
  [anana]
pineapple juice le jus d'ananas
  [jOO]
pink rose [roz]
pipe (for smoking) la pipe [peep]
  (for water) le tuyau [twee-o]
pity: it's a pity c'est dommage
  [say domahj]
pizza la pizza
place l'endroit **m** [ONdrwa]
  is this place taken? est-ce
  que cette place est prise?
  [eskuh set plass ay preez]
  at your place chez toi/vous
  [shay twa/voo]
  at his place chez lui [lwee]
plain (not patterned) uni [OOnee]
plane l'avion **m** [av-yON]
  by plane en avion
plant la plante [plONt]
plaster cast le plâtre [plahtr]
plasters les pansements **mpl**
  [pONsmON]
plastic le plastique [plass-teek]
  (credit cards) les cartes de

crédit [kart duh kray-dee]
plastic bag le sac en plastique
  [ON plass-teek]
plate l'assiette **f** [ass-yet]
platform le quai [kay]
  which platform is it for Paris?
  c'est quelle voie pour Paris?
  [say kel vwa]
play (verb) jouer [joo-ay]
  (in theatre) la pièce de théâtre
  [p-yess duh tay-atr]
playground (for children) le
  terrain de jeux [terrAN duh juh]
pleasant agréable [agray-abl]
please s'il vous plaît [seel voo
  play]
  (if using 'tu' form) s'il te plaît
  [seel tuh]
  yes please oui, merci [wee
  mairsee]
  could you please ...?
  pourriez-vous ..., s'il vous
  plaît? [pooree-ay-voo]
  please don't wait for me
  ce n'est pas la peine de
  m'attendre [suh nay pa la pen]
  pleased to meet you
  enchanté [ONshONtay]
pleasure le plaisir [plezzeer]
  my pleasure tout le plaisir
  est pour moi [too luh ... ay poor
  mwa]
plenty: plenty of ... beaucoup
  de ... [bo-koo duh]
  we've plenty of time nous
  avons largement le temps
  [noo zavON larj-mON luh tON]
  that's plenty, thanks merci, ça
  suffit [sa soofee]

pliers la pince [pANss]
plug (electrical) la prise [preez]
(for car) la bougie [boojee]
(in sink) le bouchon [booshON]
plumber le plombier [plONb-yay]
p.m.* de l'après-midi [duh lapray-meedee]
(in the evening) du soir [dOO swahr]
poached egg l'œuf poché **m** [urf poshay]
pocket la poche [posh]
point: two point five deux virgule cinq [... veergOOl ...]
there's no point ça ne sert à rien [sa nuh sair a ree-AN]
points (in car) les vis platinées [veess plateenay]
poisonous toxique
police la police
call the police! appelez la police! [aplay]
policeman l'agent de police **m** [ajON]
police station le commissariat [komeessaree-a]
policewoman la femme agent [fam ajON]
polish le cirage [seerahj]
polite poli [polee]
polluted pollué [polOO-ay]
pony le poney [ponay]
pool (for swimming) la piscine [peesseen]
poor (not rich) pauvre [pohvr]
(quality) médiocre [maydeeokr]
pop music la musique pop [mOOzeek]

pop singer le chanteur/la chanteuse de musique pop [shONturr/shONturz duh]
population la population [popOOlass-yON]
pork le porc [por]
port (for boats) le port [por]
(drink) le porto
porter (in hotel) le portier [port-yay]
portrait le portrait [portray]
Portugal le Portugal
Portuguese (adj) portugais [portOOgay]
posh (restaurant, people) chic [sheek]
possible possible [posseebl]
is it possible to ...? est-ce qu'on peut ...? [eskON puh]
as ... as possible aussi ... que possible [o-see]
post (mail) le courrier [kooree-ay]
(verb) poster [posstay]
could you post this for me? pourriez-vous me poster cette lettre? [pooree-ay-voo muh posstay set letr]
postbox la boîte aux lettres [bwat o letr]
postcard la carte postale [kart poss-tal]
poster l'affiche **f** [afeesh]
post office la poste [posst]
poste restante la poste restante
potato la pomme de terre [pom duh tair]
potato chips les chips **fpl**

[cheeps]

pots and pans les casseroles [kassuhrohl]

pottery (objects) la poterie [potree]

pound (money) la livre (sterling) [leevr (stairleeng)] (weight) la livre [leevr]

power cut la coupure de courant [koopoor duh kooroN]

power point la prise (de courant) [preez]

practise: I want to practise my French je veux m'exercer à parler français [juh vuh mexairsay a parlay]

prawns les crevettes fpl [kruhvet]

prefer: I prefer ... je préfère ... [juh prayfair]

pregnant enceinte [ONSANt]

prescription (for chemist) l'ordonnance f [ordonONss]

present (gift) le cadeau [kado]

president le président [prayzeedON]

pretty joli [jolee]

it's pretty expensive c'est plutôt cher [say plOOto shair]

price le prix [pree]

priest le prêtre [pretr]

prime minister le Premier ministre [pruhm-yay meeneestr]

printed matter l'imprimé m [ANpreemay]

priority (in driving) la priorité [preeoreetay]

prison la prison [preezON]

private privé [preevay]

private bathroom la salle de bain particulière [sal duh bAN parteekOOl-yair]

probably probablement [prob-abluhmON]

problem le problème [prob-lem]

no problem! pas de problème! [pa duh]

program(me) le programme [prog-ram]

promise: I promise je te/vous le promets [juh tuh/voo luh promay]

pronounce: how is this pronounced? comment est-ce que ça se prononce? [komON teskuh sa suh prononONss]

properly (repaired, locked etc) bien [b-yAN]

protection factor l'indice de protection m [ANdeess duh protex-yON]

Protestant protestant [-tON]

public holiday le jour férié [joor fayree-ay]

public toilets les toilettes publiques [twalet pOObleek]

pudding (dessert) le dessert [dessair]

pull tirer [teeray]

pullover le pull [pOOl]

puncture la crevaison [kruhvezzON]

purple violet [veeolay]

purse (for money) le porte-monnaie [port-monay] (US) le sac à main [mAN]

push pousser [poossay]

pushchair la poussette
[poosset]

put mettre [metr]

where can I put ...? où est-ce que je peux mettre ...?
[weskuh juh puh]

could you put us up for the night? pourriez-vous nous héberger pour la nuit?
[pooree-ay-voo noo zaybairjay poor la nwee]

pyjamas le pyjama [peejama]

Pyrenees les Pyrénées
[peeraynay]

Q

quality la qualité [kaleetay]

quarantine la quarantaine
[karONten]

quarter le quart [kar]

quayside: on the quayside sur les quais [soor lay kay]

question la question [kest-yON]

queue la queue [kuh]

quick rapide [rapeed]

that was quick tu as/vous avez fait vite [too a/voo zavay fay veet]

what's the quickest way there? quel est le chemin le plus court? [kel ay luh shuhmAN luh ploo koor]

fancy a quick drink? tu as/vous avez le temps de prendre un verre? [too a/voo zavay luh tON duh proNdr AN vair]

quickly vite [veet]

quiet (place, hotel) tranquille
[trONkeel]

quiet! silence! [seelONss]

quite (fairly) assez [assay]
(very) très [tray]

that's quite right c'est tout à fait juste [say too ta fay joost]

quite a lot pas mal [pa]

R

rabbit le lapin [lapAN]

race (for runners, cars) la course
[koorss]

racket (tennis, squash etc) la raquette [raket]

radiator (of car, in room) le radiateur [rad-yaturr]

radio la radio [ra-deeo]

on the radio à la radio

rail: by rail en train [ON trAN]

railway le chemin de fer
[shuhmAN duh fair]

rain la pluie [plwee]

in the rain sous la pluie
[soo]

it's raining il pleut [eel pluh]

raincoat l'imperméable **m**
[ANpairmay-abl]

rape le viol [veeol]

rare (steak) saignant [sen-yON]

rash (on skin) l'éruption **f**
[ayroops-yON]

raspberry la framboise
[frONbwahz]

rat le rat [ra]

rate (for changing money) le taux
[toh]

rather: it's rather good c'est assez bon [say tassay bON]

I'd rather ... je préfère ... [juh prayfair]

razor le rasoir [razwahr]

razor blades les lames de rasoir **fpl** [lahm duh razwahr]

read lire [leer]

ready prêt [pray]

are you ready? est-ce que tu es/vous êtes prêt? [eskuh too ay/voo zet]

I'm not ready yet je ne suis pas encore prêt [juh nuh swee pa zONkor]

dialogue

when will it be ready? quand est-ce que ce sera prêt? [KONteskuh suh suhra]

it should be ready in a couple of days ça devrait être prêt dans un ou deux jours [sa duhvray]

real véritable [vayreet-abl]

really vraiment [vraymON]

that's really great c'est vraiment formidable

really? (doubt) vraiment?
(polite interest) ah bon?

rearview mirror le rétroviseur [raytroveezurr]

reasonable raisonnable [rezzON-abl]

receipt le reçu [ruhsoo]

recently récemment [ray-samON]

reception (for guests, in hotel) la réception [ray-seps-yON]

at reception à la réception

reception desk le bureau de réception

receptionist le/la réceptionniste [rayseps-yoneest]

recognize reconnaître [ruhkonetr]

recommend: could you recommend ...? pourriez-vous me recommander ...? [pooree-ay-voo muh ruhkomONday]

record (music) le disque [deesk]

red rouge [rooj]

red wine le vin rouge [VAN]

refund le remboursement [rONboorss-mON]

can I have a refund? est-ce que je serai remboursé? [eskuh juh suhray rONboorsay]

region la région [rayjeeON]

registered: by registered mail en recommandé [ON ruhkomONday]

registration number le numéro d'immatriculation [noomayro deematreekoolass-yON]

relative le parent [parON]

religion la religion [ruhleejeeON]

remember: I don't remember je ne me souviens pas [juh nuh muh soov-yAN pa]

I remember je m'en souviens [juh mON]

do you remember? tu te souviens?/vous souvenez-vous? [too tuh .../voo soovnay-voo]

rent (for apartment etc) le loyer
[lwy-ay]
(verb) louer [loo-ay]
for rent à louer
rented car la voiture de
location [vwatoor duh lokass-yON]
repair (verb) réparer [rayparay]
can you repair it? est-ce que
vous pouvez réparer ça?
[eskuh voo poovay]
repeat répéter [raypaytay]
could you repeat that?
pourriez-vous répéter?
[pooree-ay-voo]
reservation la réservation
[rayzairvass-yON]
I'd like to make a reservation
je voudrais faire une
réservation [juh voodray fair]

dialogue

I have a reservation j'ai
réservé [jay rayzairvay]
yes sir, what name please?
certainement monsieur, à
quel nom s'il vous plaît?
[sairten-mON muh-syuh a kel
nON]

reserve réserver [rayzairvay]

dialogue

can I reserve a table for
tonight? j'aimerais réserver
une table pour ce soir
[jemray]
yes madam, for how many

people? certainement
madame, pour combien
de personnes? [sairten-
mON ... poor kONb-yAN duh
pairsON]
for two pour deux
and for what time? et pour
quelle heure? [kel urr]
for eight o'clock pour huit
heures
and could I have your
name please? pourrais-je
avoir votre nom s'il vous
plaît? [poorayj avwahr]
see alphabet

rest: I need a rest j'ai besoin
de repos [jay buh-zwAN duh
ruhpo]
the rest of the group le reste
du groupe [rest]
restaurant le restaurant
[restorON]

dialogue

what's the dish of the day?
quel est le plat du jour?
[kel ay luh pla doo joor?]
I'll take the 30 euro menu
je vais prendre le menu
à trente euros [juh vay
prONdr]

restaurant car le wagon-
restaurant [vagON]
rest room les toilettes [twalet]
retired: I'm retired je suis
retraité(e) [ruhtretay]

return (ticket) l'aller-retour **m** [alay-ruhtoor]

reverse charge call le PCV [pay-say-vay]

reverse gear la marche arrière [marsh aree-air]

revolting dégoûtant [daygootON]

rib la côte [koht]

rice le riz [ree]

rich (person) riche [reesh]

(food) lourd [loor]

ridiculous ridicule [reedeekool]

right (correct) juste [joost]

(not left) droit [drwa]

you were right vous aviez raison [voo zaveeay rezzON]

that's right c'est juste [say joost]

this can't be right ce n'est pas possible [suh nay pa posseebl]

right! d'accord! [dakor]

is this the right road for ...? est-ce bien la route de ...? [ess b-yAN la root]

on the right à droite [drwat]

turn right tournez à droite [toornay]

right-hand drive la conduite à droite [kONdweet a drwat]

ring (on finger) la bague [bag]

I'll ring you je vous appellerai [juh vooz apelray]

ring back rappeler

ripe (fruit) mûr [moor]

rip-off: it's a rip-off c'est de l'arnaque [say duh larnak]

rip-off prices les prix exorbitants [pree exorbeetON]

risky risqué [reeskay]

river la rivière [reev-yair]

road la route [root]

is this the road for ...? est-ce la bonne route pour aller à ...? [ess la bon root poor alay]

it's just down the road c'est tout près d'ici [say too pray dee-see]

road accident l'accident de la circulation **m** [axeedon duh la seerkoolass-yON]

road map la carte routière [kart root-yair]

roadsign le panneau de signalisation [pano duh seen-yaleezass-yON]

rob: I've been robbed j'ai été dévalisé [jay aytay dayvaleezay]

rock le rocher [roshay]

(music) la musique rock [moozeek]

on the rocks (with ice) avec des glaçons [avek day glassON]

roll (bread) le petit pain [puhtee pAN]

roof le toit [twa]

roof rack la galerie [galree]

room la chambre [shONbr]

in my room dans ma chambre [dON]

dialogue

do you have any rooms? est-ce que vous avez des chambres? [eskuh voo zavay day]

for how many people?
pour combien de
personnes? [poor kONb-yAN
duh pairson]

for one/for two pour une
personne/deux personnes

yes, we have rooms free
oui, nous avons des
chambres libres [leebr]

**for how many nights
will it be?** ce serait pour
combien de nuits? [suh
suhray – duh nwee]

just for one night pour une
nuit seulement [surlmON]

how much is it? combien
est-ce? [ess]

**100 euros with bathroom
and 80 euros without
bathroom** cent euros avec
salle de bain et quatre-
vingts euros sans salle de
bain [sal duh bAN]

**can I see a room with
bathroom?** est-ce que
je pourrais voir une
chambre avec salle de
bain? [eskuh juh pooray
vwahr]

OK, I'll take it d'accord, je
la prends [dakor juh la prON]

room service le service en
chambre [sairveess ON shONbr]

rope la corde [kord]

rosé (wine) le rosé [rozzay]

roughly (approximately) environ
[ONveerON]

round: it's my round c'est ma

tournée [say ma toornay]

roundabout (for traffic) le rond-
point [rON-pwAN]

round trip ticket l'aller-retour
m [alay-ruhtoor]

route l'itinéraire **m** [eeteenay-
rair]

what's the best route? quel
itinéraire nous conseillez-
vous? [noo kONsay-ay-voo]

rubber (material) le caoutchouc
[ka-oochoo]
(eraser) la gomme [gom]

rubber band l'élastique **m**
[aylasteek]

rubbish (waste) les ordures
[ordOOr]
(poor-quality goods) la camelote
[kamlot]

rubbish! (nonsense) n'importe
quoi! [nANport kwa]

rucksack le sac à dos [do]

rude grossier [gross-yay]

ruins les ruines **fpl** [rOOeen]

rum le rhum [rum]

rum and coke un rhum coca

run (person) courir [kooreer]

how often do the buses run?
à quels intervalles les bus
passent-ils? [kel zANtairval lay
bOOss pasteel]

I've run out of money je n'ai
plus d'argent [juh nay plOO
darjON]

rush hour les heures de pointe
[urr duh pwANt]

S

sad triste [treest]
saddle (for bike, horse) la selle [sel]
safe (not in danger) en sécurité [ON saykOOreetay]
(not dangerous) sûr [sOOr]
safety pin l'épingle de sûreté f [aypANgl duh sOOrtay]
sail la voile [vwal]
sailboard la planche à voile [plONsh a vwal]
sailboarding la planche à voile
salad la salade [sa-lad]
salad dressing la vinaigrette
sale: for sale à vendre [vONdr]
salmon le saumon [so-mON]
salt le sel
same: the same le/la même [mem]
the same as he has le/la même que lui
the same again, please la même chose, s'il vous plaît [shohz seel voo play]
it's all the same to me ça m'est égal [sa met aygal]
sand le sable [sabl]
sandals les sandales fpl [sON-dal]
sandwich le sandwich [sONd-weetch]
sanitary napkin la serviette hygiénique [eejee-ayneek]
sanitary towel la serviette hygiénique
sardines les sardines fpl
Saturday samedi [samdee]

sauce la sauce [sohss]
saucepan la casserole
saucer la soucoupe [sookoop]
sauna le sauna [sona]
sausage la saucisse [soseess]
say: how do you say ... in French? comment dit-on ... en français? [komON deet-ON]
what did he say? qu'est-ce qu'il a dit? [keskeel a dee]
he said ... il a dit ...
I said ... j'ai dit ... [jay]
could you say that again? pourriez-vous répéter? [pooree-ay-voo raypaytay]
scarf (for neck) l'écharpe f [aysharp]
(for head) le foulard [foolar]
scenery le paysage [payee-zahj]
schedule (US) l'horaire m [orair]
scheduled flight le vol de ligne [vol duh leeñ]
school l'école f [aykol]
scissors: a pair of scissors une paire de ciseaux [seezo]
scotch le whisky
Scotch tape® le scotch
Scotland l'Écosse f [aykoss]
Scottish écossais [aykossay]
I'm Scottish (man/woman) je suis écossais/écossaise [aykossez]
scrambled eggs les œufs brouillés [uh broo-yay]
scratch l'éraflure f [ayraflOOr]
screw la vis [veess]
screwdriver le tournevis [toornuhveess]

scrubbing brush la brosse [bross]

sea la mer [mair]

  by the sea au bord de la mer [o bor]

seafood les fruits de mer [frwee duh mair]

seafood restaurant le restaurant de fruits de mer

seafront le bord de la mer [bor duh la mair]

  on the seafront au bord de la mer

seagull la mouette [mwet]

search chercher [shairshay]

seashell le coquillage [kokee-yahj]

seasick: I feel seasick j'ai le mal de mer [jay luh mal duh mair]

  I get seasick je suis sujet au mal de mer [juh swee soojay]

seaside: by the seaside au bord de la mer [o bor duh la mair]

seat le siège [see-ej]

  is this anyone's seat? est-ce que cette place est prise? [eskuh set plass ay preez]

seat belt la ceinture de sécurité [sANtoor duh saykooreetay]

sea urchin l'oursin m [oorsAN]

seaweed les algues [alg]

secluded isolé [eezolay]

second (adj) second [suhgON] (of time) la seconde [suhgON d]

  just a second! une seconde!

second class (travel) en

seconde [ON suhgON d]

second floor le deuxième [duhz-yem]; (US) le premier [pruhm-yay]

second-hand d'occasion [dokaz-yON]

see voir [vwahr]

  can I see? est-ce que je peux voir? [eskuh juh puh]

  have you seen ...? est-ce que tu as/vous avez vu ...? [too a/voo zavay voo]

  I saw him this morning je l'ai vu ce matin [juh lay]

  see you! à bientôt! [b-yANto]

  I see (I understand) je vois [juh vwa]

self-catering apartment l'appartement (de vacances) m [apartmON (duh vakONss)]

self-service le self-service [-sairveess]

sell vendre [vONdr]

  do you sell ...? est-ce que vous vendez ...? [eskuh voo vONday]

Sellotape® le scotch

send envoyer [ONvwy-ay]

  I want to send this to England j'aimerais envoyer ceci en Angleterre [jemray]

senior citizen la personne du troisième âge [pairson doo trwaz-yem ahj]

separate séparé [sayparay]

separated: I'm separated je suis séparé [juh swee sayparay]

separately (pay, travel) séparément [sayparay-mON]

September septembre [septONbr]

septic infecté [ANfektay]

serious (person, situation, problem) sérieux [sayree-uh]
(illness) grave [grahv]

service charge (in restaurant) le service [sairveess]

service station la station-service [stass-yON sairveess]

serviette la serviette [sair-]

set menu le menu (à prix fixe) [muhnoo (a pree feex)]

several plusieurs [plooz-yurr]

sew coudre [koodr]
could you sew this back on? pouvez-vous recoudre ceci? [poovay-voo ruhkoodr suhsee]

sex le sexe

sexy sexy

shade: in the shade à l'ombre [lONbr]

shake: let's shake hands serrons-nous la main [sairrON-noo la mAN]

shallow (water) peu profond [puh profoN]

shame: what a shame! quel dommage! [kel domahj]

shampoo le shampoing [shONpwAN]

shampoo and set le shampoing-mise en plis [ON plee]

share (room, table etc) partager [partajay]

sharp (knife) tranchant [tronshON]
(taste, pain) piquant, âpre [apr]

shattered (very tired) épuisé [aypweezay]

shaver le rasoir [razwahr]

shaving foam la mousse à raser [razay]

shaving point la prise pour rasoirs [preez poor razwahr]

she* elle [el]

sheet (for bed) le drap [dra]

shelf l'étagère f [aytajair]

shellfish les crustacés [kroostassay]

sherry le sherry

ship le bateau [bato]
by ship en bateau

shirt la chemise [shuhmeez]

shit! merde! [maird]

shock le choc [shok]
I got an electric shock from the ... j'ai reçu une décharge en touchant ... [jay ruhsoo oon daysharj ON tooshoN]

shock-absorber l'amortisseur m [amorteessurr]

shocking scandaleux [skONdaluh]

shoe la chaussure [shoshoor]
a pair of shoes une paire de chaussures

shoelaces les lacets mpl [lassay]

shoe polish le cirage [seerahj]

shoe repairer le cordonnier [kordon-yay]

shop le magasin [magazAN]

shopping: I'm going shopping je vais faire des courses [juh vay fair day koorss]

shopping centre le centre commercial [sONtr komairs-yal]

shop window la vitrine [veetreen]

shore (of sea, lake) le rivage [reevahj]

short (time, journey) court [koor] (person) petit [puhtee]

shortcut le raccourci [rakoorsee]

shorts le short

should: what should I do? que dois-je faire? [kuh dwaj fair]

he shouldn't be long il devrait revenir bientôt [eel duhvray]

you should have told me vous auriez dû me le dire [voo zoreeay doo]

shoulder l'épaule **f** [aypol]

shout crier [kree-ay]

show (in theatre) le spectacle [spekt-akl]

could you show me? pourrais-tu/pourriez-vous me montrer? [pooray-too/pooree-ay-voo muh moNtray]

shower (in bathroom) la douche [doosh]

with shower avec douche

shower gel le gel douche

shut fermer [fairmay]

when do you shut? à quelle heure fermez-vous? [kel urr fairmay-voo]

when do they shut? à quelle heure est-ce que ça ferme? [eskuh sa fairm]

they're shut c'est fermé [say fairmay]

I've shut myself out je me

suis enfermé dehors [juh muh swee zoNfairmay duh-or]

shut up! tais-toi/taisez-vous! [tay-twa/tezzay-voo]

shutter (on camera) l'obturateur **m** [obtooraturr] (on window) le volet [volay]

shy timide [teemeed]

sick (US) malade [malad]

I'm going to be sick (vomit) j'ai envie de vomir [jay oNvee duh vomeer]

see **ill**

side le côté [kotay]

the other side of town l'autre côté de la ville

side lights les feux de position **mpl** [fuh duh pozeess-yoN]

side salad la salade [sa-lad]

side street la petite rue [puhteet roo]

sidewalk le trottoir [trotwahr]

see **pavement**

sight: the sights of ... les endroits à voir à ... [lay zoNdrwa a vwahr]

sightseeing: we're going sightseeing nous allons visiter la ville [noo zaloN veezeetay]

sightseeing tour l'excursion **f** [exkoors-yoN]

sign (roadsign etc) le panneau de signalisation [pano duh seen-yaleezass-yoN]

signal: he didn't give a signal (driver) il n'a pas mis son clignotant [eel na pa mee soN

kleen-yotON]
(cyclist) il n'a pas fait signe
qu'il allait tourner [fay seeñ
keel alay toornay]
signature la signature [seen-
yatOOr]
signpost le poteau indicateur
[poto ANdeekaturr]
silence le silence [seelONss]
silk la soie [swa]
silly idiot [eed-yo]
silver l'argent m [arjON]
silver foil le papier d'argent
[papyay]
similar semblable [sONbl-abl]
simple simple [sAN-pl]
since: since yesterday depuis
hier [duhp-wee]
  since I got here depuis que je
  suis arrivé [areevay]
sing chanter [shONtay]
singer le chanteur, la
chanteuse [shONturr, -urz]
single: a single to ... un aller
simple pour ... [alay sAN-pl]
  I'm single je suis célibataire
  [juh swee sayleebatair]
single bed le lit d'une
personne [lee dOOn pairson]
single room la chambre pour
une personne [shONbr poor OOn
pairson]
sink (in kitchen) l'évier m [ayv-
yay]
sister la sœur [surr]
sister-in-law la belle-sœur
[bel-surr]
sit: can I sit here? est-ce que
je peux m'asseoir ici? [eskuh

juh puh masswahr ee-see]
sit down s'asseoir
  sit down assieds-toi/asseyez-
  vous [ass-yay-twa/asay-ay-voo]
  is anyone sitting here? est-
  ce que cette place est prise?
  [eskuh set plass ay preez]
size la taille [tī]
ski le ski
(verb) skier [skee-ay]
  a pair of skis une paire de skis
ski boots les chaussures de ski
fpl [shohsOOr]
skiing le ski
  we're going skiing nous
  allons faire du ski [noo zalON
  fair]
ski instructor le moniteur (de
ski) [moneeturr]
ski-lift le remonte-pente
[ruhmONt-pONt]
skin la peau [po]
skin-diving la plongée sous-
marine [plONjay soo-mareen]
skinny maigre [megr]
ski-pants le fuseau [fOOzo]
ski-pass le forfait de ski
[forfay]
ski pole le bâton de ski
[bahtON]
skirt la jupe [jOOp]
ski run la piste de ski
ski slope la pente de ski [pONt]
ski wax le fart [far]
sky le ciel [s-yel]
sleep dormir [dormeer]
  did you sleep well? tu as/
  vous avez bien dormi? [too
  a/voo zavay b-yAN dormee]

I need a good sleep j'ai besoin d'une bonne nuit de sommeil [jay buh-zWAN dOOn bon nwee duh somay]

sleeper (rail) le wagon-lit [vagON-lee]

sleeping bag le sac de couchage [kooshahj]

sleeping car le wagon-lit [vagON-lee]

sleeping pill le somnifère [somneefair]

sleepy: I'm feeling sleepy j'ai sommeil [jay somay]

sleeve la manche [mONsh]

slide (photographic) la diapositive [dee-apozeeteev]

slip (under dress) la combinaison [kONbeenezzON]

slippery glissant [gleessON]

slow lent [lON]

slow down! (driving, speaking) moins vite! [mwAN veet]

slowly lentement [lONtmON]

could you say it slowly? pourriez-vous parler plus lentement? [pooree-ay-voo parlay plOO]

very slowly très lentement

small petit [puhtee]

smell: it smells ça sent mauvais [mo-vay]

smile sourire [sooreer]

smoke la fumée [fOOmay]

do you mind if I smoke? est-ce que ça vous dérange si je fume? [eskuh sa voo dayrONj see juh fOOm]

I don't smoke je ne fume pas

do you smoke? tu fumes/vous fumez? [tOO fOOm/voo fOOmay]

snack: I'd just like a snack j'aimerais manger un petit quelque chose [jemray mONjay AN puhtee kelkuh shohz]

sneeze l'éternuement m [aytairnOOmON]

snorkel le tuba

snow la neige [nej]

so: it's so good c'est tellement bien [telmON]

not so fast pas si vite!

so am I moi aussi [mwa o-see]

so do I moi aussi

so-so comme ci, comme ça [kom see, kom sa]

soaking solution (for contact lenses) la solution de trempage [solOOss-yON duh trONpahj]

soap le savon [savON]

soap powder la lessive [lesseev]

sober sobre [sobr]

sock la chaussette [sho-set]

socket (electrical) la prise de courant [preez duh koorON]

soda (water) le soda

sofa le canapé, le divan [deevON]

soft doux, f douce [doo, dooss]

soft-boiled egg l'œuf à la coque m [urf a la kok]

soft drink la boisson non-alcoolisée [bwassON nON-alkoleezay]

soft lenses les lentilles

souples **fpl** [lONtee soopl]

sole (of shoe, of foot) la semelle [suhmel]

could you put new soles on these? pourriez-vous ressemeler ces chaussures? [pooree-ay-voo ruh-suhmuhlay say shohsOOr]

some: **can I have some water/ peanuts?** j'aimerais de l'eau/ des cacahuètes, s'il vous plaît [jemray duh lo/day]

can I have some? est-ce que je peux en avoir? [eskuh juh puh ON avvwahr]

somebody, someone quelqu'un [kel-kAN]

something quelque chose [kelkuh shohz]

something to drink quelque chose à boire

sometimes parfois [parfwa]

somewhere quelque part [kelkuh par]

son le fils [feess]

song la chanson [shONsON]

son-in-law le beau-fils [bofeess]

soon bientôt [b-yANto]

I'll be back soon je reviens bientôt

as soon as possible dès que possible [day kuh]

sore: **it's sore** ça fait mal [sa fay mal]

sore throat le mal de gorge

sorry: (I'm) **sorry** je suis désolé, excusez-moi [juh swee dayzolay, eskOOzay-mwa]

sorry? (didn't understand)

pardon? [par-dON]

sort: **what sort of ...?** quel genre de ...? [kel jONr duh]

soup le potage [potahj]

sour (taste) acide [aseed]

south le sud [sOOd]

in the south dans le sud

South Africa l'Afrique du Sud **f** [afreek dOO sOOd]

South African (adj) sud-africain [sOOd afreekAN]

I'm South African (man/woman) je suis sud-africain/sud-africaine [-ken]

southeast le sud-est [sOOd-est]

South of France le Midi

southwest le sud-ouest [sOOd-west]

souvenir le souvenir

Spain l'Espagne **f** [españ]

Spanish espagnol [espan-yol]

spanner la clé anglaise [klay ONglez]

spare part la pièce de rechange [p-yes duh ruhshONj]

spare tyre le pneu de rechange [p-nuh duh ruhshONj]

spark plug la bougie [boojee]

speak: **do you speak English?** parlez-vous l'anglais? [parlay-voo]

I don't speak ... je ne parle pas ... [juh nuh parl pa]

dialogue

can I speak to Marc? j'aimerais parler à Marc [jemray parlay]

who's calling? c'est de la part de qui? [say duh la par duh kee]
it's Patricia c'est Patricia
I'm sorry, he's not in, can I take a message? désolé, il n'est pas là, est-ce que je peux prendre un message [proNdr un messahj]
no thanks, I'll call back later non merci, je rappellerai plus tard [mairsee juh rapeluhray plOO tar]
please tell him I called dites-lui que j'ai appelé, s'il vous plaît [deet-lwee kuh jay apelay seel voo play]

spearmint la menthe verte [mONt vairt]
speciality la spécialité [spayss-yaleetay]
spectacles les lunettes [lOOnet]
speed la vitesse [veetess]
speed limit la limite de vitesse [leemeet]
speedometer le compteur [kONturr]
spell: how do you spell it? comment est-ce que ça s'écrit? [komON teskuh sa saykree]
see alphabet
spend dépenser [daypONsay]
spider l'araignée f [aren-yay]
spin-dryer l'essoreuse f [esrorurz]
splinter l'écharde f [ayshard]
spoke (in wheel) le rayon [ray-ON]

spoon la cuillère [kwee-yair]
sport le sport [spor]
sprain: I've sprained my ... je me suis foulé ... [juh muh swee foolay]
spring (season) le printemps [prANtoN]
(of car, seat) le ressort [ruhsor]
square (in town) la place [plass]
stairs l'escalier m [eskal-yay]
stale (taste) pas frais, f pas fraîche [pa fray, pa fresh]
(bread) rassis [rassee]
stall: the engine keeps stalling le moteur cale sans arrêt [moturr kal sON zaray]
stamp le timbre [tANbr]

dialogue

a stamp for England, please un timbre pour l'Angleterre, s'il vous plaît
what are you sending? qu'est-ce que vous envoyez? [keskuh voo zONvwy-yay]
it's for this postcard c'est pour cette carte postale

standby le vol en stand-by [ON]
star l'étoile f [aytwal]
(in film) la star
start le début [daybOO]
(verb) commencer [komONssay]

when does it start? quand est-ce que ça commence? [kONteskuh sa kom-mONSS]

the car won't start la voiture refuse de démarrer [ruhfOOz duh daymaray]

starter (of car) le démarreur [daymarurr]

(food) l'entrée f [ONtray]

state (in country) l'état m [ayta]

the States (USA) les États-Unis [ayta-zOOnee]

station la gare [gar]

statue la statue

stay: where are you staying? où logez-vous? [oo lojay-voo]

I'm staying at ... je loge au ... [juh loj o]

I'd like to stay another two nights j'aimerais rester deux nuits de plus [jemray restay]

steak le steak

steal voler [volay]

my bag has been stolen on m'a volé mon sac [ON ma volay]

steep (hill) raide [red]

steering la direction [deereeks-yON]

step: on the steps sur les marches [sOOr lay marsh]

stereo stéréo [stayray-o]

sterling la livre sterling [leevr stairleeng]

steward (on plane) le steward

stewardess l'hôtesse de l'air f [otess]

sticking plaster le sparadrap [-dra]

still: I'm still waiting j'attends

toujours [toojoor]

is he still there? est-ce qu'il est toujours là? [eskeel ay toojoor la]

keep still! ne bouge/bougez pas! [nuh booj/boojay pa]

sting: I've been stung j'ai été piqué (par un insecte) [jay aytay peekay (par AN ANsekt)]

stockings les bas mpl [ba]

stomach le ventre, l'estomac m [vONtr, estoma]

stomach ache les maux d'estomac [mo destoma]

stone (rock) la pierre [p-yair]

stop s'arrêter [sa-retay]

to stop the car arrêter la voiture

please, stop here (to taxi driver etc) arrêtez-moi ici, s'il vous plaît [aretay-mwa ee-see]

do you stop near ...? est-ce que vous vous arrêtez près de ...? [eskuh voo voo zaretay]

stop doing that! arrêtez!

stopover la halte [alt]

storm la tempête [tON-pet]

straight: it's straight ahead c'est tout droit [say too drwa]

a straight whisky un whisky sec

straightaway tout de suite [toot sweet]

strange (odd) bizarre, étrange [aytroNj]

stranger l'étranger m, l'étrangère f [aytrONjay, -jair]

I'm a stranger here je ne suis pas d'ici [juh nuh swee pa dee-see]

strap (on watch) le bracelet [braslay]
(on dress) la bretelle [bruhtel]
(on suitcase) la sangle [sONgl]
strawberry la fraise [frez]
stream le ruisseau [rwee-so]
street la rue [rOO]
on the street dans la rue
streetmap le plan de ville [plON duh veel]
string la ficelle [feessel]
strong fort [for]
stuck coincé [kwANsay]
the key's stuck le clé est coincée
student (male/female) l'étudiant m, l'étudiante f [aytOOd-yON, -yONt]
stupid stupide [stOOpeed]
suburb le faubourg [fo-boor]
subway (US) le métro [maytro]
suddenly tout d'un coup [too dAN koo]
suede le daim [dAN]
sugar le sucre [sOOkr]
suit le costume
it doesn't suit me (colour etc) ça ne me va pas [sa nuh muh va pa]
it suits you (colour etc) ça vous va bien [b-yAN]
suitcase la valise [valeez]
summer l'été m [aytay]
in the summer en été
sun le soleil [solay]
in the sun au soleil [o]
out of the sun à l'ombre [lONbr]
sunbathe prendre un bain de soleil [prONdr AN bAN duh solay]

sunblock (cream) l'écran total m [aykrON toh-tal]
sunburn le coup de soleil [koo duh solay]
sunburnt: I'm sunburnt j'ai pris un coup de soleil [pree AN]
Sunday dimanche [deemONsh]
sunglasses les lunettes de soleil [lOOnet duh solay]
sun lounger la chaise longue [shez lON-g]
sunny ensoleillé [ONsolay-yay]
it's sunny il fait soleil [eel fay solay]
sun roof (in car) le toit ouvrant [twa oovrON]
sunset le coucher de soleil [kooshay duh solay]
sunshade le parasol
sunshine le soleil [solay]
sunstroke l'insolation f [ANsolass-yON]
suntan le bronzage [brONzahj]
suntan lotion le lait solaire [lay solair]
suntanned bronzé [brONzay]
suntan oil l'huile solaire f [weel solair]
super super [sOOpair]
we had a super time c'était super [saytay]
supermarket le supermarché [sOOpairmarshay]
supper le dîner [deenay]
supplement (extra charge) le supplément [sOOplaymON]
sure: are you sure? vous êtes sûr? [voo zet sOOr]
sure! d'accord! [dakor]

surname le nom de famille
[nON duh famee]
swearword le juron [jOOrON]
sweater le pullover
sweatshirt le sweatshirt
Sweden la Suède [swed]
Swedish (adj) suédois [swaydwa]
sweet (taste) sucré [sOOkray]
(dessert) le dessert [dessair]
sweets les bonbons **mpl**
[bONbON]
swelling l'enflure **f** [ONflOOr]
swim nager [nahjay]
I'm going for a swim je vais
me baigner [juh vay muh
benyay]
let's go for a swim allons
nous baigner
swimming costume le maillot
de bain [my-o duh bAN]
swimming pool la piscine
[peesseen]
swimming trunks le slip de
bain [sleep duh bAN]
Swiss (adj) suisse [sweess]
(man) le Suisse
(woman) la Suissesse
[sweessess]
switch l'interrupteur **m**
[ANtairOOpturr]
switch off (TV, lights) éteindre
[aytANdr]
(engine) arrêter [aretay]
switch on (TV, lights) allumer
[alOOmay]
(engine) mettre en marche
[metr ON marsh]
Switzerland la Suisse [sweess]
swollen enflé [ONflay]

T

table la table [tahbl]
a table for two une table
pour deux
tablecloth la nappe [nap]
table tennis le ping-pong
table wine le vin ordinaire
[vAN ordeenair]
tailback (of traffic) le bouchon
[booshON]
tailor le tailleur [tī-urr]
take (lead) prendre [prONdr]
(accept) accepter [axeptay]
**can you take me to the
airport?** est-ce que vous
pouvez m'emmener à
l'aéroport? [eskuh voo poovay
mONmuhnay]
do you take credit cards?
acceptez-vous les cartes de
crédit? [axeptay-voo]
fine, I'll take it d'accord, je le
prends [juh luh prON]
can I take this? (leaflet etc) je
peux le prendre? [puh]
how long does it take?
combien de temps est-ce que
ça prend? [kONb-yAN duh tON
eskuh sa prON]
it takes three hours ça prend
trois heures
is this seat taken? est-ce
que cette place est occupée?
[eskuh set plass et okOOpay]
hamburger to take away
hamburger à emporter
[ONportay]

can you take a little off here? (to hairdresser) pouvez-vous couper un peu par ici? [koopay AN puh]

talcum powder le talc

talk parler [parlay]

tall grand [grON]

tampons les tampons **mpl** [tONpON]

tan le bronzage [brONzahj]

to get a tan bronzer [brONzay]

tank (of car) le réservoir [rayzairvwahr]

tap le robinet [robeenay]

tape (cassette) la cassette (sticky) le scotch®

tape measure le mètre [metr]

tape recorder le magnétophone [man-yaytofon]

taste le goût [goo]

can I taste it? est-ce que je peux goûter? [eskuh juh puh gootay]

taxi le taxi

will you get me a taxi? pouvez-vous m'appeler un taxi? [poovay-voo maplay]

where can I find a taxi? où y a-t-il des taxis? [oo yateel]

dialogue

to the airport/to Hotel ... please à l'aéroport/à l'Hôtel ..., s'il vous plaît

how much will it be? combien est-ce que ça me coûtera? [kONb-yAN eskuh sa muh kootuhra]

about 15 euros à peu près quinze euros [puh pray]

that's just fine right here thanks vous pouvez me déposer ici, merci [muh daypozay]

taxi-driver le chauffeur de taxi

taxi rank la station de taxi [stass-yON]

tea (drink) le thé [tay]

tea for one/two please un thé/deux thés, s'il vous plaît [duh tay]

teabags les sachets de thé **mpl** [sashay duh tay]

teach: could you teach me? est-ce que vous pouvez m'apprendre? [eskuh voo poovay maprONdr]

teacher (junior) l'instituteur **m**, l'institutrice **f** [ANsteetOOturr, -treess]

(secondary) le professeur [-urr]

team l'équipe **f** [aykeep]

teaspoon la cuillère à café [kwee-yair a kafay]

tea towel le torchon à vaisselle [torshON a vess-el]

teenager l'adolescent **m**, l'adolescente **f** [-sON, -sONt]

telephone le téléphone [taylay-]

television la télévision [taylayveez-yON]

tell: could you tell him ...?

pourriez-vous lui dire ...?
[pooree-ay-voo lwee deer]

temperature (weather) la
température [tONpayratOOr]
(fever) la fièvre [fee-evr]

tennis le tennis [teneess]

tennis ball la balle de tennis
[bal]

tennis court le court de tennis
[koor]

tennis racket la raquette de
tennis [raket]

tent la tente [tONt]

term (at university, school) le
trimestre [treemestr]

terminus (rail) le terminus
[tairmeenOOss]

terrible épouvantable
[aypoovONt-abl]

terrific fantastique
[fONtasteek]

text (message) le texto
[mairsee]

than* que [kuh]
smaller than plus petit
que

thanks, thank you merci
[mairsee]
thank you very much merci
beaucoup [bo-koo]
thanks for the help merci de
m'avoir aidé
no thanks non, merci

dialogue

thanks merci
that's OK, don't mention it
il n'y a pas de quoi [eel
n-ya pa duh kwa]

that: that building ce bâtiment
[suh]
that woman cette femme
[set]
that one celui-là, **f** celle-là
[suhlwee-la, sel-la]
I hope that ... j'espère que ...
[kuh]
that's nice c'est joli [say]
is that ...? est-ce que c'est ...?
[eskuh say]
that's it (that's right) c'est ça [say
sa]

the* (singular) le, **f** la [luh]
(plural) les [lay]

theatre le théâtre [tay-atr]

their* leur [lurr]

theirs* le/la leur [luh/la lurr]

them*: I know them je les
connais [juh lay konay]
for them pour eux, **f** pour
elles [uh, el]
with them avec eux/elles
I gave it to them je le leur
ai donné [juh luh lurr ay donay]
who? – them qui? – eux/elles

then (at that time) à cette
époque [set aypok]
(after that) alors [alor]

there là
over there là-bas [la-ba]
up there là-haut [la-o]
is there ...? y a-t-il ...?
[yateel]
are there ...? y a-t-il ...?
there is ... il y a ... [eel ya]
there are ... il y a ...
there you are (giving something)
voilà [vwala]

thermometer le thermomètre [tairmometr]

Thermos flask® le thermos [tairmoss]

these*: these men ces hommes [say]

these women ces femmes

can I have these? j'aimerais ceux-ci/celles-ci, s'il vous plaît [suh-see/sel-see]

they* ils, **f** elles [eel, el]

thick épais [aypay]

(stupid) bouché [booshay]

thief le voleur, **f** la voleuse [volurr, -urz]

thigh la cuisse [kweess]

thin mince [MANss]

thing la chose [shohz]

my things mes affaires [may zafair]

think penser [poNsay]

I think so je pense que oui [juh poNss kuh wee]

I don't think so je ne crois pas [nuh krwa pa]

I'll think about it je vais y réfléchir [vay zee rayflesheer]

third party insurance l'assurance au tiers **f** [o t-yair]

thirsty: I'm thirsty j'ai soif [jay swaf]

this: this building ce bâtiment [suh]

this woman cette femme [set]

this one celui-ci, **f** celle-ci [suhlwee-see, sel-see]

this is my wife je vous présente ma femme [juh voo prayzoNt ma fam]

is this ...? est-ce que c'est ...? [eskuh say]

those: those men ces hommes [say]

those women ces femmes

which ones? – those lesquel(le)s? – ceux-là/celles-là [suhk-la/sel-la]

thread le fil [feel]

throat la gorge [gorj]

throat pastilles les pastilles pour la gorge **fpl** [pastee poor la gorj]

through par

does it go through ...? (train, bus) est-ce qu'il passe à ...? [eskeel pass]

throw lancer [loNsay]

throw away jeter [juhtay]

thumb le pouce [pooss]

thunderstorm l'orage **m** [orahj]

Thursday jeudi [juhdee]

ticket (for bus, train, plane) le billet [bee-yay]

(for cinema, cloakroom) le ticket [teekay]

dialogue

a return ticket to Dijon un aller-retour pour Dijon [alay-ruhtoor]

coming back when? avec retour à quelle date? [ruhtoor]

today/next Tuesday

aujourd'hui/mardi prochain
that will be 60 euros soixante euros, si'il vous plaît

ticket office (bus, rail) le guichet [geeshay]
tide la marée [maray]
tie (necktie) la cravate [kravat]
tight (clothes etc) serré [serray]
 it's too tight ça me serre [sa muh sair]
tights le collant [kollON]
till (cash desk) la caisse [kess]
time* le temps [tON]
 what's the time? quelle heure est-il? [kel urr eteel]
 this time cette fois [set fwa]
 last time la dernière fois
 next time la prochaine fois
 four times quatre fois
timetable l'horaire m [orair]
tin (can) la boîte [bwat]
tinfoil le papier d'aluminium [pap-yay]
tin opener l'ouvre-boîte m [oovr-bwat]
tiny minuscule [meenOOskOOl]
tip (to waiter etc) le pourboire [poorbwahr]
tired fatigué [fateegay]
 I'm tired je suis fatigué
tissues les kleenex® mpl
to: **to Strasbourg/London** à Strasbourg/Londres
 to Brittany/England en Bretagne/Angleterre [ON]

to the post office à la poste
to the bar au bar [o]
toast (bread) le pain grillé [pAN gree-yay]
today aujourd'hui [ojoordwee]
toe l'orteil m [ortay]
together ensemble [ONSONbl]
 we're together (in shop etc) nous sommes ensemble
 can we pay together? pouvons-nous payer ensemble? [poovON-noo payay]
toilet les toilettes [twalet]
 where is the toilet? où sont les toilettes? [oo sON lay]
 I have to go to the toilet j'aimerais aller aux toilettes [jemray alay o]
toilet paper le papier hygiénique [papyay eejee-ayneek]
tomato la tomate [tomat]
tomato juice le jus de tomate [jOO]
tomato ketchup le ketchup
tomorrow demain [duhmAN]
 tomorrow morning demain matin
 the day after tomorrow après-demain [apray]
toner (cosmetic) la lotion tonique [lohss-yON toneek]
tongue la langue [lON-g]
tonic (water) le schweppes®
tonight ce soir [suh swahr]
tonsillitis l'angine f [ONjeen]
too (excessively) trop [tro]
 (also) aussi [o-see]

too hot trop chaud
too much trop
me too moi aussi [mwa]
tooth la dent [dON]
toothache le mal de dents [mal duh dON]
toothbrush la brosse à dents [bross]
toothpaste le dentifrice [dONteefreess]
top: on top of ... sur ... [soor]
at the top en haut [ON o]
top floor le dernier étage [dairn-yay aytahj]
topless seins nus [saN noo]
torch la lampe de poche [lONp duh posh]
total le total [toh-tal]
touch toucher [tooshay]
tour l'excursion f [exkoors-yON]
is there a tour of ...? y a-t-il une visite guidée de ...? [yateel oon veezeet geeday duh]
tour guide le guide [geed]
tourist le/la touriste [tooreest]
tourist information office le centre d'information touristique [sONtr dANformass-yON tooreesteek]
tour operator le voyagiste [vwy-ahjeest]
towards vers [vair]
towel la serviette [sairvee-et]
town la ville [veel]
in town en ville [ON]
just out of town à la sortie de la ville
town centre le centre-ville [sONtr-]

town hall la mairie [mairee]
toy le jouet [joo-ay]
track (US) le quai [kay]
tracksuit le survêtement [soorvetmON]
traditional traditionnel [tradeess-yonel]
traffic la circulation [seerkoolass-yON]
traffic jam l'embouteillage m [ONbootay-ahj]
traffic lights les feux [fuh]
trailer (for carrying tent etc) la remorque [ruhmork]
(US) la caravane
trailer park le terrain de camping pour caravanes [terrAN duh kONpeeng poor]
train le train [trAN]
by train en train [ON]

dialogue

is this the train for ...?
est-ce que ce train va bien à ...? [eskuh suh trAN va b-yAN a]
sure oui
no, you want that platform there non, il faut que vous alliez sur ce quai là-bas [eel fo kuh voo zalee-ay soor suh kay]

trainers (shoes) les tennis fpl [tenneess]
train station la gare [gar]
translate traduire [tradweer]

could you translate that?
pourriez-vous me traduire
cela? [pooree-ay-voo muh ... suhla]

translation la traduction
[tradooks-yON]

translator le traducteur, la
traductrice [tradookturr, -treess]

trashcan la poubelle [poo-bel]

travel voyager [vwyahj-ay]
we're travelling around
nous visitons la région [noo
veezeetON la rayjeeON]

travel agent's l'agence de
voyages **f** [ajONss duh vwyahj]

traveller's cheque le chèque
de voyage [shek duh vwyahj]

tray le plateau [pla-toh]

tree l'arbre **m** [arbr]

tremendous fantastique
[fONtasteek]

trendy à la mode

trim: just a trim please (to
hairdresser) pouvez-vous me
les égaliser, s'il vous plaît?
[poovay-voo muh lay zaygaleezay]

trip le voyage [vwyahj]
(excursion) l'excursion **f**
[exkOOrs-yON]
I'd like to go on a trip to ...
j'aimerais faire une excursion
à ... [jemray fair]

trolley le chariot [sharee-o]

trouble les ennuis [ON-nwee]
I'm having trouble with ... j'ai
des problèmes de ... [jay day
prob-lem]
sorry to trouble you désolé de
vous déranger [dayzolay duh voo
dayrONjay]

trousers le pantalon [pONtalON]

true vrai [vray]
that's not true ce n'est pas
vrai

trunk le coffre [kofr]

trunks (swimming) le maillot de
bain [my-o duh bAN]

try essayer [esay-ay]
can I have a try? (at doing
something) est-ce que je peux
essayer? [eskuh juh puh]
(food) est-ce que je peux
goûter? [gootay]

try on essayer [essay-ay]
can I try it on? est-ce que je
peux l'essayer?

T-shirt le T-shirt

Tuesday mardi [mardee]

tuna le thon [tON]

Tunisia la Tunisie [tooneezee]

Tunisian tunisien [tooneez-yAN]

tunnel le tunnel [toonel]

turn: turn left/right tournez à
gauche/droite [toornay]

turn off: where do I turn off?
où dois-je bifurquer? [oo dwa-
juh beefOOrkay]
**can you turn the heating
off?** pouvez-vous arrêter le
chauffage? [aretay]

**turn on: can you turn the
heating on?** pouvez-vous
mettre le chauffage? [metr]

turning (in road) la bifurcation
[beefOOrkass-yON]

TV la télé [taylay]

tweezers la pince à épiler
[pANss a aypeelay]

twice deux fois [duh fwa]

twice as much deux fois plus [plOOss]

twin beds les lits jumeaux [lee jOOmo]

twin room la chambre à deux lits [shONbr]

twist: I've twisted my ankle je me suis tordu la cheville [juh muh swee tordOO la shuhvee]

type le type [teep]

a different type of ... une autre sorte de ... [ohtr sort duh]

typical typique [teepeek]

tyre le pneu [p-nuh]

U

ugly (person, building) laid [lay]

UK le Royaume-Uni [rwy-ohm OOnee]

ulcer l'ulcère m [OOlsair]

umbrella le parapluie [paraplwee]

uncle l'oncle m [ONkl]

unconscious sans connaissance [sON konessONss]

under (in position) sous [soo]
(less than) moins de [mwAN duh]

underdone (meat) pas assez cuit [pa zassay kwee]

underground (railway) le métro [maytro]

underpants le slip [sleep]

understand: I understand je comprends [juh kONprON]
I don't understand je ne comprends pas [pa]

do you understand? comprenez-vous? [kONpruhnay-voo]

unemployed au chômage [o shohmahj]

United States les États-Unis [aytazOOnee]

university l'université f [OOneevairseetay]

unleaded petrol l'essence sans plomb f [essONss sON plON]

unlimited mileage le kilométrage illimité [keelomaytrahj eeleemeetay]

unlock ouvrir [oovreer]

unpack défaire sa valise [dayfair sa valeez]

until jusqu'à [jOOska]
I'll wait until you're back j'attendrai jusqu'à ce que tu reviennes [jatONdray jOOss-kass kuh]

unusual inhabituel [eenabeetOOel]

up en haut [ON o]
up there là-haut [la-o]
he's not up yet (not out of bed) il n'est pas encore levé [eel nay pa zONkor luhvay]
what's up? (what's wrong?) que se passe-t-il? [kuh suh pasteel]

upmarket chic [sheek]

upset stomach l'indigestion f [ANdeejest-yON]

upside down à l'envers [a lONvair]

upstairs en haut [ON o]

urgent urgent [OOrjON]

us* nous [noo]
  with us avec nous
  for us pour nous
USA les USA [oo-ess-a]
use utiliser [ooteeleezay]
  may I use ...? puis-je me
  servir de ...? [pweej muh sairveer
  duh]
useful utile [ooteel]
usual habituel [abeetooel]
  the usual (drink etc) comme
  d'habitude [kom dabeetood]

V

vacancy: do you have any
  vacancies? (hotel) est-ce que
  vous avez des chambres?
  [eskuh voo zavay day shONbr]
vacation les vacances fpl
vaccination le vaccin [vaxAN]
vacuum cleaner l'aspirateur m
  [aspeeraturr]
valid (ticket etc) valable [val-abl]
  how long is it valid for?
  jusqu'à quand est-il valable?
  [jooska kON eteel]
valley la vallée [valay]
valuable (adj) précieux [prayss-
  yuh]
  can I leave my valuables
  here? est-ce que je peux
  laisser mes objets de valeur
  ici? [eskuh juh puh lessay may
  zobjay duh valurr ee-see]
value la valeur [valurr]
van la camionnette [kameeonet]
vanilla la vanille [vanee]

a vanilla ice cream une glace
  à la vanille [glass]
vary: it varies ça dépend [sa
  daypON]
vase le vase [vahz]
veal le veau [vo]
vegetables les légumes mpl
  [laygoom]
vegetarian le végétarien, la
  végétarienne [vayjaytaree-AN,
  -en]
vending machine le
  distributeur automatique
  [deestreebooturr otomateek]
very très [tray]
  very little for me un tout petit
  peu pour moi [AN too puhtee
  puh]
  I like it very much ça me plaît
  beaucoup [sa muh play bo-koo]
vest (under shirt) le maillot de
  corps [my-o duh kor]
via par
video (film) la vidéo [veedayo]
  (recorder) le magnétoscope
  [man-yaytoskop]
view la vue [voo]
villa la villa [veela]
village le village [veelahj]
vinegar le vinaigre [veenegr]
vineyard le vignoble [veen-
  yobl]
visa le visa [veezeetay]
visit visiter [veezeetay]
  I'd like to visit ... j'aimerais
  visiter ... [jemray]
vital: it's vital that ... il faut
  absolument que ... [eel foht
  absoloomON kuh]

119

vodka la vodka
voice la voix [vwa]
voltage le voltage [volt-ahj]
vomit vomir [vomeer]

W

waist la taille [tī]
waistcoat le gilet [jeelay]
wait attendre [atONdr]
  wait for me! attendez-moi! [atONday-mwa]
  don't wait for me ne m'attendez pas [nuh]
  can I wait until my wife/ partner gets here? est-ce que je peux attendre ma femme/ mon ami(e)? [eksuh juh puh]
  can you do it while I wait? pouvez-vous le faire tout de suite? [poovay-voo luh fair toot sweet]
  could you wait here for me? (as said to taxi driver) est-ce que vous pouvez m'attendre ici?
waiter le serveur [sairvurr], le garçon [garsON]
  waiter! garçon!
waitress la serveuse [sairvurz]
  waitress! s'il vous plaît! [seel voo play]
wake: can you wake me up at 5.30? pouvez-vous me réveiller à cinq heures trente? [poovay-voo muh rayvayay]
wake-up call le réveil téléphonique [ray-vay

taylayfoneek]
Wales le Pays de Galles [payee duh gal]
walk: is it a long walk? est-ce loin à pied? [es lwaN a p-yay]
  it's only a short walk c'est à deux pas d'ici [set a duh pa dee-see]
  I'll walk j'y vais à pied [jee vay]
  I'm going for a walk je vais faire un tour [juh vay fair AN toor]
Walkman® le walkman
wall le mur [moor]
wallet le portefeuille [portfuh-ee]
wander: I like just wandering around j'aime bien flâner [jem b-yAN flanay]
want: I want a ... je veux un ... [juh vuh]
  I don't want any ... je ne veux pas de ... [juh nuh vuh pa duh]
  we want to go home nous voulons rentrer à la maison [noo voolON]
  I don't want to non, je ne veux pas
  he wants to ... il veut ... [eel vuh]
  what do you want? que voulez-vous? [kuh voolay-voo]
ward (in hospital) la salle [sal]
warm chaud [sho]
  I'm so warm j'ai tellement chaud
was*: it was ... c'était ... [saytay]
wash laver [lavay]

can you wash these?
pouvez-vous laver ceci, s'il
vous plaît? [poovay-voo]

washer (for bolt etc) la rondelle
[rONdel]

washhand basin le lavabo

washing (clothes) la lessive
[lesseev]

washing machine la machine
à laver [lavay]

washing powder la lessive
[lesseev]

washing-up liquid le produit à
vaisselle [prodwee a vess-el]

wasp la guêpe [gep]

watch (wristwatch) la montre
[mONtr]

will you watch my things
for me? pourriez-vous me
garder mes affaires, s'il vous
plaît? [pooree-ay-voo muh garday]

watch out! attention! [atONs-
yON]

watch strap le bracelet-
montre [braslay-mONtr]

water l'eau f [o]

may I have some water?
pourriez-vous m'apporter de
l'eau, s'il vous plaît? [pooree-
ay-voo maportay]

waterproof (adj) imperméable
[ANpairmayabl]

waterskiing le ski nautique
[skee noteek]

wave (in sea) la vague [vag]

way: it's this way c'est par ici
[say par ee-see]

it's that way c'est par là

is it a long way to ...? est-

ce que c'est loin d'ici à ...?
[eskuh say lwAN dee-see]

no way! pas question!
[pa kest-yON]

dialogue

could you tell me the
way to ...? pouvez-vous
m'indiquer le chemin
pour aller à ...?
go straight on until you
reach the traffic lights
continuez tout droit
jusqu'aux feux [kONteenoo-
ay too drwa jOOsko fuh]
turn left tournez à gauche
[toornay]
take the first on the right
prenez la première à
droite [pruhnay]
see also **where**

we* nous [noo]

weak (person) faible [febl]

(drink) pas fort [pa for]

weather le temps [tON]

dialogue

what's the weather
forecast? quelles sont les
prévisions de météo?
[kels sON lay prayveez-yON duh la
maytay-o]
it's going to be fine il va
faire beau [eel va fair bo]
it's going to rain il va
pleuvoir

it'll brighten up later ça va s'éclaircir plus tard [sa va sayklairseer]

wedding le mariage [maree-ahj]
wedding ring l'alliance **f** [aleeONss]
Wednesday mercredi [mairkruhdee]
week la semaine [suhmen]
a week (from) today aujourd'hui en huit [ojoordwee ON weet]
a week (from) tomorrow demain en huit
weekend le week-end
at the weekend ce week-end
weight le poids [pwa]
weird bizarre
weirdo l'énergumène **mf** [aynairgoOmen]
welcome: welcome to ... bienvenue à ... [b-yAN-vuhnOO]
you're welcome (don't mention it) je vous en prie [juh voo zON pree]
well: I don't feel well je ne me sens pas bien [juh nuh muh sON pa b-yAN]
she's not well elle ne se sent pas bien [... sON ...]
you speak English very well vous parlez très bien l'anglais
well done! bravo!
this one as well celui-là aussi [o-see]
well well! (surprise) tiens! [tyAN]

We

dialogue

how are you? comment vas-tu/allez-vous? [komON va-tOO/alay-voo]
very well, thanks très bien, merci [tray b-yAN]

well-done (meat) bien cuit [b-yAN kwee]
Welsh gallois [galwa]
I'm Welsh (man/woman) je suis gallois/galloise [... galwahz]
were*: we were nous étions [noo zayteeON]
you were vous étiez [voo zaytee-ay]
they were ils/elles étaient [eel/el zaytay]
west l'ouest **m** [west]
in the west à l'ouest
West Indian (adj) antillais [ONteeray]
wet mouillé [mooyay]
what? quoi? [kwa]
what's that? qu'est-ce que c'est? [keskuh say]
what should I do? que dois-je faire? [kuh dwahj fair]
what a view! quelle vue magnifique! [kel]
what bus do I take? je prends quel bus?
wheel la roue [roo]
wheelchair le fauteuil roulant [fotuh-ee roolON]
when? quand? [kON]
when we get back à notre

retour [a notr ruhtoor]
when's the train/ferry? à quelle heure part le train/ferry? [kel urr par]
where? où? [oo]
I don't know where it is je ne sais pas où il est

dialogue

where is the cathedral? où est la cathédrale? [oo ay est la cathedral]
it's over there c'est par là [say]
could you show me where it is on the map? pouvez-vous me montrer où ça se trouve sur la carte?
it's just here c'est ici

which: which train? quel train? [kel]

dialogue

which one? lequel (laquelle)? [luhkel, lakel]
that one celui-là (celle-là) [suhlwee-la, sel-la]
this one? celui-ci (celle-ci)? [suhlwee-see]
no, that one non, celui-là (celle-là)

while: while I'm here pendant que je suis ici [pondoN kuh]
whisky le whisky
white blanc, f blanche [bloN, bloNsh]

white wine le vin blanc [VAN bloN]
who? qui? [kee]
who is it? qui est-ce? [ess]
the man who ... l'homme qui ...
whole: the whole week toute la semaine [toot]
the whole lot le tout [luh too]
whose: whose is this? à qui est ceci? [a kee ay suhsee]
why? pourquoi? [poorkwa]
why not? pourquoi pas? [pa]
wide large [larj]
wife: my wife ma femme [fam]
will*: will you do it for me? pouvez-vous faire ça pour moi? [poovay-voo]
wind le vent [voN]
window la fenêtre [fuhnetr]
near the window près de la fenêtre
in the window (of shop) en vitrine [oN veetreen]
window seat le siège près de la fenêtre [pray duh la fuhnetr]
windscreen le pare-brise [par-breez]
windscreen wiper l'essuie-glace m [eswee-glass]
windsurfing la planche à voile [ploNsh a vwal]
windy: it's so windy il y a beaucoup de vent [eelya bo-koo duh voN]
wine le vin [VAN]
can we have some more wine? encore un peu de vin, s'il vous plaît [oNkor AN puh]

wine list la carte des vins [kart day vAN]

wine merchant le marchand de vins [marshON duh vAN]

wine-tasting la dégustation [daygOOstass-yON]

winter l'hiver **m** [eevair]

in the winter en hiver [ON]

winter holiday les vacances d'hiver [vakONss deevair]

wire le fil de fer [feel duh fair] (electric) le fil (électrique) [aylektreek]

wish: best wishes meilleurs vœux [mayurr vuh]

with avec [avek]

I'm staying with ... j'habite chez ... [jabeet shay]

without sans [sON]

witness le témoin [taymwAN]

will you be a witness for me? voulez-vous me servir de témoin? [voolay-voo muh sairveer duh]

woman la femme [fam]

wonderful merveilleux [mairvayuh]

won't*: the car won't start la voiture ne veut pas démarrer [nuh vuh pa]

wood (material) le bois [bwa]

woods (forest) la forêt [foray]

wool la laine [len]

word le mot [mo]

work le travail [trav-ī]

I work in ... je travaille dans ... [juh trav-ī]

it's not working ça ne marche pas [sa nuh marsh pa]

world le monde [mONd]

worried inquiet, **f** inquiète [ANkee-ay, -et]

worse: it's worse c'est pire [say peer]

worst le pire [luh peer]

worth: is it worth a visit? est-ce que ça vaut le détour? [eskuh sa vo luh daytoor]

would: would you give this to ...? pourriez-vous donner ceci à ...? [pooree-ay-voo donay suhsee]

wrap: could you wrap it up? pourriez-vous me l'emballer? [pooree-ay-voo muh lONbalay]

wrapping paper le papier d'emballage [pap-yay dONbalahj]

wrist le poignet [pwAN-yay]

write écrire [aykreer]

could you write it down? pouvez-vous me l'écrire? [poovay-voo muh laykreer]

how do you write it? comment est-ce que ça s'écrit? [komON teskuh sa saykree]

writing paper le papier à lettres [pap-yay a letr]

wrong: it's the wrong key ce n'est pas la bonne clef [suh nuh pa la bon klay]

this is the wrong train ce n'est pas le bon train

the bill's wrong il y a une erreur dans la facture [eelya OOn air-rurr dON la faktOOr]

sorry, wrong number

excusez-moi, j'ai fait un mauvais numéro [exkoozay-mwa jay fay AN movay noomayro]

sorry, wrong room excusez-moi, je me suis trompé de chambre [juh muh swee troNpay]

there's something wrong with ... ... ne marche pas bien [nuh marsh pa b-yAN]

what's wrong? qu'y a-t-il? [k-yateel]

dialogue

is it here yet? est-ce que c'est arrivé? [eskuh say]

no, not yet non, pas encore [pa zoNkor]

you'll have to wait a little longer yet il vous faudra attendre encore un peu

X

X-ray les rayons X **mpl** [rayoN eex]

Y

yacht le voilier [vwal-yay]

yard* le jardin [jardAN]

year l'année **f** [anay]

yellow jaune [jo-n]

yes oui [wee]

you're not going already, are you? – yes tu ne t'en vas pas déjà, hein? – si [too nuh toN va pa day-ja AN – see]

yesterday hier [yair]

yesterday morning hier matin

the day before yesterday avant-hier [avoNt-yair]

yet encore [oNkor]

have you heard from him yet? est-ce que vous avez déjà eu de ses nouvelles? [eskuh voo zavay day-ja oo duh say noovel]

yoghurt le yaourt [ya-oor]

you* (polite or plural) vous [voo] (singular, familiar) tu [too]

this is for you c'est pour toi/vous [twa]

with you avec toi/vous

young jeune [jurn]

your* votre, pl vos [votr, vo] (singular, familiar) ton, **f** ta, pl tes [toN, ta, tay]

yours* le/la vôtre [luh/la vohtr], pl les vôtres (singular, familiar) le tien, **f** la tienne [t-yAN, t-yen], pl les tiens/tiennes

youth hostel l'auberge de jeunesse **f** [obairj duh jur-ness]

Z

zero zéro [zayro]

zip la fermeture éclair [fairmtoor ayklair]

could you put a new zip on? pourriez-vous mettre une nouvelle fermeture éclair? [pooree-ay-voo metr oon noovel]

zoo le zoo [zo]

French

→

English

Colloquialisms

The following are words you might well hear. You shouldn't be tempted to use any of the stronger ones unless you are sure of your audience.

bagnole f [ban-yol] old banger
bouffer [boofay] eat
ça craint [sa krAN] it's just terrible
ça me gonfle [sa muh gONfl] it's a pain
ça pête [sa pet] it's great
casse-toi! [kass twa] get lost!
c'est de la merde [say duh la maird] it's crap
c'est nul à chier [say nool a shee-ay] it's a load of crap
chiant [shee-ON] bloody annoying
con [kON] bloody stupid; bastard
connard m [konar] bloody idiot
dégage! [daygaj] get lost!
dégueulasse [dayguhlass] disgusting
dingue [dANg] crazy
fils de pute m [feess duh poot] son of a bitch
génial [jaynee-al] brilliant, cool
je m'emmerde [juh mONmaird] I'm bored stiff
je m'en fous! [juh mON foo] I couldn't care less
j'en ai marre! [jON-ay mar] I've had it up to here
mec m [mek] guy, bloke
merde! [maird] shit!
nana f [nana] bird, chick
on s'éclate! [ON sayklat] we're having a blast
pété [paytay] pissed
salaud m [salo] bastard
salope f [salop] bitch
ta gueule! [ta gurl] shut it!
tout baigne! [too beñ] everything's just hunky-dory!
tu déconnes? [too daykon] are you crazy?
tu m'emmerdes! [too mONmaird] you're a pain in the arse!
tu te fous de ma gueule? [too tuh foo duh ma gurl] are you taking the piss!
va te faire foutre! [va tuh fair footr] fuck off!

A

a: il/elle a he/she/it has

à [a] to; at; in; by
  à la gare at the station

abcès m [absay] abscess

abeille f [abay] bee

abonnements mpl [abonnuh-mON] season tickets

abord: d'abord [dabor] first

absolument [absolOOmON] absolutely

accélérateur m [axaylayraturr] accelerator

accélérer [axaylayray] to accelerate

accepter [axeptay] to accept

accès autorisé pour livraisons deliveries only

accès aux quais to the platforms

accès aux trains to the trains

accès interdit no entry

accès réservé au personnel staff entrance only

accès réservé aux riverains no entry except for access

accès réservé aux voyageurs munis de billets ticket holders only

accompagner [akONpan-yay] to accompany

accord: d'accord [dakor] OK
  je suis d'accord I agree

accotement non stabilisé soft verge

accueil m [akuh-ee] reception

accusé de réception m [akOOzay duh rayseps-yON] acknowledgement of receipt

achat m [a-sha] purchase
  faire des achats to go shopping

acheter [ashtay] to buy

acide [a-seed] sour

acteur m [akturr] actor

actrice f [aktreess] actress

adaptateur m [adaptaturr] adaptor

addition f [adeess-yON] bill

adolescent m [adolessON] teenager

s'adresser à ... [sadressay] ask ...
  adressez-vous à la réception ask at reception

aérogare f [a-airogar] air terminal

aéroglisseur m [a-airogleessurr] hovercraft

aéroport m [a-airopor] airport

affaires fpl [affair] things, belongings; business

affichage m [affeeshahj] display

affiche f [affeesh] poster

afficher [affeeshay] to display

affranchir [affrONsheer] to stamp

affranchissement m [affrONsheess-mON] postage

affreux [affruh] awful

afin que [afAN kuh] so that

âge m [ahj] age

agence f [ajONss] agency

agence de voyages f [duh vwyahj] travel agent's

agenda m [ajANda] diary
agent conservateur [ajON kONsairvaturr] preservative
agent de police m [duh poleess] policeman
agiter avant l'emploi shake before use
agrandissement m [agroNdeess-mON] enlargement
agréable [agray-abl] pleasant
agriculteur m [agreekOOlturr] farmer
ai: j'ai [jay] I have
aide f [ed] help
aider [ayday] to help
aiguille f [aygwee] needle
aile f [el] wing
ailleurs [ī-yur] elsewhere
aimable [aymabl] kind
aimer [aymay] to like; to love
ne pas aimer to dislike
aimerais: j'aimerais [jemray] I would like
ainsi [ANsee] so; like this
ainsi que (just) as
air m [air] air
avoir l'air [avwahr] to look
air conditionné [kondeess-yonay] air conditioning
aire de croisement f [air duh krwaz-mON] passing place
aire de repos [ruhpo] rest area
aire de service [sairveess] service area
aire de stationnement [stass-yonuh-mON] parking area
ajouter [ajootay] to add
alimentation f [aleemONtass-yon] food; grocer

alimentation générale [jaynayral] grocer
allaiter [alaytay] to breastfeed
Allemagne f [almañ] Germany
allemand [almON] German
aller [alay] to go
comment allez-vous? [komON talay voo] how are you?
s'en aller [sON] to go away
allez-vous-en! [alay-voo zON] go away!
aller chercher [shairshay] to go and get, to fetch
aller-retour m [alay ruhtoor] return/round trip ticket
aller simple m [sANpl] single ticket
aller voir [vwahr] to go and see, to go and visit
allumage m [alOOmahj] ignition
allumer [alOOmay] to light; to switch on
allumette f [alOOmet] match
allumez vos phares switch on your lights
allumez vos veilleuses switch on your sidelights/parking lights
alors [alor] then; well
alpinisme m [alpeeneess-muh] mountaineering
ambassade f [ONbasad] embassy
améliorer [amayleeooray] to improve
amende f [amoNd] fine
amener [amuhnay] to bring
amer [amair] bitter
américain [amayreekAN]

American

Amérique f [amayreek] America

ameublement m [amurbluhmON] furniture

ami m, amie f [amee] friend

amortisseur m [amorteessurr] shock-absorber

amour m [amoor] love
  faire l'amour [fair] to make love

ampoule f [ONpool] light bulb; blister

s'amuser [samOOzay] to have fun

an m [ON] year

analgésique m [an-aljayzeek] painkiller

ancien [ONss-yAN] ancient; old, former

ancien franc [frAN] old French franc (= 1 centime)

ancre f [ONkr] anchor

anémique [anaymeek] anaemic

anesthésie générale f [anestayzee jaynayral] general anaesthetic

anesthésie locale [lo-kal] local anaesthetic

angine f [ONjeen] tonsillitis

angine de poitrine [pwatreen] angina

anglais [ONglay] English

Anglais m Englishman
  les Anglais the English

Anglaise f [ONglez] Englishwoman

Angleterre f [ONgluhtair] England

année f [anay] year

anniversaire m [aneevairsair] birthday

anniversaire de mariage [maree-ahj] wedding anniversary

annuaire m [anOO-air] phone book

annulé [anOOlay] cancelled

annuler [anOOlay] to cancel

antigel m [ONtee-jel] antifreeze

antihistaminique m [ONteeheestameeneek] antihistamine

anti-insecte: la crème anti-insecte [krem ONtee-ANsekt] insect repellent

antiquaire m [ONteekair] antique shop

août [OO] August

apparaître [aparetr] to appear

appareil m [aparay] device; camera
  qui est à l'appareil? who's speaking?
  Madame ... à l'appareil Madame ... speaking
  cet appareil ne rend pas la monnaie this machine does not give change
  cet appareil rend la monnaie this machine gives change

appareil acoustique m hearing aid

appareil-photo m camera

appartement m [apartmON] flat, apartment

appartenir [apartuhneer] to belong

appeler [aplay] to call
  comment vous appelez-

vous? [komON voo zaplay-voo] what's your name?

je m'appelle ... [juh mapel] my name is ...

appendicite f [apANdeesseet] appendicitis

apporter [aportay] to bring

on peut apporter son repas you may eat your own food here

apprendre [aprONdr] to learn

s'approcher (de) [saproshay] to go/come near

appuyer [apwee-yay] to lean, to push

appuyer ici press here

appuyez pour ouvrir press to open

après [apray] after

après-demain [-duhmAN] the day after tomorrow

après-midi m afternoon

arabe (m/f) [a-rab] Arabic; Arab

araignée f [aren-yay] spider

arbre m [arbr] tree

arc-en-ciel m [arkONss-yel] rainbow

argent m [arjON] money; silver

argent massif solid silver

armoire f [armwahr] cupboard

arnaque f [arnak] rip-off, swindle

arôme m [arohm] flavour

arôme naturel/artificiel natural/artificial flavouring

arrêt m [aray] stop

arrêt d'autobus bus stop

arrêt de bus bus stop

arrêté: par arrêté préfectoral by order

arrêter [aretay] to stop; to arrest

s'arrêter to stop

arrêtez! stop!

arrêtez votre moteur switch off your engine

arrêt facultatif request stop

arrêt interdit no stopping

arrière m [aree-air] back

la roue arrière the back wheel

le siège arrière the back seat

arrivée(s) f(pl) [areevay] arrival(s)

arriver [areevay] to arrive; to happen

arrondissement m [arONdeess-mON] administrative district of Paris

arthrite f [artreet] arthritis

articles mpl [arteekl]: **les articles soldés ne sont ni repris ni échangés** no refund or exchange of reduced price goods

articles de camping camping accessories

articles de sport sports goods

articles de voyage travel accessories

articles ménagers [mayna-jay] household goods

artisanat m [arteezana] crafts

arts ménagers mpl [ar mayna-jay] household goods

as: tu as [a] you have

as-tu ...? do you have ...?

ascenseur **m** [asONsurr] lift,
  elevator
aspirateur **m** [aspeeraturr]
  hoover®
s'asseoir [sasswahr] to sit
  down
  asseyez-vous [asay-ay-voo]
  sit down
assez (de) [assay] enough;
  quite
  j'en ai assez [jON ay assay] I
  have enough; I'm fed up
assieds-toi [ass-yay-twa] sit
  down
assiette **f** [ass-yet] plate
assurance **f** [assOOrONss]
  insurance
assure la correspondance
  avec ... connects with ...
asthme **m** [ass-muh] asthma
astucieux [astOOss-yuh] clever
athée **m/f** [atay] atheist
athlétisme **m** [atlayteess-muh]
  athletics
Atlantique **m** [atlONteek]
  Atlantic
attachez vos ceintures fasten
  your seat belt
attaque **f** [atak] attack; stroke
atteindre [atANdr] to reach
attendez ici wait here
attendez-moi! wait for me!
attendez votre ticket wait for
  your ticket
attendre [atONdr] to wait
attendre la sonorité wait for
  the dialling tone
attention! [atONss-yON] look
  out!; caution!

attention à la marche mind
  the step
attention, chien méchant
  beware of the dog
attention, enfants caution,
  children
attention, fermeture
  automatique des portes
  caution, doors close
  automatically
attention, peinture fraîche wet
  paint
atterrir [ataireer] to land
attraper [atrapay] to catch
au [o] to the; at the; in the;
  by the; with
auberge **f** [obairj] inn
auberge de jeunesse [jur-ness]
  youth hostel
aucun [okAN] none, not any
au-dessous de [o-duhsoo duh]
  below
au-dessus de [o-duhssOO duh]
  above
audiophone **m** [odeeo-fon]
  hearing aid
aujourd'hui [ojoordwee] today
  aujourd'hui en huit a week
  today
auprès de [opray duh] near
auquel [okel] to which; at
  which
aurai: j'aurai [joray] I will have
aura: il/elle aura [ora] he/she/
  it will have
aurais: j'aurais/tu aurais [oray]
  I/you would have
auras: tu auras [ora] you will
  have

au revoir goodbye

aurez: vous aurez [oray] you will have

auriez: vous auriez [oree-ay] you would have

aurions: nous aurions [oree-ON] we would have

aurons: nous aurons [orON] we will have

auront: ils/elles auront [orON] they will have

aussi [o-see] also
   aussi grand que as big as
   moi aussi me too
   aussi ... que possible as ... as possible

aussitôt [o-seeto] at once
   aussitôt que as soon as

Australie f [ostralee] Australia

australien [ostralee-AN] Australian

autant (de) [otON duh] as much; as many

autobus m [otobOOss] bus

autocar m coach, bus

automne m [otON] autumn

automobiliste m/f [otomobeeleest] car driver; motorist

Au

autoradio m [otorad-yo] car radio

autoroute f [otoroot] motorway, highway
   autoroute à péage toll motorway/highway

auto-stop m [otostop] hitch-hiking
   faire de l'autostop to hitchhike

autre [ohtr] other
   un/une autre another

autre chose [shohz] something else

autres destinations other destinations

autres directions other destinations

Autriche f [otreesh] Austria

autrichien [otreeshee-AN] Austrian

aux [o] to the; at; in the; by the; with

auxquel(le)s [okel] to which; at which; in which; by which

avaler [avalay] to swallow

avance: d'avance [davONss] in advance
   en avance early

avancer [avONsay] to move forward, to advance

avant m [avON] front

avant before
   avant JC BC

avant-hier [avON-tee-air] the day before yesterday

avec [avek] with

averse f [avairss] shower

aveugle [avurgl] blind

avez: vous avez [voo zavay] you have
   avez-vous ...? do you have ...?

avion m [av-yON] plane
   par avion by airmail

avis m [avee] notice

avocat m [avoka] lawyer

avoir* [avwahr] to have

avons: **nous avons** [noo zavON]
we have

avril [avreel] April

ayant [ay-yON] having

B

bac **m** ferry

bagages **mpl** [bagahj] luggage
  faire ses bagages to pack

bagages à main [MAN] hand
  luggage

bagarre **f** [ba-gar] fight

bagnole **f** [ban-yol] car (familiar
  word)

bague **f** [bag] ring

baignade dangereuse danger,
  do not swim here

baignade interdite no
  swimming

se baigner [suh ben-yay] to go
  swimming

baignoire **f** [beñ-wahr] bathtub

bain **m** [BAN] bath

bains douches municipaux
  public baths

baiser **m** [bezzay] kiss

baiser to screw

bal **m** dance
  bal du 14 juillet open air
  dance on the French
  national holiday

balade **f** [bal-ad] walk, stroll

se balader [suh baladay] to go
  for a stroll

baladeur **m** [baladurr] personal
  stereo

balcon **m** [balkON] balcony

balle **f** [bal] ball

balles [bal] francs (familiar word)

ballon **m** [balON] ball; balloon

bande d'arrêt d'urgence hard
  shoulder

bande magnétique **f** [man-
  yayteek] tape

bande médiane [mayd-yan]
  central reservation

banlieue **f** [bON-l-yuh] suburbs

banque **f** [bONK] bank

barbe **f** [barb] beard

barque **f** [bark] small boat

barrière **f** [baree-air] fence

barrière de dégel road closed
  to heavy vehicles during
  thaw

bas **mpl** [ba] stockings

bas low
  en bas [ON] downstairs

baskets **fpl** [bass-ket] trainers

bateau **m** [bato] boat

bateau à rames [ram] rowing
  boat

bateau à vapeur [vapurr]
  steamer

bateau à voile [vwahl] sailing
  boat

bateau-mouche [-moosh]
  pleasure boat on the Seine

bâtiment **m** [bateemON]
  building

batterie **f** [batree] battery

se battre [suh batr] to fight

baume après-shampoing
  m [bohm apray-shONpwan]
  conditioner

bd boulevard

BD (bande dessinée) **f** [bay-day

(bONd desseenay)] comic strip

beaucoup [bo-koo] a lot; much
beaucoup de ... a lot of ...

beau, f belle [bo, bel]
beautiful; fine
il fait beau the weather is
good

beau-fils m [-feess] son-in-law

beau-père m [-pair] father-
in-law

bébé m [bay-bay] baby

belge [belj] Belgian

Belgique f [beljeek] Belgium

belle [bel] beautiful

belle-fille f [-fee] daughter-
in-law

belle-mère f [-mair] mother-
in-law

béquilles fpl [baykee] crutches

besoin: j'ai besoin de ... [jay
buhzwAN duh] I need ...

bibliothèque f [beebleeo-tek]
library

bibliothèque municipale
public library

bicyclette f [beesseeklet]
bicycle

bien [b-yAN] well, fine

bien du/de la/des many, a
lot of

bien portant [portON] in good
health

bien que [kuh] although

bien sûr [soor] of course

bientôt [b-yanto] soon
à bientôt see you later

bienvenue! [b-yAN-vuhnoo]
welcome!

bienvenue sur notre réseau
welcome to our network

bijouterie f [beejootuhree]
jeweller's

bijoux mpl [beejoo] jewellery

billet m [bee-yay] ticket

billet de banque [bONk]
banknote, bill

billets tickets; (bank)notes,
bills

billet Section Urbaine ticket
valid for suburban train and
métro and all RER

billets internationaux
international tickets

billets périmés used tickets

blaireau m [blairo] shaving
brush

blanc, f blanche [blON, blONsh]
white

blanchisserie f [blONsheesree]
laundry

blessé [blessay] injured; hurt

blessure f [blessoor] wound

bleu [bluh] blue

bleu m bruise

boire [bwahr] to drink

bois m [bwa] wood

boîte f [bwat] box; can;
nightclub

boîte à/aux lettres [letr]
letterbox

boîte de nuit [nwee] nightclub

boîte de vitesses [veetess]
gearbox

bol m bowl

bombe f [bONb] bomb

bon [bON] good
bon! right!, OK!

bon anniversaire! happy

birthday!

bon appétit! enjoy your meal!

bon après-midi! have a good afternoon!

bonbon m [bON-bON] sweet, candy

bondé [bONday] crowded

bonde f [bONd] plug

bonjour [bONjoor] hello; good morning

bon marché [bON marshay] cheap

bonne année! [bon anay] happy New Year!

bonne chance! [shONss] good luck!

bonne journée! [joornay] have a good day!

bonne nuit [nwee] good night

bonne route! [root] safe journey!

bonnet de bain m [bonay duh bAN] bathing cap

bonsoir [bONswahr] good evening

bon voyage! have a good trip!

bord m [bor] edge
  au bord de la mer [o] at the seaside

borne f [born] kilometre (familiar word)

botte f [bot] boot

bottin m [botAN] telephone directory

bouche f [boosh] mouth

bouché [booshay] blocked

boucherie f [booshree] butcher's

boucherie-charcuterie [-sharkootree] butcher's (also selling pâté and sausages)

boucherie chevaline horsemeat butcher

bouchon m [booshON] cork; stopper; traffic jam

bouclé [booklay] curly

boucles d'oreille fpl [bookl doray] earrings

bouée f [boo-ay] buoy

bouffe f [boof] grub, food

bouger [boojay] to move

bougie f [boojee] candle; spark plug

bouillotte f [boo-ee-yot] hot-water bottle

boulangerie f [boolONjree] baker's

boulangerie-pâtisserie baker's and cake shop

boules fpl [bool] (French-style) bowling

boules Quiès® [kee-ess] earplugs

boulevard périphérique m ring road

bourré [booray] pissed

boussole f [boossol] compass

bouteille f [bootay] bottle

boutique f small shop

boutique de mode clothes boutique

boutique hors-taxe [or tax] duty free shop

bouton m [bootON] button; spot

boxe f [box] boxing

BP (boîte postale) PO Box

bras m [bra] arm

brasserie f pub/bar/café serving food
brave [brahv] good; brave
bref brief
Bretagne f [bruhtañ] Brittany
bricolage m [breekolahj] do-it-yourself, DIY (supplies)
bricoler [breekolay] to do DIY
briller [bree-yay] to shine
briquet m [breekay] lighter
brise f [breez] breeze
britannique British
brocante secondhand goods
broche f [brosh] brooch
bronchite f [brONsheet] bronchitis
bronzage m [brONzahj] suntan
bronzer [bronzay] to tan
se bronzer to sunbathe
brosse f [bross] brush
brosse à cheveux [shuhvuh] hairbrush
brosse à dents [dON] toothbrush
brosser [brossay] to brush
brouillard m [broo-ee-yar] fog
brouillard fréquent risk of fog
bruit m [brwee] noise
brûler [broolay] to burn
brûlure f [broolOOr] burn
brume f [broom] mist
brun [brAN] brown
brushing m [brwee-yoN] blow-dry
bruyant [brwee-yoN] noisy
bu [boo] drunk
buffet à volonté unlimited buffet
bureau m office
bureau d'accueil [dakuh-ee]

reception centre
bureau de poste [posst] post office
bureau des objets trouvés [objay troovay] lost property office
bureautique f office automation
butagaz m camping gas
buvette f [boovet] refreshment room; refreshment stall
buvez: vous buvez [boovay] you drink
buvons: nous buvons [boovON] we drink

C

ça* [sa] it; that
ça alors! well really!; I don't believe it!
ça va? how's things?
ça va it's OK, I'm OK; that's fine
ça va mieux I'm feeling better; things are better
cabas m [kaba] shopping bag
cabine f [kabeen] cabin
cette cabine peut être appelée au numéro: ... incoming calls can be made to this phonebox using the following number: ...
cabine téléphonique phone box
cabines d'essayage fitting rooms
cabinet dentaire m dentist's surgery

cabinet médical doctor's surgery

cacher [kashay] to hide

cacher [kashair] kosher

cachet m [kashay] tablet

caddie m (supermarket) trolley

cadeau m [kado] present, gift

cadeaux-souvenirs gift shop

cafard m [kafar] cockroach
j'ai le cafard I feel a bit down

café m [kafay] coffee, black coffee; café, bar

café complet [kONplay] continental breakfast

cahier m [ky-yay] notebook; exercise book

caisse f [kess] till, cash desk

caisse d'épargne [dayparñ] savings bank

caissier m cashier

calculette f [kalOOlet] calculator

calendrier m [kalONdree-ay] calendar

calmant m [kalmON] tranquillizer

caméra f [kamayra] cine-camera; (TV) camera

camion m [kam-yON] lorry

camionnette f [kam-yonet] van

campagne f [kONpañ] countryside
à la campagne in the country

camping m [kONpeeng] camping; campsite

camping-car m mobile home

camping-caravaning site for camping and caravans

camping interdit no camping

canadien [kanadee-AN] Canadian

canif m [kaneef] penknife

canne à pêche f [kan a pesh] fishing rod

canoë m [kano-ay] canoe; canoeing

canton m [kONtON] administrative district of Switzerland

caoutchouc m [ka-oochoo] rubber

capitaine m [kapeeten] captain

capot m [kapo] bonnet, (US) hood

car m coach, bus

car for, because

caravane f caravan

carburateur m carburettor

cardiaque: être cardiaque to have a heart condition

carie f [karee] caries

carnet m [karnay] book (of tickets)

carnet d'adresses [dadress] address book

carnet de tickets [teekay] book of tickets

carnet de timbres [tANbr] book of stamps

carrefour m [karfoor] crossroads, intersection

carrefour dangereux dangerous crossroads/intersection

carrosserie f garage that does bodywork repairs

carte f [kart] card; map; pass

carte d'anniversaire birthday card

carte de crédit [kraydee] credit card

carte d'embarquement [ONbarkmON] boarding pass

carte de réduction [raydOOx-yON] card entitling the holder to price reductions

carte de visite [veezeet] (business) card

carte d'identité [eedONteetay] ID card

carte grise [greez] car registration book

carte orange [orONj] season ticket for transport in Paris and its suburbs

carte postale [poss-tal] postcard

carte refusée card rejected

carte routière [root-yair] road map

carte verte [vairt] green card

carton m [kartON] box; cardboard

cascade f [kaskad] waterfall

casquette f [kasket] cap

cassé [kassay] broken

casser [kassay] to break

casserole f saucepan

cauchemar m [kohsh-mar] nightmare

cause f [kohz] cause
à cause de because of

CCP (compte de chèques postaux) giro account

ce* [suh] this; that; it

ce serait [suhray] it would be

ceci [suhsee] this

cédez le passage give way, yield

ceinture f [sANtOOr] belt

ceinture de sécurité [saykOOreetay] seat belt

cela [suhla] that

célèbre [saylebr] famous

célibataire m [sayleebatair] bachelor

célibataire single

celle-ci [sel-see] this one

celle-là [-la] that one

celles-ci [sel-see] these

celles-là those

celui-ci [suhlwee-see] this one

celui-là that one

cendrier m [sONdree-ay] ashtray

cent [sON] hundred

centime m [sONteem] centime (1/100 franc)

centre m [sONtr] centre

centre commercial shopping centre

centre culturel arts centre

centre sportif sports centre

centre-ville city centre

cependant [suhpONdON] however

ce que [suh kuh] what

ce qui [kee] what

certain [sairtAN] sure, certain; some

ces* [say] these

c'est [say] it is; that's
c'est ça that's it

c'est-à-dire [setadeer] that is

to say

cet [set] this; that

c'était [saytay] it was

cette* [set] this; that

ceux-ci* [suh-see] these

ceux-là* those

CFF (Chemins de fer fédéraux) Swiss railways

chacun [shakAN] each one; everyone

chaîne f [shen] chain; channel; stereo

chaise f [shez] chair

chaise longue deck chair

chaleur f [shalurr] heat

chambre f [shONbr] room; bedroom

chambre à air inner tube

chambre à coucher [kooshay] bedroom

chambre à deux lits [duh lee] twin room

chambre pour deux personnes [pairson] double room

chambre pour une personne [OOn] single room

chambres à louer rooms to let

champ m [shON] field

chance f [shONss] luck; chance

change m [shONj] change; exchange; currency exchange

change de devises currency exchange

changement à ... change at ...

changer [shonjay] to change

se changer to change

changer de train to change trains

changer de vitesse to change gear

changeur de monnaie m change machine

chanson f [shONsON] song

chanter [shONtay] to sing

chantier m roadworks; building site

chantilly f [shontee-yee] whipped cream

chapeau m [shapo] hat

chapeau de soleil [solay] sun hat

chapellerie f hat shop

chaque [shak] each, every

charcuterie f [sharkOOtree] delicatessen; cold meat, sausages, salami, pâtés etc

chariot m [sharee-o] trolley

chariot obligatoire you must take a trolley

charter m charter flight

chasse gardée hunting preserve

chat m [sha] cat

châtain [shatAN] chestnut, brown

château m [shato] castle; mansion

château fort fortified castle

chaud [sho] warm, hot

chauffage m [shofahj] heating

chauffage central [sON-tral] central heating

chauffard! [shofar] learn to drive!

chauffe-eau m [shohf-o] water

heater

chaussée déformée uneven road surface

chaussée glissante slippery road surface

chaussée rétrécie road narrows

chaussée verglacée icy road

chaussettes fpl [sho-set] socks

chaussures fpl [sho-sOOr] shoes

chaussures de ski ski boots

chaussures de tennis gym shoes

chauve [shohv] bald

CH (Confédération Helvétique) Switzerland

chemin m [shuhmAN] path

chemin de fer [duh fair] railway

chemise f [shuhmeez] shirt

chemise de nuit [duh nwee] nightdress

chemiserie menswear

chemisier m [shuhmeez-yay] blouse

chèque m [shek] cheque, (US) check

les chèques ne sont acceptés qu'à partir de 100 F cheques accepted for amounts over 100F only

les chèques ne sont pas acceptés we do not accept cheques

chèque de voyage [duh vwyahj] traveller's cheque

chéquier m [shaykee-ay] cheque book

cher [shair] expensive; dear

chercher [shairshay] to look for

cheveux mpl [shuhvuh] hair

cheville f [shuhvee] ankle

chez [shay] at; among

chez Nadine at Nadine's

faites comme chez vous make yourself at home

chez Marcel/Mimi (name of bar etc) Marcel's/Mimi's

chien m [shee-AN] dog

les chiens doivent être tenus en laisse dogs must be kept on a leash

choc m [shok] shock

chocolat à croquer m [shokola a krokay] plain chocolate

chocolat au lait [o lay] milk chocolate

chocolatier m chocolate shop

choisir [shwazeer] to choose

choix m [shwa] choice

chômage: au chômage [o shohmahj] unemployed

chose f [shohz] thing

Chronopost® express mail

chute de neige f [shOOt duh nej] snowfall

chute de pierres falling rocks

ciel m [see-el] sky; heaven

cigare m [seegar] cigar

cimetière m [seemt-yair] cemetery

cinémathèque f film theatre, movie theater

cinglé m [sANglay] nutter, nutcase

cinq [sANk] five

cinquante [sANkONt] fifty

cinquième [sANk-yem] fifth

cintre **m** [SANtr] coathanger

cirage **m** [seerahj] shoe polish

circuit touristique tourist route

circulation **f** [seerkOOlass-yON] traffic

circulation alternée single line traffic

circuler [seerkOOlay] to run
  circule le ... runs on ...
  ne circule pas le samedi/ dimanche does not run on Saturdays/Sundays

circulez! move along!

circulez sur une file single line traffic

cire pour voiture **f** [seer poor vwatOOr] car wax

cirque **m** [seerk] circus

ciseaux **mpl** [seezo] scissors

cité universitaire **f** university halls of residence

clair clear
  bleu clair light blue

classe **f** [klass] class

clé **f** [klay] key

clé anglaise [ONglez] wrench

clignotant **m** [kleen-yotON] indicator

climat **m** [kleema] climate

climatisation **f** [kleemateezass-yON] air-conditioning

climatisé air-conditioned

clinique **f** [kleeneek] clinic

cloche **f** bell

clôture électrifiée electric fence

clou **m** [kloo] nail

cochon **m** [koshON] pig

code de la route **m** [kod duh la root] highway code

code postal [poss-tal] postcode, zip code

coffre **m** [kofr] boot, (US) trunk

coiffer [kwafay] to comb
  se coiffer to do one's hair

coiffeur **m**, coiffeuse **f** [kwafurr, -urz] hairdresser

coiffeur pour dames [poor dam] ladies' hairdresser

coiffeur pour hommes [om] men's hairdresser, barber's

coiffure **f** [kwafOOr] hairstyle; hairdresser's

coin **m** [kwAN] corner

coincé [kwANsay] stuck

col **m** collar; (mountain) pass
  col fermé pass closed
  col ouvert pass open
  col roulé [roolay] polo neck (jumper)

colis **m** [kolee] parcel, package

colis France parcels for France only

collant **m** [kolON] tights

colle **f** [kol] glue

collectionner [kolex-yonay] to collect

collier **m** [kol-yay] necklace

colline **f** [koleen] hill

combien? [kONb-yAN] how many?, how much?

commander [komONday] to order

comme [kom] like; as; how

commencer [komONsay] to begin

comment? [komON] how?; pardon?; sorry?

comment allez-vous? [talay-voo] how are you?

comment ça va? [sa] how are things?

comment vas-tu? [va-too] how are you?

commerçant m [komairsON] shopkeeper

commissariat m [komeessaree-a] police station

commissariat de police police station

commotion cérébrale f [komoss-yON sayray-bral] concussion

communication f [kom00neekass-yON] call

communication internationale international call

communication interurbaine long-distance call

communication locale local call

communication urbaine local call

compagnie aérienne f [kompan-yee a-ayree-en] airline

comparer [kONparay] to compare

compartiment fumeurs smoking compartment

compartiment non-fumeurs non-smoking compartment

complet m [kONplay] suit

complet full, no vacancies

complètement [kONpletmON] totally

compliqué [kONpleekay] complicated

composer le numéro dial the number

composez sur le clavier numérique le montant choisi pour la vignette enter selected value of postage label on numerical keyboard (francs, comma, centimes)

composez votre code confidentiel à l'abri des regards indiscrets enter your PIN without letting anybody see it

composition contents

composition du train order of cars

compostage: le compostage des billets est obligatoire tickets are valid only if punched

compostez votre billet validate/punch your ticket in the machine

comprendre [kONproNdr] to understand; to include

comprimé m [kONpreemay] tablet

comprimé effervescent effervescent tablet

compris [kONpree] included

comptable m [kONtabl] accountant

comptant: payer comptant [kONtON] pay cash

compteur m [kONturr] speedometer

con m [kON] stupid idiot; stupid bastard

concessionnaire **m** agent

concierge **m/f** caretaker

conditions d'enneigement snow conditions

conditions pour skier skiing conditions

conducteur **m** [kONdOOkturr] driver

conductrice **f** [kONdOOktreess] driver

conduire [kONdweer] to drive

confirmer [kONfeermay] to confirm

confiserie **f** confectioner, sweet shop

congé annuel **m** annual holiday

congélateur **m** [kONjaylaturr] freezer

connaître [konetr] to know

conseiller [kONsay-yay] to advise

conserver: se conserve au moins ... après la date-limite de vente keeps for at least ... after the sell-by date

conserver au frais (et au sec) keep in a cool (dry) place

conservez votre ticket sur vous keep your ticket with you

conservez votre titre de transport jusqu'à la sortie keep your ticket till you leave the station

consigne **f** [kONseeñ] left luggage, baggage checkroom

consigne automatique left luggage lockers

consommation **f** [kONsomass-yON] drink

consommation au comptoir drink at the bar

consommation en salle drink in the lounge

consommer avant le ... eat by ..., best before ...

constipé [kONsteepay] constipated

consulat **m** [kONsOOla] consulate

contacter [kONtaktay] to contact

contagieux [kONtah-jyuh] contagious

contenir [kONtuhneer] to contain

ne contient pas de ... contains no ...

content [kONtON] pleased

contenu contents

continuer [kONteenOO-ay] to continue, to go on

contraceptif **m** contraceptive

contractuel **m** traffic warden

contraire **m** [kONtrair] opposite

contre [kONtr] against

contre les ... for ...

contre-indications contra-indications

contrôle des bagages **m** baggage security check

contrôle des passeports passport control

contrôles radar radar speed checks

convoi exceptionnel long vehicle

copain m [kopAN] pal, mate; boyfriend

copine f [kopeen] friend; girlfriend

coquillage m [kokee-ahj] shell

Corail m intercity train

cor au pied m [o p-yay] corn

corde f rope

cordonnerie f cobbler's

cordonnier m cobbler, shoe repairs

corps m [kor] body

correspondance f [koresspONdONss] connection

correspondance Porte d'Orléans all stops on the line to Porte d'Orléans

Corse f [korss] Corsica

costume m suit

côté m [kotay] side

  à côté de next to

  mettre de côté to put aside

côte f [koht] coast; rib

Côte d'Azur French Riviera

côté non stabilisé soft verge

coton m [kotON] cotton

coton hydrophile [eedrofeel] cotton wool, absorbent cotton

cou m [koo] neck

couche f [koosh] nappy

coucher: aller se coucher [alay suh kooshay] to go to bed

  au coucher seulement only when you go to bed

couchette f couchette; reclining seat; bunk bed

coude m [kood] elbow

coudre [koodr] to sew

couette f [kwet] continental quilt; bunch (in hair)

couler [koolay] to sink; to run

couleur f [koolurr] colour

couloir bus et taxis bus and taxi lane

coup m [koo] blow, knock; stroke

  tout d'un coup suddenly

coup de fil phonecall

coup de soleil [solay] sunburn

coupe f [koop] haircut

coupe de cheveux [duh shuhvuh] haircut

couper [koopay] to cut

coupure f [koopOOr] cut

coupure de courant [duh kooroN] power cut

cour court; courtyard

courageux [koorahj-uh] brave

courant d'air m [kooroN dair] draught

courant dangereux dangerous current

courir [kooreer] to run

courrier m [kooree-ay] mail; letters and postcards

courrier recommandé registered mail

courroie du ventilateur f [koorwa dOO vONteelaturr] fan belt

cours du change m [koor dOO shONj] exchange rate

course f [koorss] race

  faire des courses to go shopping

course automobile racing track

court [koor] short
court de tennis m tennis court
cousin m, cousine f [koozAN, -een] cousin
couteau m [kooto] knife
coûter [kootay] to cost
coutume f [kootoom] custom
couture f dressmaking; couture
couvent m [koovON] convent
couvercle m [koovairkl] lid
couvert [koovair] covered; overcast
couverts mpl [koovair] cutlery
couverts à poisson fish cutlery
couverture f [koovairtoor] blanket
couverture chauffante [shohfONt] electric blanket
couvre-lit m [koovr-lee] bedspread
cracher [krashay] to spit
crachin m [krashAN] drizzle
craindre [krAndr] to fear
crampe f [krONp] cramp
crâne m [krahn] skull
cravate f tie
crayon m pencil
crédit ... unités ... units remaining, credit ...
crème de beauté f [botay] cold cream
crème démaquillante [daymakee-yONt] cleansing cream
crème hydratante [eedratONt] moisturizer
crémerie f dairy

crêperie f [krepuhree] pancake restaurant
crevaison f [kruhvezzON] puncture
crevé [kruhvay] knackered; punctured
cric m jack
crier [kree-ay] to shout
crise f [kreez] fit, attack; crisis
crise cardiaque heart attack
crise de foie [duh fwa] upset stomach
crise d'épilepsie epileptic fit
croire [krwahr] to believe
croisement m [krwazmON] junction, intersection
croisière f [krwaz-yair] cruise
crosse de golf f golf club
CRS (Compagnie républicaine de sécurité) f [say-air-ess] riot police; m riot policeman
cuiller f, cuillère f [kwee-yair] spoon
cuillère à café teaspoon
cuillère à dessert dessert spoon
cuillère à soupe soup spoon
cuillerée f spoonful
cuir m [kweer] leather
cuisine f kitchen; cooking
cuisiner [kweezeenay] to cook
cuisinier m [kweezeen-yay] cook
cuisinière f [kweezeen-yair] cooker; cook
cuisse f [kweess] thigh; leg (of chicken)
cycles cycle shop
cyclisme m [seekleess-muh] cycling

cycliste **m/f** [seekleest] cyclist

cyclotourisme **m** cycle touring

cystite **f** [seess-teet] cystitis

D

daim **m** [dAN] suede

dame **f** [dam] lady

dames ladies' (toilets); draughts, checkers

dancing **m** [dONseeng] dance hall, night club

danger **m** [dONjay] danger

danger de mort danger of death

dangereux [dONjuhruh] dangerous

dans [dON] in; into

danse **f** [dONss] dance; dancing

danser [dONsay] to dance

date **f** [dat] date

date de naissance [nessONss] date of birth

date limite de vente sell-by date

de [duh] of; from

debout [duhboo] standing

début **m** beginning

débutant **m** beginner

décembre [daysONbr] December

décider [dayseeday] to decide

déclarer [dayklaray] to declare, to state

décoller [daykolay] to take off

déconseillé aux personnes sensibles unsuitable for people of a nervous disposition

décontracté [daykONtraktay] casual; laid-back

découpez suivant le pointillé cut along the dotted line

découvrir [daykoovreer] to discover

décrire [daykreer] to describe

décrochez lift the receiver

déçu [daysoo] disappointed

dedans [duhdON] inside

défaire sa valise [dayfair] to unpack

défectueux [dayfektoo-uh] faulty

défendu [dayfONdoo] forbidden

défense de ... [dayfONss] ... forbidden, no ..., do not ...

défense d'afficher stick no bills

défense de déposer des ordures no litter, no dumping

défense d'entrer no entry

défense de fumer no smoking

défense de laisser des bagages dans le couloir bags must not be left in the corridor

défense de marcher sur la pelouse keep off the grass

défense de parler au conducteur do not talk to the driver

défense de ... sous peine d'amende ... will be fined

défense de stationner no parking

défense de traverser les voies

it is forbidden to cross the
railway/railroad lines

dégagé clear

dégoûtant [daygootON]
disgusting

degré m [duhgray] degree

dégueulasse [daygurlass]
disgusting

dégustation (de vin) f
[daygOOstass-yON] wine tasting

dégustation gratuite free
wine-tasting

dehors [duh-or] outside

dehors! get out!

déjà [dayja] already

déjeuner m [dayjuhnay] lunch;
breakfast

delco m distributor

délicieux [dayleess-yuh]
delicious

deltaplane m [-plan] hang-
gliding

demain [duhmAN] tomorrow

à demain see you tomorrow

demander [duhmONday] to ask

demandez à la caisse ask at
the cash desk

démangeaison f [daymONjezzON]
itch

démaquillant m [daymakee-yON]
skin cleanser

se démaquiller [daymakee-yay]
to remove one's make-up

démarrer [daymaray] to start
up

demi [duhmee] half

demi-litre m half a litre

demi-heure f [-urr] half an
hour

demi-journée f [-joornay] half
a day

demi-pension f [-pONss-yON]
half board, American plan

demi-tour m U-turn

dent f [dON] tooth

dentier m [dONt-yay] dentures,
false teeth

dentifrice m [dONteefreess]
toothpaste

dentiste m/f [dONteest] dentist

dépanneuse f [daypanurz]
breakdown lorry

département m [daypartmON]
administrative district of
France

départementale f
[daypartmONtal] B road

départ(s) departure(s)

dépasser [daypassay] to pass

se dépêcher [suh daypeshay] to
hurry

dépêchez-vous! hurry up!

dépendre: ça dépend [sa
daypON] it depends

dépenser [daypONsay] to
spend

dépliant m [dayplee-ON] leaflet

dépression (nerveuse) f
[daypress-yON nairvurz] nervous
breakdown

déprimé [daypreemay]
depressed

depuis (que) [duhpwee (kuh)]
since

**dérangement: en
dérangement** out of order

déranger [dayrONjay] to disturb

ça vous dérange si ...? [sa

voo dayrONj] do you mind
if ...?

déraper [dayrapay] to skid

dermatologue m/f [dairmatolog]
dermatologist

dernier [dairn-yay] last

l'année dernière last year

derrière [dairyair] behind

derrière m bottom

des* [day] of the; from the;
some

des biscuits some biscuits

dès [day] from

dès que as soon as

désagréable [dayzagray-abl]
unpleasant

désastre m [dayzastr] disaster

descendre [duhsONdr] to go
down; to get off

se déshabiller [suh dayzabee-yay]
to undress

désinfectant m [dayzANfektON]
disinfectant; antiseptic

désirer [dayzeeray] to want, to
wish for

désolé: je suis désolé
[dayzolay] I'm sorry

desquels [daykel] of which;
from which

dessert m [desair] dessert

dessert ... stops at ...

dessin m [duhsAN] drawing

dessiner [duhseenay] to draw

dessous [duhsoo] underneath;
under it

dessus [duhsoo] above; on
top; on it

destinataire m/f addressee;
consignee

détaxe à l'exportation f tax
refund on export goods

détendre: se détendre [suh
daytONdr] to relax

détester [daytestay] to hate

deux [duh] two

deuxième étage m [duhz-yem
aytahj] second floor, (US)
third floor

devant [duhvON] in front of;
in front

**développement de pellicules/
photos** film processing

développer [dayvlopay] to
develop

devenir [duhvuhneer] to become

déviation f diversion

devises étrangères fpl [duhveez
aytrONjair] foreign currency

devoir m [duhvwahr] duty

devoir to have to

devrai: je devrai [duhvray] I
will have to

devrais: je/tu devrais [duhvray]
I/you should

devras: tu devras [duhvra] you
will have to

devrez: vous devrez [duhvray]
you will have to

devriez: vous devriez [duhvree-
ay] you should

diabétique diabetic

diamant m [dee-amON] diamond

diapositive f [dee-apozeeteev]
slide

diarrhée f [dee-aray] diarrhoea

dictionnaire m [deex-yonair]
dictionary

diététique health food

Dieu m [d-yuh] God
différent [deefayrON] different
difficile [deefeesseel] difficult
Diligo® pre-stamped parcel, for France only
diluer [deelOO-ay] to dissolve
diluer dans un peu d'eau dissolve in water
dimanche [deemONsh] Sunday
dimanches et jours fériés Sundays and public holidays
dîner m [deenay] dinner
dîner to have dinner
dîner-spectacle dinner during the show (in cabaret)
dingue [dAN-g] crazy
dire [deer] to say; to tell
directeur m [deerekturr] manager; director; headteacher
direction f [deerex-yON] steering; direction
dis: je/tu dis [dee] I/you say
disent: il/elles disent [deez] they say
disons: nous disons [deezON] we say
disparaître [deesparetr] to disappear
disquaire m [deeskair] record shop
disque m [deesk] record
disque compact compact disc
disque obligatoire parking disk compulsory
dissolvant m [deessolvON] nail-polish remover
Distingo® envelope with pre-printed address box
distributeur automatique de billets m ticket machine
distributeur (automatique) de billets (de banque) cash machine, ATM
distributeur de boissons drinks vending machine
dit [dee] says; said
dites: vous dites [deet] you say
divorcé [deevorsay] divorced
divorcer [deevorsay] to get a divorce
dix [deess] ten
dix-huit [deez-weet] eighteen
dixième [deez-yem] tenth
dix-neuf [deez-nuhf] nineteen
dix-sept [deesset] seventeen
d'occasion [dokaz-yON] second-hand
docteur m [dokturr] doctor
doigt m [dwa] finger
dois: je/tu dois [dwa] I/you must
doit: il/elle doit [dwa] he/she/it must
doivent: ils/elles doivent [dwav] they must
dolmen m megalithic tomb
domicile m home address
dommage: c'est dommage [domahj] it's a pity
donc [dONK] then, therefore
donner [donay] to give
dont [dON] of which; whose
dormir [dormeer] to sleep
dos m [doh] back
dose pour adultes/enfants

dose for adults/children

douane f [dwan] Customs

doubler [dooblay] to overtake

douce [dooss] soft; sweet

douche f [doosh] shower

douleur f [doolurr] pain

douloureux [doolooruh] painful

douter [dootay] to doubt

doux, f douce [doo, dooss] soft; sweet

douzaine f [doozen] dozen

douze [dooz] twelve

drap m [dra] sheet

drapeau m [drapo] flag

draps de lit mpl [dra duh lee] bed linen

drogue f [drog] drug

droguerie f [drogree] shop selling selling non-prescription medicines, toiletries and household goods

droit [drwa] straight

droit m right

droite f [drwat] right
à droite (de) on the right (of)

drôle funny

du* [doo] of the; from the; some
du vin some wine

dû: j'ai dû [doo] I had to; I must have

duquel [dookel] of which; from which

dur [door] hard

durer [dooray] to last; to keep

durée de conservation ... keeps for ...

E

eau f [o] water

eau de Javel [duh javel] bleach

eau non potable not drinking water

eau potable drinking water

échanger [ayshONjay] to exchange

échange/remboursement exchange/refund

échantillon gratuit – ne peut être vendu free sample – not for sale

échecs mpl [ayshek] chess

écharpe f [aysharp] scarf

échelle f [ayshel] ladder

école f [aykol] school

école de langues [duh lON-g] language school

économique [aykonomeek] economy; economy-rate

Écopli® m [aykoplee] economy-rate letter for France

écossais [aykossay] Scottish

Écosse f [aykoss] Scotland

écouter [aykootay] to listen (to)

écrire [aykreer] to write

écrou m [aykroo] nut

édifice public m [aydeefeess pOObleek] public building

édredon m [aydruhdON] duvet

égal [aygal] equal
ça m'est égal I don't mind

égaliser [aygaleezay] to equalize; to trim

église f [aygleez] church

élastique m [aylasteek] rubber band

électricité f [aylektreesseetay] electricity

électroménager m household appliances

électrophone m [aylektrofon] record player

élever [ayluhvay] to raise; to lift up

elle* [el] she; her; it

elle-même [el-mem] herself; speaking

elles* [el] they; them

emballer [ONbalay] to wrap

embarquement (immédiat) boarding (now)

embouteillage m [ONbootay-ahj] traffic jam

embranchement m [ONbrONshmON] fork

embranchement d'autoroutes motorway junction

embrasser [ONbrassay] to kiss

embrayage m [ONbray-ahj] clutch

émission f [aymeess-yON] programme

emmener [ONmuhnay] to give a lift to; to take away

Empire [ONpeer] Napoleon's reign (1804-14)

emplacement m [ONplassmON] site

emplacement réservé no parking

employer [ONplwy-yay] to use; to employ

emporter [ONportay] to take away

emprunter [ONprANtay] to borrow

empruntez le passage souterrain use the underpass

en [ON] in; to; by

  en 1945 in 1945

  en France in France

  en bas [ba] downstairs

  en haut [o] upstairs

  en cas d'incendie in the event of fire

  en cas d'urgence in an emergency

  en cas d'affluence ne pas utiliser les strapontins do not use fold-down seats when the train is crowded

  en face de opposite

enceinte [ONSANt] pregnant

enchanté [ONshONtay] pleased to meet you

encolure f [ONkolŒr] collar size

encore [ONkor] again; still

  encore plus beau even more beautiful

  encore une bière another beer

endommager [ONdoma-jay] to damage

endormi [ONdormee] asleep

enfant m/f [ONfoN] child

enfin [ONfAN] at last

enflé [ONflay] swollen

enjoliveur m [ONjoleevurr] hub cap

enlever [ONluhvay] to take away; to remove

ennuyer [ON-nwee-yay] to

bother; to bore

s'ennuyer to be bored

ennuyeux [ON-nwee-yuh] annoying; boring

énorme [aynorm] enormous

énormément [aynormaymON] enormously

enregistrement des bagages m check-in

enrhumé: je suis enrhumé [ONrOOmay] I've got a cold

enseignant m [ONsen-yON] teacher

enseigner [ONsen-yay] to teach

ensemble [ONsONbl] together

ensoleillé [ONsolay-yay] sunny

ensuite [ONsweet] afterwards

entendre [ONtONdr] to hear

enterrement m [ONtairmON] funeral

entier [ONteeyay] whole

entièrement [ONtee-yairmON] entirely

entorse f [ONtorss] sprain

entracte m interval

entraînement m [ONtrenmON] training

entre [ONtr] between; among

entrée f [ONtray] entrance, way in; entrée

entrée à l'avant entry at the front

entrée des artistes stage door

entrée de service tradesman's entrance

entrée gratuite admission free

entrée interdite no admittance, no entry

entrée libre admission free

entrejambe m inside leg measurement; crutch

entrer [ONtray] to go in; to come in; to enter

vous entrez dans un espace non fumeur you are entering a no smoking area

entrez! [ONtray] come in!

entrez sans frapper enter without knocking

entrez sans sonner enter without ringing the bell

envers [ONvair] to, towards

envie: j'ai envie de [ONvee] I feel like

environ [ONveerON] about

envoi d'un objet recommandé avec/sans avis de réception mailing of a registered item with/without receipt note

envoi recommandé m recorded delivery

envoyer [ONvwy-ay] to send

épais [aypay] thick

épaule f [aypol] shoulder

épeler [ayplay] to spell

épicerie f [aypeesree] grocer's

épicerie fine delicatessen

épingle f [aypANgl] pin

épingle de nourrice [duh nooreess] safety pin

épouse f [aypooz] wife

épouser [aypoozay] to marry

épouvantable [aypoovONtabl] terrible

épuisé [aypweezay] exhausted

équipage m [aykeepahj] crew

équipe f [aykeep] team

équipements sportifs sporting

facilities

équitation f [aykeetass-yON] horse riding

erreur f [air-rurr] mistake

éruption f [ayrOOps-yON] rash

es: tu es [ay] you are

escale f [eskal] stop-over

escalier m [eskal-yay] stairs

escalier roulant [roolON] escalator

Espagne f [españ] Spain

espagnol [espan-yol] Spanish

espèce de con! [espess duh kON] you stupid bastard!

espérer [espayray] to hope

espoir m [espwahr] hope

esquimau m [eskeemo] ice cream on a stick, ice lolly

essayer [essay-ay] to try; to try on

essence f [essONss] petrol, gas

essieu m [ess-yuh] axle

essuie-glace m [ess-wee-glass] windscreen wiper

est: il/elle est [ay] he/she/it is

est m east

à l'est de east of

est-ce que ...? [eskuh] to form questions

est-ce que vous pensez ...? do you think ...?

est-ce qu'il y a ...? [eskeel ya] is there ...?; are there ...?

estomac m [estoma] stomach

et [ay] and

et ... et both ... and

étage m [aytahj] floor

1er étage first floor, (US) second floor

étage inférieur lower floor

étage supérieur upper floor

étang m [aytON] pond

étant [aytON] being

état m [ayta] state

États-Unis mpl [ayta zoonee] United States

été m [aytay] summer

été been

éteignez vos phares switch off your lights

éteignez vos veilleuses switch off your sidelights/parking lights

éteindre [aytANdr] to switch off

éteint [aytAN] switched off; out

s'étendre [saytONdr] to lie down; to extend

éternuer [aytairnoo-ay] to sneeze

êtes: vous êtes [et] you are

étiquette f label

étoile f [aytwal] star

étonnant [aytonON] astonishing

étranger m [aytrONjay] foreigner

à l'étranger abroad

étranger foreign

étranger service prioritaire overseas priority mail

être* [etr] to be

étroit [aytrwa] narrow; tight

études fpl [aytood] studies

étudiant m, **étudiante** f [aytood-yON, -yONt] student

étudier [aytood-yay] to study

eu [oo] had

européen [urropay-AN] European

eux* [uh] them

s'évanouir [sayvanweer] to faint

évidemment [ayveedamON] obviously

évident [ayveedON] obvious

évier m [ayv-yay] sink

exagérer [exajayray] to exaggerate

examiner [exameenay] to examine

excédent de bagages m excess baggage

excès de vitesse m speeding

s'excuser [sexkOOzay] to apologize

excusez-moi [exkoozay mwa] sorry; excuse me

exemple m [exONpl] example
par exemple for example

exiger [exeejay] to demand

exigez votre reçu ask for a receipt

expliquer [expleekay] to explain

exposition f exhibition; exposure

exprès [expray] deliberately
par exprès [express] special delivery

express m ordinary fast train

extincteur m [extANkturr] fire extinguisher

F

fabriqué en/au ... made in ...

fâché [fashay] angry

facile [fasseel] easy

façon f [fassON] way

de façon que so that

facteur m postman

facultatif optional; request

faible [febl] weak

faim: j'ai faim [fAN] I'm hungry

faire* [fair] to do; to make
ça ne fait rien [san fay ree-AN] it doesn't matter

faisons: nous faisons [fuhzON] we do; we make

fait: il/elle fait [fay] he/she/it does; he/she/it makes

fait did; made

faites: vous faites [fet] you do; you make

faites attention! be careful!

faites l'appoint have the right change ready

faites vérifier votre niveau d'huile have your oil checked

fait main hand-made

falaise f [falez] cliff

falloir [falwahr] to be necessary
il va falloir ... it will be necessary to ...

famille f [fameel] family

fard à paupières m [far a pohp-yair] eye-shadow

fatigué [fateegay] tired

fauché [fohshay] broke

fausse [fohss] wrong

faut: il faut que je/vous ... [eel fo kuh] I/you must ...

faute f [foht] mistake; fault

fauteuil roulant m [fotuh-ee roolON] wheelchair

faux, f fausse [fo, fohss] wrong

faux numéro wrong number

favori favourite

FB (franc belge) Belgian franc

félicitations! [fayleesseetass-yON] congratulations!

femelle [fuhmel] female

femme f [fam] woman; wife

femme d'affaires [dafair] businesswoman

femme de chambre [duh shONbr] chambermaid

fenêtre f [fuhnetr] window

fer m [fair] iron
  fer à repasser [ruhpassay] iron

ferai: je ferai [fuhray] I will do; I will make

fera: il/elle fera [fuhra] he/she/it will do; he/she/it will make

feras: tu feras [fuhra] you will do; you will make

ferez: vous ferez [fuhray] you will do; you will make

fermé [fairmay] closed
  fermé jusqu'au ... closed until ...
  fermé le ... closed on ...

ferme f [fairm] farm

fermer [fairmay] to close

fermer à clé [klay] to lock

fermer la grille [gree] close the outside door

fermeture annuelle f annual holiday, annual closure

fermeture automatique des portes doors close automatically

fermeture éclair f [fairmuhtoor ayklair] zip

fermeture hebdomadaire le lundi closed on Mondays

fermez le volet svp please close the flap

ferons: nous ferons [fuhrON] we will do; we will make

feront: ils/elles feront [fuhrON] they will do; they will make

fête f [fet] party; feast day

fête des vendanges [vONdONj] grape harvest festival

fête de village [veelajh] village fair

fête nationale 14 July (national holiday)

feu m [feu] fire
  vous avez du feu? [voo zavay dOO] have you got a light?

feuille f [fuh-ee] leaf

feux arrière mpl [fuh aree-yair] rear lights

feux d'artifice fireworks

feux de camp interdits no campfires

feux de position sidelights

feux de signalisation traffic lights

février [fayvree-ay] February

fiancé engaged

se fiancer [suh fee-ONsay] to get engaged

fibres naturelles natural fibres

ficelle f [feessel] string

fier [fee-air] proud

fièvre f [fee-evr] fever
  avoir de la fièvre to have a

temperature
fil m [feel] thread
fil de fer [duh fair] wire
file f [feel] lane
fille f [fee] girl; daughter
film en VO m film in the
  original language
fils m [feess] son
filtre m [feeltr] filter
fin f [fAN] end
fin fine
fin d'autoroute end of
  motorway
fin de ... end of ...
fin de série oddment
finir [feeneer] to finish
fleur f [flurr] flower
fleuriste m [flurreest] florist's
foire f [fwahr] fair
foire à la brocante [brokONt]
  street market for antiques
  and bric-à-brac
fois f [fwa] time
  une fois once
  à la fois at the same time
folle [fol] mad
fonctionnaire m/f [fONks-yonair]
  civil servant
fond m [fON] bottom
  au fond de at the bottom
  of
fond de teint [duh tAN]
  foundation cream
fonds m [fON] fund; funds
fontaine f [fONten] fountain
font: ils/elles font [fON] they
  do; they make
footing m jogging
forêt f [foray] forest

forme: en forme [form] fit
formellement interdit strictly
  prohibited
formez le ... dial ...
formidable [formeedabl] great
formulaire m [formOOlair] form
fort [for] strong; loud; loudly;
  very
fou, f folle [foo, fol] mad
foulard m [foolar] scarf
foule f [fool] crowd
foulure f [foolOOr] sprain
four m [foor] oven
fourchette f [foorshet] fork
fournitures de bureau office
  supplies
fourreur m furrier
fous: je m'en fous [juh mON foo]
  I don't give a damn
  fous le camp! [kON] get
  lost!
foutre [footr] to put; to do
  allez vous faire foutre! [alay
  voo fair] go to hell!
fr (franc) franc
fraîche [fresh] fresh
frais mpl [fray] charges
frais, f fraîche [fray, fresh]
  fresh
franc m [frON] franc
français [frONsay] French
Français m Frenchman
Française f [frONsez] French
  woman
franc suisse [sweess] Swiss
  franc
frapper [frapay] to hit
frappez avant d'entrer knock
  before entering

frein **m** [frAN] brake

frein à main [mAN] handbrake; (US) parking brake

freiner [frenay] to brake

frein moteur: utilisez votre frein moteur engage lower gear

frère **m** [frair] brother

fret **m** [fray] freight

frigo **m** fridge

frisé [freezay] curly

froid [frwa] cold

fromager **m** [fromajay], fromages [fromahj] cheese shop

front **m** [frON] forehead

frontière **f** [frONt-yair] border

frotter [frotay] to rub

FrS (franc suisse) Swiss franc

fuite **f** [fweet] leak

fumée **f** [foomay] smoke

fumer [foomay] to smoke

fumeurs [foomurr] smokers

fusible **m** [foozeebl] fuse

fusil **m** [foozee] gun

G

gagner [gan-yay] to win; to earn

galerie **f** gallery; roof rack; circle

galerie d'art [dar] art gallery

gallois [galwa] Welsh

gallo-romain civilization following Roman conquest of Gaul

ganterie **f** glove shop

gants **mpl** [gON] gloves

garçon **m** [garson] boy; waiter

garder [garday] to keep

gare **f** [gar] train station

gare routière [root-yair] bus station

se garer [suh garay] to park

gare SNCF [ess-en-say-ef] French train station

gas-oil **m** diesel

gauche **f** [gohsh] left

à gauche (de) on the left (of)

gaucher [gohshay] left-handed

Gaulois Gauls (original inhabitants of France)

gazole **m** diesel

gel **m** [jel] frost; gel

gelé [juhlay] frozen

gelée **f** [juhlay] frost

geler [juhlay] to be freezing

gélule **f** [jaylool] capsule

gênant [jenON] embarrassing

gendarme **m** policeman

gendarmerie **f** police station

gendre **m** [jONdr] son-in-law

gêner [jenay] to embarrass; to hinder

généralement [jaynayralmON] generally

généraliste **m/f** [jaynayraleest] GP, family doctor

génial! [jayn-yal] great!, fantastic!

genou **m** [juhnoo] knee

gens **mpl** [jON] people

gentil [jONtee] kind; nice

gérant **m** [jayrON] manager

gilet **m** [jeelay] cardigan

gilet de corps [duh kor] vest

gîte m rural holiday accommodation

gîte et petit déjeuner [jeet ay puhtee dayjuhnay] bed and breakfast

glacier m [glassee-ay] ice cream shop; glacier

glissant [gleessON] slippery

Golfe de Gascogne m Bay of Biscay

gomme f [gom] rubber, eraser

gorge f [gorj] throat

goût m [goo] taste

goûter [gootay] to taste

goûter m tea (meal)

gouttes fpl [goot] drops

grâce à [grass] thanks to

grand [grON] large; tall; great

Grande-Bretagne f [grONd-bruhtañ] Great Britain

grandes lignes main lines

grande surface f [sOOrfass] superstore

grandes vacances fpl [grONd vakONss] summer holidays

grand magasin m [magazAN] department store

grand-mère f [grON-mair] grandmother

grand-père m [-pair] grandfather

gras m [gra] fat

gras, f grasse [gra, grass] greasy

gratuit [gratwee] free

grave [grahv] serious; deep

gravillons loose chippings

grec, f grecque [grek] Greek

grêle f [grel] hail

grippe f [greep] flu

gris [gree] grey

gros [gro] big; fat

grossier [gross-yay] rude

grotte f [grot] cave

groupe sanguin m [groop sONGAN] blood group

guêpe f [gep] wasp

guère [gair] hardly

guérir [gay-reer] to heal, to cure; to recover

guerre f [gair] war

gueule de bois f [gurl duh bwa] hangover

guichet m [geeshay] ticket office; box office; counter

guichet automatique cash dispenser, ATM

guichet fermé position closed

guide touristique m/f [geed tooreesteek] tourist guide

gymnase m [jeemnaz] gymnasium

gynécologue m/f [jeenaykolog] gynaecologist

H

habillé [abeeyay] formal; dressed

habiller [abeeyay] to dress
s'habiller to get dressed

habiter [abeetay] to live

habitude f [abeetOOd] habit
d'habitude usually

habituel [abeetOOel] usual

s'habituer à [sabeetOO-ay] to get

used to
haïr [a-eer] to hate
hall d'arrivée m arrival hall, arrivals
hall (de) départ departures, departure hall
hall de gare station concourse
halte stop
hameau m [amo] hamlet
hanche f [ONsh] hip
handicapé [ONdeekapay] disabled
hasard: par hasard [azar] by chance
haut [o] high
en haut upstairs
hauteur limitée à ... maximum height ...
herbe f [airb] grass
heure f [urr] hour; time
quelle heure est-il? [kel urr ayteel] what time is it?
à l'heure on time
3 heures de l'après-midi 3 p.m.
5 heures du matin 5 a.m.
11 heures du soir 11 p.m.
heure limite d'enregistrement check-in deadline
heures d'affluence rush hour
heures des levées collection times
heures de visite visiting hours
heures d'ouverture opening times
heureusement [urrurzmON] fortunately

heureux [ur-ruh] happy
hexagone: l'hexagone m France (colloquial name)
hier [yair] yesterday
hippisme m [eepeess-muh] horse-riding
histoire f [eestwahr] history; story
hiver m [eevair] winter
HLM (habitation à loyer modéré) f [ash-el-em] council flat, public housing unit
hollandais [olONday] Dutch
homme m [om] man
homme d'affaires [dafair] businessman
hommes [om] gents, men's room
honnête [onet] honest
honteux [ONtuh] ashamed
hôpital m [opeetal] hospital
hoquet m [okay] hiccups
horaire m [orair] timetable, schedule
horaire d'ouverture opening times
horloge f [orloj] clock
horlogerie f watchmaker's
horlogerie-bijouterie watchmaker and jeweller's
horodateur m parking meter, pay and display
hors-bord m [or-bor] outboard motorboat
hors de [or duh] out of
hors saison off season
hors service out of order
hors taxes [tax] duty-free

hôtel **m** [otel] hotel

hôtel de ville [duh veel] town hall, city hall

hôtesse de l'air **f** [otess] air hostess

huile **f** [weel] oil

huile solaire suntan oil

huit [weet] eight

huitième [weet-yem] eighth

humeur **f** [OOmurr] mood

humide [OOmeed] damp

humidité **f** [OOmeedeetay] dampness

hypermarché **m** [eepairmarshay] supermarket; hypermarket

I

■

I tourist information

ici [ee-see] here

idée **f** [eeday] idea

il* [eel] he; it

île **f** [eel] island

il est interdit de ... ... is prohibited

il est interdit de déposer des ordures no litter, no tipping

il est interdit de donner à manger aux animaux do not feed the animals

il est interdit de marcher sur les pelouses keep off the grass

il n'y a pas ... [eel nya pa] there isn't ...; there aren't ...

il n'y a pas de quoi! [duh kwa] don't mention it!

ils* [eel] they

il y a ... [eelya] there is ...;

there are ...

il y a trois jours three days ago

est-ce qu'il y a ...? [eskeel ya] is there ...?; are there ...?

imbécile! [ANbayseel] idiot!

immédiatement [eemaydee-atmON] immediately

immeuble **m** [eemurbl] block (of flats); building

impasse dead end

imperméable **m** [ANpairmay-abl] raincoat

imprimé printed matter

incroyable [ANkrwyabl] incredible

indicatif **m** [ANdeekateef] dialling code, area code; country code

indiquer [ANdeekay] to indicate, to point out

s'infecter [sANfektay] to become infected

infirmerie **f** [ANfeermuhree] infirmary

infirmière **f** [ANfeerm-yair] nurse

informations **fpl** [ANformass-yON] news; information

informatique **f** [ANformateek] information technology; computing

informer [ANformay] to inform

infraction **f** [ANfrax-yON] offence

insérer le jeton insert token

insérez votre carte insert your card

insolation **f** [ANsolass-yON] sunstroke

insomnie **f** [ANsomnee]

insomnia

institut de beauté m [ANsteetoo duh botay] beauty salon

instrument de musique m [ANstroomoN duh moozeek] musical instrument

insupportable [ANsooportabl] obnoxious

interdiction de ... [ANtairdeex-yoN] no ...

interdiction de fumer no smoking

interdiction de marcher sur la voie do not walk on the track

interdiction de parler au conducteur do not speak to the driver

interdiction de stationner no parking

interdit [ANtairdee] forbidden, prohibited

interdit à tous véhicules no access to any vehicle

interdit aux forains et aux nomades no gypsies

interdit aux mineurs no admittance to minors

interdit aux moins de ... ans children under ... not admitted

interdit aux voyageurs no access for passengers; staff only

intéressant [ANtayressoN] interesting

s'intéresser à [sANtayressay] to be interested in

intérieur: à l'intérieur [ANtayree-urr] inside

interrupteur m [ANtairoopturr] switch

intoxication alimentaire f [ANtoxeekass-yoN aleemoNtair] food poisoning

introduire [ANtrodweer] to introduce; to insert

introduire carte ou composer numéro libre insert card or dial freephone number

introduire les pièces ici insert coins here

introduisez une pièce de 2 francs et tournez la poignée insert a 2 franc coin and turn the handle

introduisez votre pièce ici insert coin here

invité m [ANveetay] guest

inviter [ANveetay] to invite

irai: j'irai [eeray] I will go

ira: il/elle ira [eera] he/she/it will go

iras: tu iras [eera] you will go

irez: vous irez [eeray] you will go

irlandais [eerloNday] Irish

Irlande du Nord f [eerloNd doo nor] Northern Ireland

irons: nous irons [eeroN] we will go

iront: ils/elles iront [eeroN] they will go

issue de secours emergency exit, fire escape

italien [eetalyAN] Italian

itinéraire m [eeteenayrair] route

itinéraire bis alternative route

itinéraire conseillé
recommended route

itinéraire de délestage
alternative route

itinéraire obligatoire
compulsory route (for
heavy vehicles etc)

ivre [eevr] drunk

ivresse f [eevress] drunkenness

J

jaloux [jaloo] jealous

jamais [jamay] never; ever

jambe f [jONb] leg

janvier [jONvee-ay] January

jardin m [jardAN] garden

jardin public public gardens,
park

jardin zoologique zoo

jauge f [johj] gauge

jaune [jo-n] yellow

je* [juh] I

jean m jeans

j'écoute [jaykoot] speaking

jetable [juhtahbl] disposable

jeter [juhtay] to throw (away)

jeton m [juhtON] token

jeu m [juh] game

jeu de société board game

jeudi [juhdee] Thursday

jeun: le matin à jeun first
thing in the morning on an
empty stomach

jeune [jurn] young

jeune femme f [fam] young
woman

jeune fille f [fee] girl

jeune homme m [om] young
man

jeux mpl [juh] games

jeux électroniques computer
games

jeux interdits aux moins
de 16 ans use of gaming
machines forbidden for
those under 16

joindre [jwANdr] to join

joli [jolee] pretty

jouer [joo-ay] to play

jouet m [joo-ay] toy

jour m [joor] day

jour férié [fayree-ay] public
holiday

journal m [joornal] newspaper

journaux newspapers,
stationer

journée f [joornay] day

journée continue open all day

journées à tarif réduit cheap
travel days

jours de semaine uniquement
weekdays only

jours impairs odd dates of the
month (parking allowed)

jours ouvrables weekdays

jours pairs/impairs parking
allowed only on even/odd
days of the month

joyeuses Pâques! [jwy-urz pak]
happy Easter!

juif, f juive [jweef, jweev] Jewish

juillet [jwee-yay] July

juin [jwAN] June

juive [jweev] Jewish

jumeaux mpl [joomo] twins

jumelé [joomuhlay] twinned

jumelles fpl [joomel]

binoculars; twins

jupe f [j∞p] skirt

jupon m [j∞poN] petticoat

jusqu'à (ce que) [j∞ska(ss kuh)] until

jusque [j∞sk] up to, as far as; till

juste [j∞st] fair; right

K

kermesse f [kairmess] fair

kiosque à journaux m newspaper stand

klaxon m horn

klaxonner [klaxonay] to hoot

K-way® m [ka-way] cagoule

L

l'* the; him; her; it

la* the; her; it

là [la] there

là-bas [laba] over there

lac m lake

lacets mpl [lassay] shoe laces

laid [lay] ugly

laine f [len] wool

laisser [lessay] to let; to leave

lait m [lay] milk

laiterie dairy (Switzerland)

lait solaire [solair] suntan lotion

lame de rasoir f [lahm duh razwahr] razor blade

lampe de poche f [loNp duh posh] torch

lancer [loNsay] to throw

landau m [loNdo] pram

langue f [loN-g] tongue; language

laque f [lak] hair spray

laquelle [lakel] which one

large [larj] wide

lavabo m washbasin

lavage à la main hand wash

lavage du pare-brise screen wash

lave-auto m [lav-oto] car wash

laver [lavay] to wash

se laver to wash, to have a wash

laverie automatique f [lavree otomateek] launderette, laundromat

laver séparément wash separately

lave-vaisselle m [lav-vess-el] dish washer

lavoir m [lavwahr] wash house

lavomatic m launderette, laundromat

layette f babywear

le* [luh] the; him; it

leçon f [luhsoN] lesson

lecteur de cassettes m [lekturr] cassette player

lendemain m [loNduhmaN] the next day

lent [loN] slow

lentement [loNtuhmoN] slowly

lentilles de contact fpl [loNtee duh] contact lenses

lentilles dures [d∞r] hard lenses

lentilles semi-rigides [-reejeed] gas-permeable lenses

lentilles souples [soopl] soft

Le

lenses

lequel [luhkel] which one
les* [lay] the; them
lesquel(le)s [laykel] which ones
lessive f [lesseev] washing powder; washing
  faire la lessive do the washing
lettre f [letr] letter
leur* [lurr] their; (to) them
  le/la leur theirs
leurs* [lurr] their
  les leurs theirs
lever [luhvay] to lift, to raise
  se lever to get up
levier de vitesses m [luhv-yay duh veetess] gear lever
lèvre f [levr] lip
lézard m [layzar] lizard
libellez votre chèque à l'ordre de ... please make out your cheque to ...
librairie f [leebrairee] bookshop, bookstore
libre [leebr] free, vacant
libre-service self-service
libre-service affranchissement self-service stamping facility
libre-service bancaire autobank, ATM
lieu m [l-yuh] place
ligne f [leeñ] line
  la ligne est encombrée the line is busy
lignes de banlieue suburban lines
lime à ongles f [leem a ONgl] nailfile

limitation de vitesse f [leemeetass-yON duh veetess] speed limit
limite de validité des billets expiry of validity of tickets
lin m [lAN] linen
linge de maison m [lANj duh mezzON] household linen
lingerie f underwear
linge sale m [lANj sal] laundry
lire [leer] to read
liste f [leest] list
lit m [lee] bed
lit de camp [kON] campbed
lit d'enfant [dONfON] cot
literie f [leetuhree] bedding
lit pour deux personnes [duh pairson] double bed
lit pour une personne [OOn] single bed
lits superposés mpl [lee sOOpairpozay] bunk beds
living m living room
livraison f [leevrezzON] delivery
livraison à domicile home deliveries
livraisons interdites de ... à ... no deliveries between ... and ...
livre f [leevr] pound
livre m book
livres et journaux books and newspapers
livre sterling f pound sterling
localité f [lokaleetay] place
location f [lokass-yON] rental; theatre tickets
location à la semaine charge per week

location de ... ... for hire
location de bateaux [bato] boat hire
location de vélos [vaylo] bicycles for hire/rent
location de voitures [vwatOOr] car hire/rental
loft m warehouse conversion
logement m [lojmON] accommodation
loger [lojay] to stay
loges des artistes artists' dressing rooms
logiciel m [lojeess-yel] software
loi f [lwa] law
loin [lwAN] far away
 plus loin further
loisirs mpl [lwazeer] free time, leisure
Londres [lONdr] London
long, f longue [lON, lON-g] long
longtemps [lONtON] a long time
longue [lON-g] long
longueur f [lONgurr] length
lorsque [lorskuh] when
louer [loo-ay] to rent
 à louer to let, for rent, for hire
lourd [loor] heavy; rich; muggy
loyer m [lwy-ay] rent
lui* [lwee] him; to him; to her
lui-même [-mem] himself; speaking
lumière f [lOOm-yair] light
lundi [lANdee] Monday
lune f [lOOn] moon
lunettes fpl [lOOnet] glasses
lunettes de soleil [duh solay] sunglasses
lycée m [leessay] secondary school

M

M, M° (métro) underground
M (Monsieur) Mr
m'* (to) me; myself
ma* my
machine à écrire f [aykreer] typewriter
machine à laver [lavay] washing machine
mâchoire f [mashwahr] jaw
Mademoiselle [mad-mwazel] Miss
magasin m [magazAN] shop, store
magasin d'alimentation grocery store
magasin de chaussures shoe shop
magasin de disques record shop
magasin de vins et spiritueux off-licence, liquor store
magasin diététique health food store
magnétoscope m [man-yaytoskop] video recorder
mai [may] May
maigre [megr] skinny
maigrir [megreer] to lose weight
maillot de bain m [my-o duh bAN] swimming costume
main f [mAN] hand
maintenant [mANtnON] now

mairie f [mairee] town hall

mais [may] but

maison f [mezzON] house

à la maison at home

la maison n'accepte pas les chèques we do not accept cheques

la maison ne fait pas crédit we do not give credit

maison de la culture arts centre

maison des jeunes youth club

maison d'hôtes [doht] guesthouse

mal m pain; trouble; harm

mal badly; wrongly

se faire mal à la main to hurt one's hand

avoir mal au cœur to feel sick

ça fait mal it hurts

malade [malad] ill

maladie f [maladee] disease

mal de gorge m [gorj] sore throat

mal de mer [duh mair] seasickness

mal de tête [tet] headache

mal d'oreilles [doray] earache

mal du pays [payee] homesickness

mâle [mahl] male

malentendu m [malONtONdOO] misunderstanding

malgré [malgray] in spite of

malheureusement [malurr-urzmON] unfortunately

maman f [mamON] mum

Manche f [mONsh] English

Channel

manche f sleeve

mandat postal m [mONda posstal] postal order

manette du signal d'alarme pull for alarm

manger [mONjay] to eat

manquer [mONkay] to miss

... me manque [muh mONk] I miss ...

manteau m [mONto] coat

manuel de conversation m [mONOOel duh konvairsass-yON] phrase book

maquillage m [makee-ahj] make-up

se **maquiller** [makee-ay] to put one's make-up on

marchand m [marshON] shopkeeper; merchant; dealer

marchand de légumes greengrocer

marchand de vins wine merchant

marchandise: les marchandises dangereuses sont interdites dangerous items are prohibited

marche f [marsh] walking; step; march; running, working

marché m [marshay] market

marche arrière [aree-air] reverse gear

marcher [marshay] to walk; to work, to function

ça marche? OK?

mardi [mardee] Tuesday

marée f [maray] tide

mari m [maree] husband

mariage m [maree-ahj] wedding

marié [maree-ay] married

se marier (avec) [suh maree-ay] to get married, to marry

maroquinerie f leather goods

marque déposée registered trademark

marrant [marON] funny

marre: j'en ai marre (de) [jON ay mar] I'm fed up (with)

marron [marON] brown

mars [marss] March

marteau m [marto] hammer

massepain m [massuhpAN] marzipan

matelas m [matuhla] mattress

matin m [matAN] morning
le matin in the morning

mauvais [mo-vay] bad

maux de dents mpl [mo duh dON] toothache

maux d'estomac stomach ache

me* [muh] me; to me; myself

mec m bloke, guy

mécanicien m [maykaneess-yAN] mechanic

mèches fpl [mesh] highlights

médecin m [maydsAN] doctor

médicament m [maydeekamON] medicine

Méditerranée f [maydeetairanay] Mediterranean

méduse f [maydOOz] jellyfish

meilleur [mayurr] better
le meilleur the best
meilleur que better than

meilleurs vœux! [vuh] best wishes!

mélanger [maylONjay] to mix

même [mem] even; same
le/la même the same

ménage: faire le ménage [maynahj] to do the housework

mener [muhnay] to lead

menhir m [mayneer] standing stone

mentir [mONteer] to lie

menton m [mONtON] chin

menu à ... F set menu costing ... francs

mer f [mair] sea

mercerie f haberdasher's, (US) notions store

merci [mairsee] thank you; no thank you

merci beaucoup [bo-koo] thank you very much

merci de votre visite thanks for your visit

merci, pareillement [paraymON] thank you, the same to you

mercredi [mairkruhdee] Wednesday

merde! [maird] shit!

mère f [mair] mother

merveilleux [mairvay-uh] wonderful

mes* [may] my

messe f [mess] mass

messieurs [mess-yuh] gentlemen; gents, men's rest room

mesure f [muhzOOr] measure
à mesure que as

sur mesure to measure

météo f [maytay-o] weather forecast

métier m [maytee-ay] job

mètre m [metr] metre

métro m [maytro] underground, subway

mettre [metr] to put

se mettre à to begin to

meublé m [murblay] furnished accommodation

meubles mpl [murbl] furniture

Midi m South of France

midi m midday

mien*: le mien [luh m-yAN] mine

mienne*: la mienne [m-yen] mine

mien(ne)s*: les mien(ne)s [m-yAN, m-yen] mine

mieux [m-yuh] better

le mieux (the) best

mignon, mignonne [meen-yON, meen-yon] sweet, cute

milieu m [meel-yuh] middle

mille m [meel] thousand

million f [meel-yON] million

mince [mANss] thin

minuit m [meen-wee] midnight

miroir m [meer-wahr] mirror

mis [mee] put

mise en fourrière immédiate illegally parked cars will be removed

mise en marche automatique, placez vos mains sous le volet starts automatically, place your hands under the flap

Mlle (Mademoiselle) Miss

Mme (Madame) Mrs

mobylette f [mobeelet] moped

mode f [mod] fashion

à la mode fashionable

mode d'emploi directions for use

modèle m [mo-del] model; design; style

modes ladies' fashions

moi [mwa] me

moi-même [mwa-mem] myself

moindre [mwANdr] smaller; less; lesser

le moindre the smallest; the slightest

moins: à moins que [mwAN kuh] unless

au moins at least [o]

moins (de) less

le moins (the) least

mois m [mwa] month

moitié f [mwatee-ay] half

à moitié prix [pree] half-price

molle [mol] soft

mollet m [molay] calf

mon* [mON] my

monde m [mONd] world

tout le monde [too luh] everyone

moniteur m, **monitrice** f [moneeturr, -treess] instructor

monnaie f [monay] change

monsieur m [muhss-yuh] gentleman, man

Monsieur sir

montagne f [mONtañ] mountain

montant m [mONtoN] amount

montant exact exact change

monter [mONtay] to go up; to get in

montre f [mONtr] watch

montrer [mONtray] to show

monument aux morts war memorial

moquette f [moket] carpet

morceau m [morso] piece

mordre to bite

morsure f [morsoor] bite

mort f [mor] death

mort dead

mosquée f [moskay] mosque

mot m [mo] word

moteur m [moturr] engine

moto f motorbike

mou, f molle [moo, mol] soft

mouche f [moosh] fly

mouchoir m [moosh-wahr] handkerchief

mouillé [mooyay] wet

mourir [mooreer] to die

mousse à raser f [razay] shaving foam

moustique m [moosteek] mosquito

mouton m [mootON] sheep

mur m [moor] wall

mûr [moor] ripe

musée m [moozay] museum; art gallery

musée d'art [dar] art gallery

muséum m [moozay-om] natural history museum

musique f [moozeek] music

musulman [moozoolmON] Muslim

myope [mee-op] shortsighted

N

nager [nahjay] to swim

naître [netr] to be born

nana f [nana] bird, girl

nappe f [nap] tablecloth

natation f [natass-yON] swimming

nationalité f [nass-yonaleetay] nationality

nature f [natoor] nature
  yaourt nature natural yoghurt

naturel [natoorel] natural

naturellement [natoorelmON] naturally, of course

navette f [navet] shuttle service

navette de l'aéroport airport bus

ND (Notre Dame) Our Lady

né born

néanmoins [nay-ONmwAN] nevertheless

ne ... aucun [nuh ... okAN] no, not any, none

nécessaire [naysessair] necessary

négatif m [naygateef] negative

ne ... guère [gair] hardly

neige f [nej] snow

neiger [nejay] to snow

ne ... jamais [jamay] never

ne ... ni neither ... nor

ne ... nulle part [nool par] nowhere, not ... anywhere

ne ... pas* [pa] not

ne pas ... do not ...

ne pas **affranchir** freepost, do not affix stamp

ne pas **avaler** do not swallow

ne pas **congeler** do not freeze

ne pas **dépasser ... comprimés par jour** do not take more than ... tablets a day

ne pas **dépasser la dose prescrite** do not exceed the prescribed dose

ne pas **déranger** do not disturb

ne pas **essorer** do not spin dry

ne pas **laisser à la portée des enfants** keep out of the reach of children

ne pas **repasser** do not iron

ne pas **se pencher au dehors** do not lean out of the window

ne pas **se pencher par la fenêtre** do not lean out of the window

ne pas **... sous peine d'amende** ... will be fined

ne pas **tordre** do not wring

ne pas **toucher à ...** do not touch ...

ne **... personne** [pairson] nobody, not anybody

ne **... plus** [ploo] no more, no longer

ne **... que** [kuh] only

ne **quittez pas** [nuh keetay pa] hold the line, hold on

ne **... rien** [ree-AN] nothing, not anything

ne rien **jeter dans les WC** do not flush objects down the toilet

ne rien **jeter par la fenêtre** do not throw anything out of the window

ne tirer **la poignée qu'en cas de danger** pull handle only in case of emergency

nerveux [nairvuh] nervous

n'est-ce pas? [ness-pa] didn't he/she/it?; isn't it?; isn't that so?

nettoyage à sec dry cleaning; dry clean only

nettoyer [net-wy-ay] to clean

neuf, f neuve [nuhf, nuhv] new

neuf nine

neveu m [nuhvuh] nephew

neuvième [nuhv-yem] ninth

névralgies headaches

névrosé [nayvrozay] neurotic

nez m [nay] nose

ni neither

ni **... ni ...** neither ... nor ...

nids-de-poule potholes

nièce f [nee-ess] niece

nocturne late night opening

Noël [no-el] Christmas

noir [nwahr] black

noir et blanc black and white

nom m [noN] name

nom de famille [duh famee] surname, family name

nom de jeune fille [jurn fee] maiden name

nommer: se nommer [suh nomay] to be called

non [noN] no; not

non-fumeurs [-foomurr] no smoking

non merci [mairsee] no thank you

nord m [nor] north

au nord de north of

nos* [no] our

note f [not] bill; note

notez le numéro de votre emplacement make a note of the number of your parking space

notre* [notr] our

nôtre*: le/la nôtre [luh/la nohtr] ours

nôtres*: les nôtres ours

n'oubliez pas de composter votre billet do not forget to punch/validate your ticket

n'oubliez pas le guide don't forget to tip the guide

n'oubliez pas votre reçu don't forget your receipt

nourriture f [nooreetoor] food

nous* [noo] we; (to) us

nous acceptons les cartes de crédit credit cards welcome

nous n'acceptons pas les chèques cheques not accepted

nouveau, f nouvelle [noovo, -vel] new

de nouveau again

nouveau franc new French franc (100 old francs)

Nouvel An m [oN] New Year

nouvelle [noovel] new

nouvelles fpl [noovel] news

novembre [no-voNbr] November

nu [noo] naked

nuage m [noo-ahj] cloud

nuageux [noo-ahjuh] cloudy

nuit f [nwee] night

nul [nool] no; lousy

nulle part [nool par] nowhere

numéro m [noomayro] number

numéro de téléphone phone number

numéro direct direct dialling

numérotez dial

numéro vert freephone

nu-pieds mpl [noo-p-yay] flip-flops

O

objectif m [objekteef] lens; objective

objets trouvés mpl [objay troovay] lost property office, lost and found

objets volumineux large parcels/packages

oblitérez votre billet punch your ticket

obtenir [obtuhneer] to get

obturateur m [obtooraturr] shutter

occasion f [okaz-yoN] opportunity; occasion; bargain

d'occasion second-hand

occupé [okoopay] engaged; occupied; busy

s'occuper de [sokoopay] to take care of

octobre [oktobr] October

oculiste m/f [okuleest] eye specialist

odeur f [odurr] smell

œil m [uh-ee] eye

office à ... service at ...

office du tourisme tourist office

offre spéciale special offer

offrir [ofreer] to offer; to give

oiseau m [wazo] bird

ombre f [ONbr] shade
à l'ombre in the shade

ombre à paupières [pohp-yair] eye shadow

on* [ON] one; someone; you; they; people; we

oncle m [ONkl] uncle

ondulé [ONdoolay] wavy

ongle m [ONgl] nail

ont: ils/elles ont [ON] they have

onze [ONz] eleven

opérer [opayray] to operate

ophtalmologue m/f ophthalmologist

opticien m [opteess-yAN] optician

optimiste optimistic

optique optician's

or m gold

or massif solid gold

orage m [orahj] thunderstorm

orageux [orahjuh] stormy

orchestre m [orkestr] orchestra; stalls

ordinaire [ordeenair] ordinary; equivalent of two-star petrol

ordinateur m [ordeenaturr] computer

ordonnance f [ordonONss] prescription

ordures fpl [ordoor] litter; refuse; filth

oreille f [oray] ear

oreiller m [oray-yay] pillow

oreillons mpl [orayON] mumps

organiser [organeezay] to organize

orteil m [ortay] toe

os m [oss] bone

oser [ozay] to dare

ou [oo] or
ou bien [b-yAN] or else

où [oo] where

oublier [ooblee-ay] to forget

ouest m [west] west
à l'ouest de west of

oui [wee] yes

outil m [ootee] tool

ouvert [oovair] open

ouvert de ... à ... open from ... to ...

ouverture f [oovairtoor] opening

ouverture des guichets hours of opening

ouvre-boîte m [oovr-bwat] tin-opener

ouvre-bouteille m [-bootay] bottle-opener

ouvreuse f [oovrurz] usherette

ouvrier m [oovree-ay] (factory) worker

ouvrir [oovreer] to open

ouvrir ici open here

P

pages jaunes fpl [pahj jo-n] yellow pages

paire f [pair] pair

palais m [palay] palace

pâle [pahl] pale

panier m [pan-yay] basket

panier (à provisions) shopping basket

panne f [pan] breakdown

en panne [ON] out of order; broken down

tomber en panne [tONbay] to break down

panneau de signalisation m roadsign

pansement m [pONssmON] bandage

pansement adhésif [adayzeef] Elastoplast®, Bandaid®

panser [pONsay] to dress

pantalon m [pONtalON] trousers, (US) pants

pantoufles fpl [pONtoofl] slippers

papa m dad

papeterie f stationer's; stationery

papier m [pap-yay] paper

papier à lettres writing paper

papier collant [kolON] Sellotape®, Scotch tape®

papier d'aluminium [dalOOmeenee-um] aluminium foil

papier d'emballage [dONbalahj] wrapping paper

papier hygiénique [eejee-ayneek] toilet paper

papiers papers; litter

papiers, s'il vous plaît your identity papers, please

papillon m [papee-yON] butterfly

Pâques [pak] Easter

paquet m [pakay] package, packet

par by; through

parachute ascensionnel m [assONsee-onel] parascending

parachutisme m parachuting

parages: dans les parages [dON lay parahj] in the vicinity

paraître [paretre] to seem; to come out, to be published

parapluie m [paraplwee] umbrella

parc m park

parce que [parss-kuh] because

parcmètre m parking meter

parcotrain m parking for train users

pardessus m [par-duhsoo] overcoat

par-dessus over

par-dessous [-duhsoo] under

pardon [par-dON] excuse me, pardon (me); thank you

pare-brise m [par-breez] windscreen

pare-chocs m [-shok] bumper

parents mpl [parON] parents; relatives

paresseux [paressuh] lazy

parfait [parfay] perfect

parfois [parfwa] sometimes

parfum m [parfAN] perfume
parfumerie f perfume and cosmetics shop
parking m [parkeeng] car park, parking lot
parking à étages [aytahj] multi-storey car park, parking garage
parking courte durée short-term car park
parking longue durée long-term car park
parking non gardé unsupervised parking
parking payant paying car park
parking privé private car park
parking public public car park
parking réservé aux clients de l'hôtel parking for hotel guests only
parking souterrain underground car park
parking surveillé car park with attendant
parler [parlay] to speak
parler ici talk here
parmi among
pars: je/tu pars [par] I/you leave, I/you go away
part f [par] piece; share
à part except
de la part de from; on behalf of
de la part de qui? [duh kee] who shall I say is calling?
partager [partahjay] to share
parterre m stalls
partir [parteer] to leave

partout [partoo] everywhere
pas* [pa] not
pas de ... no ...
pas de remboursement we cannot give cash refunds
pas encore not yet
passage à niveau m [passahj a neevo] level crossing, (US) railroad crossing
passage à niveau gardé/non gardé manned/unmanned level crossing
passage clouté pedestrian crossing
passage interdit no entry
passage piétons pedestrian crossing
passage protégé priority road
passager m [passahjay] passenger
passage souterrain underpass
passeport m [pass-por] passport
passer [passay] to pass
qu'est-ce qui se passe? [keskee suh pass] what's happening?
passer par to go through
passerelle f gangway
passe-temps m [pass-tON] pastime
passionnant [pass-yonON] exciting
passionné de [pass-yonay] very keen on
pastilles pour la gorge fpl [pastee poor la gorj] throat pastilles

patientez svp please wait
patinage m [pateenahj] skating
patiner [pateenay] to skate
patinoire f [pateenwahr] ice rink
patins à glace mpl [patAN a glass] ice skates
patron m [pa-trON] boss; owner
pauvre [pohvr] poor
payer [pay-ay] to pay
payer comptant to pay cash
payez à la caisse pay at the cash desk
payez à la sortie pay on your way out
payez à l'ordre de ... payable to ...
payez ici pay here
pays m [payee] country
paysage m [payee-zahj] scenery
Pays de Galles m [payee duh gal] Wales
PCV m [pay-say-vay] collect call, reverse charge call
péage m [payahj] toll
peau f [po] skin
pêche f [pesh] fishing; peach
pêche interdite no fishing
pêcher [peshay] to fish
pêche sous-marine underwater fishing
peigne m [peñ] comb
se peigner [suh pen-yay] to comb one's hair
peindre [pANdr] paint
peine: à peine [pen] hardly
ce n'est pas la peine it's not worth it; it's not necessary
peinture f [pANtoor] painting
peinture fraîche wet paint

pelle f [pel] spade
pellicule f film
pelouse f [puhlooz] lawn
pénalité pour abus penalty for misuse
pendant [pONdON] during
pendant que while
penser [pONsay] to think
pension f [pONs-yON] guesthouse
pension complète [kONplet] full board
pension de famille guesthouse
pente f [pONt] slope
perdre [pairdr] to lose
se perdre to get lost
père m [pair] father
périphérique m [payreefayreek] ring road
permanente f [pairmanONt] perm
permettre [pairmetr] to allow
permis [pairmee] allowed
permis de conduire m [duh kONdweer] driving licence, driver's license
perruque f [pairook] wig
personne f [pairson] person
personne nobody
personne ne sait ... nobody knows ...
personnes handicapées disabled
peser [puhzay] to weigh
pétanque f [paytONk] French bowling game
petit [puhtee] small
petit ami m [tamee] boyfriend
petit déjeuner m [dayjuhnay]

breakfast

petite amie f [tamee] girlfriend

petite cuillère f teaspoon

petite-fille f [puhteet-fee] granddaughter

petit-fils m [puhtee-feess] grandson

petits-enfants mpl [puhtee-zONfON] grandchildren

peu: peu de ... [puh] few ...

un peu (de) a bit (of)

peur f [purr] fear

de peur que for fear that

j'ai peur (de) I'm afraid (of)

peut-être [puht-etr] maybe

peut: il/elle peut [puh] he/she/it can

il peut y avoir ... there may be ...

peuvent: ils/elles peuvent [puhv] they can

peux: je/tu peux [puh] I/you can

phallocrate m [falokrat] male chauvinist pig

phare m [far] headlight; lighthouse

phare antibrouillard [ONtee-broo-yar] fog lamp

pharmacie f [farmassee] chemist's, pharmacy

pharmacie de garde duty chemist/pharmacy, late-night chemist

pharmacie de service duty chemist

photographe m photographer; camera shop

photographie f [foto-grafee]

photograph

photographier [foto-grafyay] to photograph

photomètre m [foto-metr] light meter

pièce f [p-yess] coin; room; part

la pièce each, apiece

pièce de théâtre [duh tay-atr] play

pièces de rechange [ruhshONj] spare parts

pièces détachées [daytashay] parts

pièces rejetées reject coins

pied m [p-yay] foot

à pied on foot

pierre f stone

piéton m [p-yaytON] pedestrian

piétons passez en deux temps pedestrians cross in two stages

pile f [peel] battery; pile

pilote m [peelot] pilot

pilule f [peelool] pill

pince f [pANss] pliers; clip

pince à épiler [aypeelay] tweezers

pince à linge [lANj] clothes peg

pince à ongles [ONgl] nail clippers

pinceau m [pANso] paint brush

piquant [peekON] hot, spicy

piquer [peekay] to sting

piqûre f [peekoor] injection; bite

piqûre d'insecte [dANsekt] insect bite

pire [peer] worse

le pire worst

piscine f [peesseen] swimming pool

pissoir m public urinal

piste balisée f [baleezay] marked ski path

piste cyclable [seeklabl] cycle path

piste de ski ski track, piste

piste pour débutants [dayb00t0N] nursery slope

place f [plass] seat; square

place principale [prANseepal] main square

placer [plassay] to place

place réservée aux ... this seat is intended for ...

place(s) assise(s) seat(s)

places debout standing passengers

places libres spaces free (in car park)

plafond m [plaf0N] ceiling

plage f [plahj] beach

plaindre: se plaindre [suh plANdr] to complain

plaire [plair] to please

plaisanterie f [plezz0Ntree] joke

plaît: s'il vous plaît [seel voo play] please

plan m [pl0N] map

planche de surf f [pl0Nsh] surfboard

planche à voile [vwal] sailboard

plancher m [pl0Nshay] floor

plan de métro underground map

plan de ville map of the town

plan du quartier map of the district

plan du réseau network map

planning familial m [pla-neeng] family planning

plante f [pl0Nt] plant

plaque minéralogique f [meenayralojeek] number plate

plat m [pla] dish

plat flat

plateau m tray

plateaux-repas light meals served on trains

plâtre m plaster; plaster cast

plats à emporter take-away meals

plein [plAN] full
  faire le plein to fill up

pleurer [plurray] to cry

pleut: il pleut [pluh] it's raining

pleuvoir [pluhvwahr] to rain

plombage m [pl0Nbahj] filling

plombier m plumber

plongée f [pl0Njay] diving

plongée interdite no diving

plongée sous-marine skin-diving

plonger [pl0Njay] to dive

pluie f [plwee] rain

plupart: la plupart de [pl00par duh] most of

plus [pl00] more
  plus jamais never again
  plus de ... more; no more ...
  plus ... que ...-er than
  le plus [pl00ss] (the) most

plusieurs [pl00z-yurr] several

plutôt [pl00to] rather

pluvieux [plOOv-yuh] rainy

PMU betting on horses

pneu m [p-nuh] tyre

pneu crevé [kruhvay] flat tyre

pneu de rechange [duh ruhshONj] spare tyre

poche f [posh] pocket

poche en plastique plastic bag

poêle f [pwal] frying pan

poids m [pwa] weight

poids lourds [pwa loor] heavy vehicles

poids maximum maximum weight

poids net net weight

poignée f [pwan-yay] handle

poignet m [pwan-yay] wrist

point de rencontre m [pwAN duh rONkONtr] meeting point

point de vue [vOO] viewpoint

point noir accident blackspot; blackhead

point panoramique viewpoint

point phone pay-phone

pointure f [pwANtOOr] shoe size

poissonnerie f fishmonger

poitrine f [pwatreen] chest; breast

poli [polee] polite

police f police

police de l'aéroport airport police

police de la route traffic police

police du port harbour police

police secours emergency police

politique f politics

politique political

pollué [polOO-ay] polluted

pommade f [pomahd] ointment

pompiers mpl [pONp-yay] fire brigade

poney m pony

pont m [pON] bridge; deck

pont à péage [payahj] toll bridge

port de pêche m [por duh pesh] fishing port

porte f [port] door; gate

porte-bébé m [-baybay] carry-cot

portefeuille m [portfuh-ee] wallet

porte-jarretelles fpl suspenders

porte-monnaie m [port-monay] purse

porter [portay] to carry

bien se porter to be well

portes automatiques automatic gates

portier m [port-yay] porter

portière f [port-yair] door

portillon automatique m automatic gate

posologie directions for use, dosage

posséder [possayday] to own; to possess

poste f [posst] post office

poste de police m police station

poster [postay] to post

poste restante poste restante, (US) general delivery

pot m [po] jug

pot d'échappement [dayshapmON] exhaust

poterie f [potree] pottery
poubelle f [poobel] dustbin
poudre f [poodr] powder
pouls m pulse
poumons mpl [poomON] lungs
poupée f [poopay] doll
pour [poor] for
pourboire m [poorbwahr] tip
pourboire interdit please do not tip
pour cent [sON] per cent
pour entrer ..., to enter ...
pour ouvrir appuyer push to open
pour que [kuh] in order that, so that
pourquoi [poorkwa] why
pourrai: je pourrai [pooray] I will be able
pourra: il/elle pourra [poora] he/she/it will be able
pourras: tu pourras [poora] you will be able
pourrez: vous pourrez [pooray] you will be able
pourri [pooree] rotten
pourrons: nous pourrons [poorON] we will be able
pourront: ils/elles pourront [poorON] they will be able
pourtant [poortON] however
pour tous renseignements, s'adresser à ... for enquiries, please see ...
pourvu que [poorvoo kuh] provided that
pousser [poossay] to push
poussette f pushchair
poussez [poossay] push

pouvoir m [poovwahr] power
pouvoir to be able to
pratique practical
précautions d'emploi instructions for use
préfecture f [prayfektOOr] regional administrative headquarters
préfecture de police police headquarters
préféré [prayfayray] favourite
préférence f [prayfayrONss] preference
préférer [prayfayray] to prefer
premier m [pruhm-yay] first floor; (US) second floor
premier first
première f first class; première
premier étage first floor, (US) second floor
premiers secours mpl [pruhm-yay suhkoor] first aid
premiers soins [swAN] first aid
prendre [prONdr] to take; to catch
à prendre à jeun to be taken on an empty stomach
à prendre après les repas to be taken after meals
à prendre au coucher to be taken at bedtime
à prendre avant le coucher to be taken before going to bed
à prendre avant les repas to be taken before meals
à prendre ... fois par jour to be taken ... times a day

Pr

181

prendre ... comprimés à la fois take ... pills at a time

prendre ... comprimés ... fois par jour take ... pills ... times a day

prenez: vous prenez [pruhnay] you take

prenez un caddy take a trolley/cart

prenez un chariot take a trolley/cart

prenez un jeton à la caisse buy a token at the cash desk

prenez un panier take a basket

prenez un ticket take a ticket

prénom m [praynON] Christian name, first name

prenons: nous prenons [pruhnON] we take

préparer [prayparay] to prepare, to get ready

préparez votre monnaie have your change ready

presbyte [prezbeet] long-sighted

prescrire [preskreer] to prescribe

près de [pray duh] near

présenter [prayzONtay] to introduce; to present

préservatif m [prayzairvateef] condom

presque [presk] almost

pressing m dry-cleaner's

pression f [press-yON] pressure; draught beer

pression de l'air air pressure

pression des pneus tyre pressure

prêt [pray] ready

prêt-à-porter ready-to-wear clothes

prêter [pretay] to lend

prêtre m [pretr] priest

prier [pree-ay] to ask; to pray

je vous en prie [juh voo zON pree] don't mention it, you're welcome

prière f [pree-air] prayer

prière de ... please ...

prière de frapper avant d'entrer please knock before entering

prière de ne pas déranger please do not disturb

prière de ne pas faire de bruit après 22 heures please do not make any noise after 10 p.m.

prière de ne pas fumer please do not smoke

prière de ne pas toucher please do not touch

prière de refermer la porte please close the door

prière de s'essuyer les pieds avant d'entrer please wipe your feet

prière de tenir les chiens en laisse please keep dogs on a lead

primeurs fruit shop, greengrocer's

principal [prANseepal] main

printemps m [prANtON] spring

prioritaire [pree-oreetair] priority; priority-rate;

having right of way

priorité f [pree-oreetay] right of way; priority

priorité à droite right of way for traffic coming from the right

pris [pree] taken

prise f [preez] plug; socket

prise en charge minimum charge

prise multiple [mOOlteepl] adaptor

privé [preevay] private

prix m [pree] price; fee; prize

prix cassés reduced prices

prix coûtant at cost price

prix des places ticket prices

prix par jour price per day

prix par personne price per person

prix par semaine price per week

prix réduit reduced price

prix sacrifiés prices slashed

probablement [prob-abluhmON] probably

prochain [proshAN] next

à la prochaine [proshen] see you soon

prochaine levée next collection

prochaine séance à ... heures next performance at ...

produits de beauté cosmetics

produits d'entretien household cleaning materials

produits naturels health food

produit toxique poison

professeur m [professurr] teacher; lecturer; professor

profond [profON] deep

profondeur f [profONdurr] depth

promenade f walk

promenades à cheval horse riding

promener: aller se promener [alay suh promnay] to go for a walk

promettre [promtr] to promise

promotion: en promotion on special offer

prononcer [pronONsay] to pronounce

propre [propr] clean; own

propriétaire m/f [propee-aytair] owner

propriété privée private property

propriété privée défense d'entrer private property, keep out; no trespassing

prospectus m brochure

protège-couches mpl [protej-koosh] nappy-liners

protéger [protejay] to protect

provenance: en provenance de (arriving) from

prudence f [prOOdONss] caution

prudent [prOOdON] careful

P & T (Postes et Télécommunications) post office (with telephone)

PTT (Postes, Télégraphes, Téléphones) [pay-tay-tay] post office (with telephone)

pu: il a pu [pew] he was able to

public m [poobleek] audience; public

puce f [pewss] flea

puis [pwee] then

puisque [pweess-kuh] since

pull(over) m sweater

pure laine vierge pure new wool

puzzle m [poosl] jigsaw

PV (procès verbal) m [pay-vay] parking ticket

Q

quai m [kay] platform; track; quay

quand [kon] when

quand même [mem] anyway; all the same

quant à [konta] as for

quarante [karont] forty

quart m [kar] quarter

quartier m [kart-yay] district

quatorze [katorz] fourteen

quatre [katr] four

quatre-vingt-dix [katr-van-deess] ninety

quatre-vingts [katr-van] eighty

quatrième [katree-em] fourth

que [kuh] that; what; than; who(m); which

que ...? what ...?

que désirez-vous? what would you like?

quel [kel] which

quelque chose [kelkuh shohz] something

quelque part [par] somewhere

quelque(s) [kelkuh] some

quelques-uns [kelkuh-zan] some, a few

quelqu'un [kelkan] somebody

qu'est-ce que ...? [keskuh] what ...?

qu'est-ce que vous avez dit? what did you say?

qu'est-ce qu'il y a? [keskeel ya] what's the matter?

qu'est-ce qui ...? [keskee] what ...?

queue f [kuh] tail; queue

faire la queue to queue

qui [kee] who

quincaillerie f [kan-ky-ree] ironmonger, hardware store

quinzaine f [kanzen] fortnight; about fifteen

quinze [kanz] fifteen

quitter [kitay] to leave

ne quittez pas [nuh kitay pa] hold the line

quoi? [kwa] what?

quoique [kwa-kuh] although

R

rabais m [rabay] discount, reduction

raccourci m [rakoorsee] shortcut

raccrochez: ne raccrochez pas [nuh rakroshay pa] hold the line

raccrochez svp replace the receiver

radiateur m [rad-yaturr] heater; radiator

radio(graphie) f X-ray

raide [red] steep; straight

raison f [rezzON] reason

  avoir raison [avwahr] to be right

raisonnable [rezzonabl] sensible; reasonable

ralentir [ralONteer] to slow down

ralentisseurs speed bumps; rumble strip

ralentissez slow down

rallonge f [ralONj] extension lead

rame f [ram] train (on underground)

randonnée f [rONdonay] rambling; hike; trekking; ride; trip; hill-walking

ranger [rONjay] to tidy; to put away

rapide [rapeed] fast

rapide m inter-city train

rappel m reminder, reminder sign

rappeler [rapuhlay] to call back

  se rappeler to remember, to recall

raquette de tennis f tennis racket

rarement [raruhmON] seldom

se raser [suh razay] to shave

rasoir m [razwahr] razor

rasoir électrique electric shaver

rater [ratay] to miss

RATP (Régie autonome des transports parisiens) Paris public transport company

ravi de faire votre connaissance [ravee duh fair votr konessONss] how do you do, nice to meet you

ravissant [raveessON] lovely

rayon m [rayON] spoke; department

rayon jouets toy department

rayons X mpl [rayON eex] X-ray

récépissé m [raysaypeessay] receipt

recette f [ruhset] recipe

recevoir [ruhsuhvwahr] to receive; to have guests

recharge f [ruhsharj] refill

réchaud à gaz m [rayshoh] camping gas stove

réclamations fpl [rayklamass-yON] complaints; faults service

recommander [ruhkomONday] to recommend

  envoyer une lettre en recommandé to send a letter by recorded delivery

reconnaissant [ruhkonessON] grateful

reconnaître [ruhkonetr] to recognize

reçu m [ruhsoo] receipt

réductions familles nombreuses special rates for large families

regarder [ruhgarday] to look (at); to watch

régime m [rayjeem] diet

  être au régime to be on a

diet
règlement m [reglmON] regulation
règles fpl [regl] period
rein m [rAN] kidney
reine f [ren] queen
reins mpl [rAN] back
relâche closed
relais routier m [ruhlay root-yay] transport café (often quality restaurant)
relevez lift up
remarquer [ruhmarkay] to notice
remboursement m [rONboorsmON] refund
rembourser [rONboorsay] to refund
remercier [ruhmairs-yay] to thank
remettez mes amitiés à ... [ruhmetay may zameet-yay] give my regards to ...
remise f [ruhmeez] reduction
remonte-pente m [ruhmONt-pONt] ski lift; ski tow
remorque f [ruhmork] trailer
remorquer [ruhmorkay] to tow
remplir [rONpleer] to fill in, to fill
rencontrer [rONkONtray] to meet
rendez-vous m appointment
prendre rendez-vous to make an appointment
rendre [rONdr] to give back, to return; to make
se rendre à to go to
renouveler [ruhnoovuhlay] to renew

renseignements mpl [rONsen-yuhmON] information; directory enquiries
renseignements internationaux international directory enquiries
renseigner [rONsen-yay] to inform
se renseigner to find out; to enquire
rentrer [rONtray] to return
rentrer à la maison to go home
renverser [rONvairsay] to knock over
réparations fpl [rayparass-yON] repairs
réparer [rayparay] to repair
repas m [ruhpa] meal
repasser [ruhpassay] to iron; to come back
répéter [raypaytay] to repeat
répondre [raypONdr] to answer
réponse f [raypONss] answer
repos m [ruhpo] rest
reposer: se reposer [suh ruhpozay] to take a rest
représentant m [ruhprayzONtON] agent
représentation f [ruhprayzONtass-yON] representation; performance
reprise f [ruhpreez] revival; renewal; resumption
RER (Réseau express régional) m [air-uh-air] fast, limited-stop metro line in Paris
résa f [rayza] reservation ticket on TGV

réservation obligatoire booking essential

réservé [rayzairvay] reserved

réservé au personnel staff only

réservé aux clients patrons only

réservé aux clients de l'hôtel hotel patrons only

réservé aux membres de l'équipage reserved for the crew, crew only

réserve de chasse hunting preserve

réserver [rayzairvay] to book, to reserve

réservoir m [rayzairwahr] tank

respectez le silence de ces lieux please respect the sanctity of this place

respectez les pelouses please do not walk on the grass

respirer [respeeray] to breathe

responsable [respONsabl] responsible

resquilleur m [reskeeyurr] fare dodger

ressembler à [ruhsONblay] to look like

ressort m [ruhsor] spring

restaurant de poisson fish restaurant

restauration à votre place meal served at your seat (1st class only)

reste m [rest] rest

rester [restay] to stay

resto m restaurant

restoroute m roadside café

retard m [ruhtar] delay

en retard late

retardé [ruhtarday] delayed

retirer [ruhteeeray] to withdraw

retirez votre argent take your money

retirez votre carte remove your card

retirez votre reçu (d'opération) take your receipt

retour m [ruhtoor] return

de retour dans une heure back in an hour

retourner [ruhtoornay] to return

retrait de colis et lettres recommandées collection of parcels and recorded delivery letters

retrait des bagages m [ruhtray day bagahj] baggage claim

retrait d'espèces cash withdrawal

retraité(e) m/f [ruhtretay] old-age pensioner

retraits withdrawals

rétroviseur m [raytroveezurr] rearview mirror

réunion f [ray-OOn-yON] meeting

réussir [rayOOsseer] to succeed

rêve m [rev] dream

réveil m [rayvay] alarm clock; waking up

réveillé [rayvay-yay] awake

réveiller [rayvay-yay] to wake

se réveiller to wake up

revenir [ruhvuhneer] to come back

revêtement temporaire temporary road surface

revue f magazine
rez-de-chaussée m [rayd-shoh-say] ground floor, (US) first floor
RF (République française) French Republic
rhume m [rOOm] cold
rhume des foins [day fwAN] hay fever
riche [reesh] rich
rideau m [reedo] curtain
rien [ree-AN] nothing
de rien you're welcome
rien à déclarer nothing to declare
rire [reer] to laugh
risque d'avalanche danger of avalanche
rivage m [reevahj] shore
rive f [reev] bank
riverains autorisés no entry except for access, residents only
rivière f river
RN (route nationale) f [air-en] national highway
robe f [rob] dress
robe de chambre [duh shONbr] dressing gown
robinet m [robeenay] tap
rocher m [roshay] rock
roi m [rwa] king
Roi-Soleil [solay] Louis XIV (The Sun King)
roman m [romON] novel
roman Romanesque
rond [rON] round
rond-point m [-pwAN] roundabout, (US) traffic

circle
ronfler [rONflay] to snore
rose f [roz] rose
rose pink
rôtisserie f [roteesree] steak-house
roue f [roo] wheel
roue de secours [duh suhkoor] spare wheel
rouge [rooj] red
rouge à lèvres m [rooj a levr] lipstick
rougeole f [roojol] measles
roulez au pas drive at walking pace
roulez sur une file single lane traffic
rousse [rooss] red-haired
route f [root] road; route
route barrée road closed; road blocked
route départementale secondary road
route du vin route taking in vineyards, wine route
route nationale [nass-yonal] national highway, main road
routier m [root-yay] truck; truck-driver; roadside café
roux, f rousse [roo, rooss] red-haired
Royaume-Uni m [rwy-ohm OOnee] United Kingdom
RU (Royaume Uni) UK
rubéole f [rOObayol] German measles
rue f [rOO] street
rue commerçante [komairsONt]

shopping street
rue piétonne [p-yayton] pedestrian precinct
rue piétonnière [p-yayton-yair] pedestrian precinct
ruisseau m [rweesso] stream

S

SA (société anonyme) [ess-ah] Ltd, Inc
sa* his; her; its
sable m [sabl] sand
sables mouvants quicksand
sac m bag
sac à dos [doh] rucksack
sac à main [MAN] handbag, (US) purse
sac de couchage [duh kooshahj] sleeping bag
sac en plastique [ON plasteek] plastic bag
saignement m [sen-yuhmON] bleeding
saigner [sen-yay] to bleed
sais: je/tu sais [say] I/you know
je ne sais pas I don't know
saison f [sezzON] season
en haute saison in the high season
sait: il/elle sait [say] he/she knows
salaud [salo] bastard
sale [sal] dirty
salé [salay] salty; savoury
salle à manger f [sal a mONjay] dining room
salle climatisée [kleemateezay]

dining room with air conditioning
salle d'attente [datONt] waiting room
salle de bain [duh bAN] bathroom
salle de cinéma [duh seenayma] cinema
salon m [salON] lounge
salon de coiffure [duh kwafOOr] hairdressing salon
salon d'essayage [dessayahj] fitting room
salon de thé [duh tay] tearoom
salon privé [preevay] private lounge
salut! [salOO] hi!; cheerio!
samedi [samdee] Saturday
SAMU (Service d'Aide Medicale d'Urgence) m [samOO] emergency medical service
sang m [sON] blood
sanisette f [saneezet] automated public toilet on the street
sanitaires mpl [saneetair] toilets and showers
sans [sON] without
sans agent de conservation contains no preservatives
sans alcool non-alcoholic
sans doute [doot] undoubtedly
sans issue no through road, dead end
sans plomb lead-free
santé! [sontay] cheers!; bless you!

189

santé f health
en bonne santé healthy, in good health
bon pour la santé healthy
SARL (société à responsabilité limitée) Ltd, Inc
satellite m [-eet] section of airport terminal; satellite
sauf [sohf] except; safe
sauf indication contraire du médecin unless otherwise stated by your doctor
sauf le ... except on ...
sauf riverains access only
saurai: je saurai [soray] I will know
saura: il/elle saura [sora] he/she/it will know
sauras: tu sauras [sora] you will know
saurez: vous saurez [soray] you will know
saurons: nous saurons [soroN] we will know
sauront: ils sauront [soroN] they will know
sauter [sotay] to jump
sauvage [sovahj] wild
savoir [savwahr] to know
savon m [savoN] soap
scandaleux [skoNdaluh] shocking
se* [suh] him; to him; himself; her; to her; herself; each other
séance f [say-oNss] showing
seau m [so] bucket
sec, f sèche [sek, sesh] dry
sèche-cheveux m [sesh-shuhvuh] hair dryer

sécher [sayshay] to dry
second m [suhgoN] second floor, (US) third floor
seconde f [suhgoNd] second; second class
secours m [suhkoor] help
au secours! [oh] help!
secours de montagne [duh moNtañ] mountain rescue
Secours routier français [root-yay] French motoring organization
secrétaire m/f [suhkraytair] secretary
sécurité: en sécurité [oN saykooreetay] safe
séduisant [saydweezoN] attractive
sein m [saN] breast
au sein de within
seize [sez] sixteen
seizième: le seizième [sez-yem] the 16th arrondissement, up-market area of Paris
séjour m [sayjoor] stay
self m self-service restaurant
selle f [sel] saddle
selon [suhloN] according to
sels de bain mpl [sel duh baN] bath salts
semaine f [suhmen] week
par semaine per week
semblable [soNblabl] similar
sembler [soNblay] to seem
semelle f [suhmel] sole
semi-remorque m [suhmee-ruhmork] articulated lorry
sens m [soNss] direction

sens giratoire [jeeratwahr] roundabout; (US) traffic circle

sensible [sONseebl] sensitive

sens interdit one-way street; no entry

sens unique one-way street

sentier m [sONt-yay] path

sentier balisé marked footpath

sentiment m [sONteemON] feeling

sentir [sONteer] to feel; to smell

séparé [sayparay] separate

séparément [sayparaymON] separately

sept [set] seven

septembre [septONbr] September

septième [set-yem] seventh

serai: je serai [suhray] I will be

sera: il/elle sera [suhra] he/she/it will be

serais: je/tu serais [suhray] I/you would be

seras: tu seras [suhra] you will be

serez: vous serez [suhray] you will be

sérieux [sayree-uh] serious

seriez: vous seriez [suhree-ay] you would be

serions: nous serions [suhree-ON] we would be

serons: nous serons [suhrON] we will be

seront: ils/elles seront [suhrON] they will be

serpent m [sairpON] snake

serrez à droite keep to the right

serrure f [sair-rOOr] lock

serveur m [sairvurr] waiter

serveuse f [sairvurz] waitress

servez-vous please take one

service m [sairveess] service; service charge; ward; department

service! not at all! (Switzerland)

service après vente after-sales service

service de retouches alteration/tailoring service

service des urgences casualty department

service d'urgence emergency ward, emergencies

service non-stop 24-hour service

serviette f [sairvee-et] towel; briefcase; serviette, napkin

serviette (de table) serviette, napkin

serviette de toilette [twalet] towel

serviette hygiénique [eejee-ayneek] sanitary towel/napkin

servir [sairveer] to serve

se servir to help oneself

se servir de to use

ses* [say] his; her; its

seul [surl] alone; single; only

seulement [surlmON] only

sexe m [sex] sex

shamp(o)oing m [shONpwAN]

shampoo

shamp(o)oing - mise en plis [meez ON plee] shampoo and set

si if; so; yes

SIDA m [seeda] AIDS

siècle m [see-ekl] century

siège m [see-ej] seat

sien*: le sien [luh s-yAN] his; hers; its

sienne*: la sienne [s-yen] his; hers; its

sien(ne)s*: les sien(ne)s [s-yAN, s-yen] his; hers; its

signal d'alarme m alarm; emergency lever

signer [seen-yay] to sign

signifier [seen-yeefee-ay] to mean

silence m [seelONss] silence

silencieux [seelONssee-uh] silent

s'il te plaît [seel tuh play] please; excuse me

s'il vous plaît [seel voo play] please; excuse me

simple [SANpl] simple; mere

sinon [seenON] otherwise

sirop pour la toux m [too] cough medicine

site historique m [seet eestoreek] place of historical interest

six [seess] six

sixième [seez-yem] sixth

ski m ski; skiing
faire du ski to go skiing

ski de descente [duh dessONt] downhill skiing

ski de fond [fON] cross-country skiing

skier [skee-ay] to ski

ski nautique waterski

slip m [sleep] pants, underpants

slip de bain [duh BAN] swimming trunks

snack m snack bar

SNCB (Société Nationale des Chemins de Fer Belges) f [ess-en-say-bay] Belgian railways/railroad

SNCF (Société Nationale des Chemins de Fer Français) f [ess-en-say-ef] French railways/railroad

société f [sos-yay-tay] company; society

sœur f [surr] sister

soi [swa] oneself

soie f [swa] silk

soif: j'ai soif [jay swaf] I'm thirsty

soigner [swan-yay] to treat, to nurse, to tend

soir m [swahr] evening
le soir in the evening
ce soir tonight

soirée f [swahray] evening; evening performance

soirée privée private party

sois [swa] be

soit ... soit ... [swa] either ... or ...

soixante [swassONt] sixty

soixante-dix [-deess] seventy

sol m ground

soldé [solday] reduced

solde: en solde [ON sold] reduced

solder [solday] to sell at a reduced price

soldes fpl [sold] sale

soldes d'été [daytay] summer sale

soleil m [solay] sun
  au soleil in the sun

sombre [sONbr] dark

sommeil: j'ai sommeil [jay somay] I'm sleepy

sommes: nous sommes [som] we are

sommet m [somay] summit

somnifère m [somneefair] sleeping pill

son* [sON] his; her; its

son m sound

sonnette f bell

sonnette d'alarme alarm bell

sonnette de nuit night bell

sont: ils/elles sont [sON] they are

sorte f [sort] sort
  de sorte que so that

sortie f [sortee] exit, way out

sortie de camions vehicle exit

sortie de secours emergency exit

sortie piétons exit for pedestrians

sortir [sorteer] to go out; to take out

SOS Femmes [ess-o-ess fam] Women's Aid Centre

SOS Médecin [mayd-sAN] 24-hour emergency medical service found in large towns

souci m [soossee] worry

se faire du souci (pour) to worry (about)

soucoupe f [sookoop] saucer

soudain [soodAN] suddenly

souffrant [soofrON] unwell

souffrir [soofreer] to be in pain; to suffer
  souffrir de to suffer from

souhait: à vos souhaits [soo-ay] bless you

souhaiter [soo-ettay] to wish (for)

souliers mpl [sool-yay] shoes

sourcil m [soorseel] eyebrow

sourd [soor] deaf

sourire [sooreer] to smile

souris f [sooree] mouse

sous [soo] under

sous réserve de toute modification subject to modifications

sous-sol m basement

sous-titré [-teetray] subtitled

sous-titres mpl [-teetr] subtitles

sous-vêtements mpl [-vetmON] underwear

soutien-gorge m [soot-yAN-gorj] bra

souvenir: se souvenir de [suh soovuhneer duh] to remember

souvent [soovON] often

soyez [swy-yay] be

soyez le bienvenu [luh b-yAN-vuhnoo] welcome

sparadrap m [sparadra] plaster, Bandaid®

spécialement [spays-yalmON] especially

spectacle m [spektakl] show

spéléologie f pot-holing

sports d'hiver mpl [spor deevair] winter sports

stade m [stad] stadium

stage m [stahj] training course

standardiste m/f [stONdardeest] operator

starter m choke

station de métro f [stass-yON duh maytro] underground/subway station

station de taxis taxi rank

stationnement à durée limitée restricted parking

stationnement alterné parking on alternate sides of the street on 1st-15th and 16th-31st of the month

stationnement en épis interdit no angle parking

stationnement gênant no parking please

stationnement interdit no parking

stationnement limité à 30 minutes parking restricted to 30 minutes

stationnement payant pay to park here

stationnement réglementé limited parking

stationnement toléré 2 minutes parking for 2 minutes only

stationner [stass-yonay] to park

station-service f [stass-yON-sairveess] petrol/gas station

station thermale [tairmahl] spa

stérilet m [stayreelay] IUD, coil

strapontin m [strapontAN] fold-down seat

studio m flatlet

stylo m [steelo] pen

stylo à bille [bee] biro®

stylo-feutre [furtr] felt-tip pen

su [soo] known

substance dangereuse dangerous substance

sucette f [soosset] lollipop

sucré [sookray] sweet

sud m [sood] south
au sud de south of

suffire [soofeer] to be sufficient
ça suffit [sa soofee] that's enough

suis: je suis [swee] I am

Suisse f [sweess] Switzerland

suisse Swiss

Suisse romande [romOnd] French-speaking Switzerland

suivant [sweevON] next

suivre [sweevr] to follow
faire suivre to forward

sujet: au sujet de [o soojay duh] about

super m [soopair] 4 star petrol; (US) premium (gas)

super! great!

supermarché m [soopairmarshay] supermarket

supplément m [sooplaymON] extra charge, supplement

supporter [sooportay] to

tolerate, to stand; to support

supposer [soopozay] to suppose

sur [soor] on

sûr [soor] sure; safe; reliable

surgelé [soorjelay] frozen

surgelés mpl frozen food

surnom m [soornON] nickname

surprenant [soorpruhnON] surprising

surtout [soortoo] above all; especially

surveillant m [soorvayON] supervisor; guard

surveillant de plage [duh plahj] lifeguard

survêtement de sport m [soorvetmON duh spor] tracksuit

SVP (s'il vous plaît) please

sympa [sANpa] nice

sympathique [sANpateek] nice

syndicat d'initiative m [sANdeeka deeneess-yateev] tourist information centre

T

t'* (to) you; yourself

ta* your

tabac m [taba] tobacco; tobacconist and newsagent (also sells stamps)

tabac-journaux m newsagent, tobacco store and news vendor (also sells stamps); newspaper kiosk

tableau m [tablo] painting

tableau de bord [duh bor] dashboard

tache f [tash] stain

taille f [tī] size; waist

tailleur m [tī-urr] tailor; lady's suit

taisez-vous [tezzay-voo] shut up

tais-toi [tay-twa] shut up

talc m talcum powder

talon m [talON] heel

talon-minute heel bar

tandis que [tONdee kuh] whereas; while

tant (de) [tON] so much; so many

tant mieux [m-yuh] so much the better

tant pis [pee] too bad

tant que as long as

tante f [tONt] aunt

tapis m [tapee] rug

tapis roulant [roolON] moving walkway; baggage carousel

tard [tar] late

tarif m [tareef] price

tarif des consommations price list

tarif normal first-class mail

tarif réduit reduced fare; second-class mail

tarifs postaux postage rates

tarifs postaux intérieurs inland postage rates

tarifs postaux pour l'étranger overseas postage rates

tasse f [tass] cup

taureau m [toro] bull

taux m [toh] rate

taux à l'achat buying rate

taux à la vente selling rate
taux de change [duh shONj] exchange rate
taxis - tête de station taxi rank, queue here
TCF (Touring club de France) m [tay-say-ef] French automobile association
te* [tuh] (to) you; yourself
TEE (Trans-Europe-Express) m [tay-uh-uh] first class trans-European express
teint m [tAN] complexion
teint dyed
teinte f [tANt] colour, shade
teinturerie f [tANtOOr-uhree] dry cleaner's
teinturier m [tANtOOree-ay] dry cleaner's
télé f [taylay] TV
télécarte f [taylay-kart] phonecard
télécartes en vente ici phonecards sold here
télécopie f fax
téléférique m [taylayfayreek] cable car
téléphone à carte m cardphone
téléphone interurbain long-distance telephone
téléphoner (à) [taylayfonay] to phone
télésiège m [taylaysee-ej] chairlift, ski lift
téléski m ski tow
Télétel® free computerized service available in post offices instead of the

phonebook
téléviseur m [taylayveezurr] television set
tellement [telmON] so
tellement de so much; so many
tel(s) such
témoin m [taymwAN] witness
tempête f [tONpet] storm
tempête de neige [duh nej] snowstorm
temple m [tONpl] Protestant church
temps m [tON] time; weather
de temps en temps from time to time
tenez votre droite keep to the right
tenir [tuhneer] to hold; to keep
tennis fpl [tenneess] trainers
tente f [tONt] tent
terminer [tairmeenay] to finish
terrain m [terrAN] pitch, field, ground
terrain de camping [duh kONpeeng] campsite
terrain pour caravanes [poor karavan] caravan site
terre f [tair] earth
tes* [tay] your
tête f [tet] head
tête de station taxi rank, queue here
TGV (Train à grande vitesse) m [tay-jay-vay] high-speed train
théière f [tay-air] teapot
tiède [t-yed] lukewarm
tien*: le tien [luh t-yAN] yours
tienne*: la tienne [t-yen] yours

à la tienne! your health!

tiennent: ils/elles tiennent [t-yen] they hold

tien(ne)s*: les tien(ne)s [t-yAN, t-yen] yours

tiens: je/tu tiens [t-yAN] I/you hold

tient: il/elle tient [t-yAN] he/she/it holds

timbre m [tANbr] stamp

timbres de collection collectors' stamps

tir m [teer] shooting

tire-bouchon m [teer-booshON] corkscrew

tirer [teeray] to pull; to shoot

tirez [teeray] pull

tissu m [teessOO] material

tissus fabrics

titre de transport ticket

toi* [twa] you

toilette: faire sa toilette [twalet] to have a wash

toilettes fpl [twalet] toilets; (US) rest room

les toilettes sont dans la cour the toilet is in the back yard

toit m [twa] roof

tomber [tONbay] to fall

tomber en panne [ON pan] to break down

tomber en panne d'essence to run out of petrol

tomber malade to fall ill

ton* [tON] your

tonalité f [tohnaleetay] dialling tone

tonnage limité weight limit

tonnerre m [tonair] thunder

torchon à vaisselle m [torshON a vess-el] tea towel

tort: avoir tort [avvwahr tor] to be wrong

tôt [toh] early

toucher [tooshay] to touch

toujours [toojoor] always; still

tour m tour; turn

tour f tower

tour de hanches m [duh ONsh] hip measurement

tour de poitrine [pwatreen] bust/chest measurement

tour de taille [tī] waist measurement

tour en voiture [vwatOOr] drive

tourner [toornay] to turn

tournevis m [toornuhvee] screwdriver

tous [too] all; every

tous les deux both of them

tous les jours every day

tous les jours sauf ... every day except ...

tous les matins every morning

tousser [toossay] to cough

tout [too] everything; all; every

pas du tout not at all

en tout altogether

à tout à l'heure! [a toota lurr] see you later!

tout à fait [too ta fay] entirely; altogether

tout compris [kONpree] all inclusive

tout de suite [toot sweet]

immediately
tout droit [drwa] straight ahead
toute [toot] all; every
  toute la journée all day
toutefois [tootfwa] however
toute personne prise en flagrant délit de vol sera poursuivie all shoplifters will be prosecuted
toutes [toot] all; every
toutes directions all directions
toutes opérations all transactions
toutes taxes comprises inclusive of taxes
tout le monde [too luh mONd] everyone
toux f [too] cough
traduction f [tradOOx-yON] translation
traduire [tradweer] to translate
train m [trAN] train
  un train peut en cacher un autre there may be another train hidden behind this one
  être en train de faire quelque chose to be doing something
train à supplément train for which you must pay a supplement
train auto-couchettes motorail
train direct direct train
train en partance pour ... train leaving for ...
train omnibus slow train
train rapide express train

trains au départ departures
train supplémentaire extra train
traitement m [tretmON] (course of) treatment
traitement de texte word processing; word processor
traiteur m [treturr] delicatessen
tranche f [trONsh] slice
tranquille [trONkeel] quiet
transactions avec l'étranger overseas business
transpirer [trONspeeray] to sweat
travail m [travi] work
travailler [travi-ay] to work
travaux mpl [travo] roadworks; building work
traversée f [travairsay] crossing
traverser [travairsay] to cross, to go through
treize [trez] thirteen
trembler [trONblay] to tremble
trente [trONt] thirty
très [tray] very
  très bien, merci [b-yAN] very well, thank you
tribunal m [treebOOnal] court
tricot m [treeko] knitting; jumper
tricoter [treekotay] to knit
tricots knitwear
triste [treest] sad
trois [trwa] three
troisième [trwaz-yem] third
tromper [trONpay] to deceive
  se tromper to be wrong
  se tromper de numéro to dial the wrong number
trop [tro] too; too much

trop de too much/many

trottoir m [trotwahr] pavement; (US) sidewalk

trou m [troo] hole

trouver [troovay] to find

truc m [trook] thing

TTC (toutes taxes comprises) inclusive of tax

tu* [too] you

tuer [too-ay] to kill

tunnel de lavage m [toonel duh lavahj] car-wash

tutoyer [tootwy-ay] to use the familiar 'tu' form

tuyau m [twee-yo] pipe

TVA (taxe sur la valeur ajoutée) f [tay-vay-ah] VAT

TV par câble f [tay-vay par kahbl] cable TV

U

UE f [oo-uh] EU, European Union

ulcère m [oolsair] ulcer

un* [AN] a; one

une* [OON] a; one

unité f [ooneetay] unit

urgence f [oorjONss] emergency

urinoir m [ooreenwahr] public urinal

usage: l'usage des WC est interdit pendant l'arrêt du train en gare do not use the toilet while the train is in a station

usage externe for external use

usine f [oozeen] factory

ustensiles de cuisine cooking utensils

utile [ooteel] useful

utilisateur m [ooteeleezaturr] user

utiliser [ooteeleezay] to use

utiliser avant ... use before ...

utilisez un stylo à bille et appuyez fortement use a ball-point pen and write firmly

V

va: il/elle va he/she/it goes

comment ça va? [komON sa] how are you?

il va bien [eel va b-yAN] he's well

il va mal he's not well

le bleu me va bien blue suits me

vacances fpl [vakONss] holiday, vacation

vacances annuelles annual holiday

vaccin m [vaxAN] vaccination

vache f [vash] cow

vachement [vashmON] bloody, damn(ed)

vagin m [vajAN] vagina

vague f [vag] wave

vague de chaleur [duh shalurr] heatwave

vais: je vais [vay] I go

vaisselle f [vess-el] crockery

faire la vaisselle to do the washing up

valable [val-abl] valid

valable jusqu'au ... valid

until ...
validez [valeeday] validate
valise f [valeez] suitcase
vallée f [valay] valley
valoir [valwahr] to be worth
varappe f [varap] rock climbing
variable [varee-abl] changeable
varicelle f [vareessel] chickenpox
vase m [vahz] vase
vas: tu vas [va] you go
vas-y [va-zee] go on
vaut: il vaut [vo] it is worth
véhicule m [vay-eekool] vehicle
vélo m [vaylo] bike
  faire du vélo to cycle
vélomoteur m [-moturr] moped
vendanges fpl [vONdONj] wine harvest
vendangeur: on demande des vendangeurs grape pickers wanted
vendeur m, **vendeuse** f [vONdurr, -urz] shop assistant; salesman; saleswoman
vendre [vONdr] to sell
  à vendre for sale
vendredi [vONdruhdee] Friday
vendu uniquement sur ordonnance sold on prescription only
venir [vuhneer] to come
  venir de faire quelque chose to have just done something
  faire venir to send for
vent m [vON] wind
vente f [vONt] sale; selling rate

en vente ici available here
ventes hors taxes à bord duty free sales aboard
vent fort strong wind
ventilateur m [vONteelaturr] fan
ventre m [vONtr] stomach
verglas m [vairgla] black ice
vérifier [vayreef-yay] to check
vérifiez votre monnaie check your change
vernis à ongles m [vairnee a ONgl] nail polish
verrai: je verrai [vairray] I will see
verra: il/elle verra [vairra] he/she/it will see
verras: tu verras [vairra] you will see
verre m [vair] glass
verre à eau [o] tumbler
verre à vin [VAN] wineglass
verrez: vous verrez [vairray] you will see
verrons: nous verrons [vairrON] we will see
verront: ils/elles verront [vairrON] they will see
verrou m [vairroo] bolt
verrouiller [vairoo-yay] to bolt; to lock
vers m [vair] verse
vers towards; about
versement m [vairss-mON] payment, deposit
verser [vairsay] to pay; to pour
version originale f [vairss-yON oreejeenal] in the original language
vert [vair] green

vessie f [vessee] bladder

veste f [vest] jacket

vestiaire m [vestee-air] cloakroom; (US) checkroom; changing room

vêtements mpl [vetmON] clothes

vêtements dames ladies' fashions

vêtements enfants children's wear

vêtements femmes ladies' wear

vêtements hommes menswear

vêtements messieurs menswear

vétérinaire m [vaytayreenair] vet

veuf m [vurf] widower

veuillez ... [vuh-ee-yay] please ...

veuillez établir votre chèque à l'ordre de ... please make cheques payable to ...

veuillez éteindre votre moteur please switch off engine

veuillez fermer la porte please close the door

veuillez libérer votre chambre avant midi please vacate your room by 12 noon

veuillez patienter please wait

veuillez patienter, nous traitons votre demande please wait, your request is being processed

veulent: ils/elles veulent [vurl] they want

veut: il/elle veut [vuh] he/she/it wants

cela veut dire ... that means ...

veuve f [vurv] widow

veux: je/tu veux [vuh] I/you want

vexer [vexay] to offend

vidange f [veedONj] oil change

vide [veed] empty

vide-ordures m [-ordOOr] garbage chute

vie f [vee] life

vieille [v-yay] old

vieille ville f [veel] old town

viendrai: je viendrai [v-yANdray] I will come

viendra: il/elle viendra [v-yANdra] he/she/it will come

viendras: tu viendras [v-yANdra] you will come

viendrez: vous viendrez [v-yANdray] you will come

viendrons: nous viendrons [v-yANdrON] we will come

viendront: ils/elles viendront [v-yANdrON] they will come

viennent: ils/elles viennent [v-yen] they come

viens: je/tu viens [v-yAN] I/you come

vient: il/elle vient [v-yAN] he/she/it comes

vieux, f vieille [v-yuh, v-yay] old

vignette f [veen-yet] road tax disc; postage label

vignettes montant au choix select postage labels to required value

vignoble m [veen-yobl] vineyard

vilebrequin m [veelbruhkAN] crankshaft

ville f [veel] town

en ville in town; to town

ville jumelée avec ... twin town ...

vingt [VAN] twenty

vins et spiritueux wine merchant

viol m [veeol] rape

violet [veeolay] purple

violon m [veeolON] violin

virage m [veerahj] bend

virage dangereux dangerous bend

virages sur ... km bends for ... km

virement m [veermON] transfer

vis f [vee] screw

visage m [veezahj] face

viseur m [veezurr] viewfinder

visite guidée f [veezeet geeday] guided tour

visiter [veezeetay] to visit

visitez ... visit ...

vite [veet] quick; quickly

vitesse f speed; gear

vitesse limitée à ... speed limit ...

vitre f [veetr] window

vitrine f [veetreen] shop window

vivant [veevON] alive

vivre [veevr] to live

VO (version originale) [vay-o] in the original language

vœux: meilleurs vœux [may-yurr vuh] best wishes

voici [vwa-see] here is; here

are; here you are

voie f [vwa] platform; track; lane

par voie orale orally

voie ferrée railway

voie pour véhicules lents crawler lane

voilà [vwala] here is; here are; there you are

le voilà there he is

voile f [vwal] sail; sailing

voilier m [vwal-yay] sailing boat

voir [vwahr] to see

voisin m, voisine f [vwazAN, -zeen] neighbour

voiture f [vwat00r] car; coach; carriage

en voiture by car

voiture de queue rear car

voiture de tête front car

voix f [vwa] voice

vol m flight; theft

volant m [volON] steering wheel

vol à voile [vwal] gliding

vol direct direct flight

voler [volay] to steal; to fly

volets mpl [volay] shutters

voleur m [volurr] thief

volley m [volay] volleyball

vols intérieurs mpl [vol zANtayree-urr] domestic flights

vols internationaux [zANtairnass-yono] international flights

vomir [vomeer] to be sick, to vomit

vont: ils/elles vont [vON] they go

vos* [vo] your

votre* [votr] your

vôtre*: le/la vôtre [luh/la vohtr]
  yours
  à la vôtre! cheers!

vôtres*: les vôtres [lay vohtr]
  yours

voudraient: il/elles voudraient
  [voodray] they would like

voudrais: je/tu voudrais
  [voodray] I/you would like

voudrait: il/elle voudrait
  [voodray] he/she/it would
  like

voudriez: vous voudriez
  [voodree-ay] you would like

voudrions: nous voudrions
  [voodree-ON] we would like

voulez: que voulez-vous?
  [kuh voolay-voo] what do you
  want?
  voulez-vous ...? do you
  want ...?
  voulez-vous un reçu? do you
  want a receipt?

vouloir [voolwahr] to want

vouloir dire [deer] to mean

voulu [voolOO] wanted

vous* [voo] you; (to) you
  vous désirez? can I help
  you?

vous êtes ici you are here

vouvoyer [voovwy-ay] to use
  the polite 'vous' form

voyage m [vwy-ahj] trip,
  journey

voyage d'affaires [dafair]
  business trip

voyage de noces [duh noss]
  honeymoon

voyage organisé [organeezay]
  package tour

voyager [vwy-ahjay] to travel

voyageur m [vwy-ahjurr]
  traveller

voyagiste m [vwy-ahjeest] tour
  operator

vrai [vray] true; real
  à vrai dire actually

vraiment [vraymON] really

vu [vOO] seen

vue f [vOO] view

W

wagon m [vagON] carriage

wagon-lit [-lee] sleeper,
  sleeping car

wagon-restaurant [-restorON]
  dining car

WC mpl [vay-say] toilet, rest
  room

Y

y [ee] there; it
  y a-t-il ...? [yateel] is there
  ...?; are there ...?

yeux mpl [yuh] eyes

Z

zéro [zayro] zero

zone bleue f [zon bluh]
  restricted parking area

zone piétonne [p-yayton]
  pedestrian precinct

zone piétonnière [p-yaytonair]
  pedestrian precinct

Menu
Reader:
Food

Essential Terms

bread le pain [pAN]
butter le beurre [burr]
cup la tasse [tass]
dessert le dessert [desair]
fish le poisson [pwassON]
fork la fourchette [foorshet]
glass le verre [vair]
knife le couteau [kooto]
main course le plat principal [pla prANseepal]
meat la viande [veeONd]
menu la carte [kart]
pepper le poivre [pwahvr]
plate l'assiette f [ass-yet]
salad la salade [sa-lad]
salt le sel
set menu le menu (à prix fixe) [muhnOO (a pree feex)]
soup le potage [potahj]
spoon la cuillère [kwee-yair]
starter l'entrée f [ONtray]
table la table [tahbl]

another ..., please encore ..., s'il vous plaît [ONkor ..., seel voo play]
excuse me! (to call waiter/waitress) pardon [par-dON]
could I have the bill, please? l'addition, s'il vous plaît [adeess-yON seel voo play]

abats [aba] offal

abricot [abreeko] apricot

agneau [an-yo] lamb

aiguillette de bœuf [ay-gwee-yet duh burf] slices of rump steak

ail [i] garlic

ailloli [i-olee] garlic mayonnaise

à la broche [ala brosh] roasted on a spit

à l'ail [ala] with garlic

à la jardinière [ala jardeen-yair] with assorted vegetables

à l'ancienne [alONs-yen] traditional style

à la normande [ala normONd] in cream sauce

à la provençale [ala provONsahl] cooked in olive oil with tomatoes, garlic and herbs

alose [aloze] shad (fish)

amande [amONd] almond

ananas [anana] pineapple

anchois [ONshwa] anchovies

andouillette [ONdoo-yet] small, spicy tripe sausage

anguille [ONgwee] eel

araignée de mer [aren-yay duh mair] spider crab

arête [aret] fishbone

artichaut [artee-sho] artichoke

asperge(s) [aspairj] asparagus

aspic de volaille [vol-i] chicken in aspic

assaisonnement [assezonuhmON] seasoning; dressing

assiette anglaise [ass-yet ONglez] selection of cold meats

aubergine aubergine, eggplant

au choix ... [o shwa] choice of ...

aux câpres [o kapr] in caper sauce

avocat [avoka] avocado

baba au rhum [o rum] rum baba

baguette stick of bread, French stick

banane [banan] banana

bananes flambées [banan flONbay] bananas flambéd in brandy

barbue [barbew] brill (fish)

bâtard [batar] a half-size French stick (250g)

bavaroise [bavarwaz] light mousse

bavette à l'échalote [bavet a layshalot] grilled beef with shallots

béarnaise [bay-arnez] with béarnaise sauce (sauce made from egg yolks, butter and herbs)

beaufort [bofor] hard cheese from Savoie

bécasse [baykass] woodcock

béchamel [bayshamel] white sauce, béchamel sauce

beignet [ben-yay] fritter, doughnut

beignet aux pommes [o pom] apple fritter

betterave [betrahv] beetroot; (US) red beet

beurre [burr] butter

beurre d'anchois [dONshwa] anchovy paste

beurre d'estragon [destragON] tarragon butter

beurre noir [nwahr] dark melted butter

bien cuit [b-yan kwee] well done (meat)

bifteck [beeftek] steak

bifteck de cheval [duh shuhval] horsemeat steak

biscuit de Savoie [beess-kwee duh savva] sponge cake

bisque d'écrevisses [beesk daykruhveess] freshwater crayfish soup

bisque de homard [duh omar] lobster bisque

bisque de langoustines [lONgoosteen] saltwater crayfish soup

blanquette de veau [blONket duh vo] veal stew

bleu [bluh] very rare; rare; blue

bleu d'Auvergne [dovairn] blue cheese from Auvergne

bœuf [burf] beef

bœuf à la ficelle [feesel] beef cooked in stock

bœuf bourguignon [boor-geen-yON] beef cooked in red wine

bœuf en daube [ON dohb] beef casserole

bœuf miroton [meerotON] boiled beef with onions

bœuf mode [mod] beef stew

with carrots

boisson [bwassON] drink

bolet [bolay] boletus (mushroom)

bouchée à la reine [booshay ala ren] vol au vent

boudin [boodAN] black pudding

boudin blanc [blON] white pudding

boudin noir [nwahr] black pudding

bouillabaisse [booyabess] spicy fish soup from the Midi

bouilli [boo-yee] boiled

bouillon [booyON] stock

bouillon de légumes [duh laygOOm] vegetable stock

bouillon de poule [pool] chicken stock

boulette [boolet] meatball

bouquet rose [bookay roz] prawns

boutargue [bootarg] smoked fish roe

braisé [brezay] braised

brandade de morue [brONdad duh morOO] cod and potatoes, mashed

brioche [bree-osh] round bun

brochet [broshay] pike

brochette [broshet] kebab

brugnon [broon-yON] nectarine

cabillaud [kabee-yo] cod

cacahuètes [kaka-wet] peanuts

caille [kī] quail

cake fruit cake

cal(a)mar squid

canapé [kanapay] small open sandwich, canapé

canard [kanar] duck

canard à l'orange [lorONj] duck in orange sauce

canard aux cerises [o suhreez] duck with cherries

canard aux navets [o navay] duck with turnips

canard laqué [lakay] Chinese roast duck, Peking duck

canard rôti [rotee] roast duck

caneton [kantON] duckling

cantal [kONtal] hard cheese from Auvergne

câpres [kapr] capers

carbonnade [karbonad] stew made with beef, onions and beer

cardon [kardON] cardoon, vegetable similar to celery

cari [karee] curry

carotte [karot] carrot

carottes râpées [rapay] grated carrots (with vinaigrette)

carottes Vichy carrots in butter and parsley

carpe [karp] carp

carré d'agneau [karray dan-yo] rack of lamb

carrelet [karlay] plaice

carte [kart] menu

carvi [karvee] caraway

casse-croûte [kass-kroot] sandwich; snack

cassis [kasseess] blackcurrant

cassoulet [kassoolay] casserole with pork, sausages and beans

céleri (en branches) [selree (ON broNsh)] celery

céleri rave [rahv] celeriac

céleri rémoulade [raymoolad] celeriac in mayonnaise and mustard dressing

cèpe [sep] cep (mushroom)

cerise [suhreez] cherry

cerises à l'eau de vie [lo duh vee] cherries in brandy

cervelas [sairvuhla] saveloy (highly seasoned sausage made from brains)

cervelle [sairvel] brains

chabichou [shabeeshoo] goats' and cows' milk cheese

champignon [shONpeen-yON] mushroom

champignons de Paris [duh paree] white button mushrooms

champignons à la grecque [grek] mushrooms in olive oil, tomatoes and herbs

chanterelle chanterelle (mushroom)

charlotte dessert consisting of layers of fruit, cream and biscuits

chasselas [shassla] white grape

châtaigne [shateñ] sweet chestnut

chausson aux pommes [shohsON o pom] apple turnover

cheval [shuhval] horse

chèvre [shevr] goats' milk cheese

chevreuil [shevruh-ee] venison

chicorée [sheekoray] endive, chicory

chicorée frisée [freezay] curly lettuce

chiffonnade d'oseille [sheefonad dozay] sorrel cooked in butter

chips [sheeps] crisps, (US) potato chips

chocolatine [shokolateen] chocolate puff pastry

chou [shoo] cabbage

chou à la crème cream puff

choucroute [shookroot] sauerkraut with sausages and smoked ham

chou-fleur [shooflurr] cauliflower

chou-fleur au gratin [o gratAN] cauliflower cheese

chou rouge [shoo rooj] red cabbage

choux de Bruxelles [duh brOO-sel] Brussels sprouts

ciboulette [seeboolet] chives

cigarette [seegaret] kind of finger biscuit (eg to serve with ice cream)

citron [seetrON] lemon

citron vert [vair] lime

civet de lièvre [seevay duh lee-evr] jugged hare

clafoutis [klafootee] batter pudding with fruit

cochon de lait [koshON duh lay] sucking pig

cocktail de crevettes [kruhvet] prawn cocktail

cœur [kurr] heart

cœur d'artichaut [darteesho] artichoke heart

coing [kwAN] quince

colin [kolAN] hake

compote [kONpot] stewed fruit

compris [kONpree] included

comté [kONtay] hard cheese from the Jura area

concombre [kONkONbr] cucumber

confit de canard [kONfit duh kanar] duck preserve

confit d'oie [kONfee dwa] goose preserve

confiture [kONfeetoor] jam

confiture d'orange [dorONj] marmalade

congre [kONgr] conger eel

consommé [kONsommay] clear soup made from meat or chicken

consultez aussi l'ardoise other suggestions on the slate

consultez notre carte des desserts have a look at our dessert menu

coq au vin [kok o vAN] chicken in red wine

coque [kok] cockle

coquelet [koklay] young cockerel, poult

coquilles Saint-Jacques [kokee SAN jak] scallops

côte de porc [koht duh por] pork chop

côtelette [kotlet] chop

côtelette de porc [duh por] pork chop

cotriade bretonne [kotree-ad bruhton] fish soup from Brittany

coulis [koolee] creamy sauce or soup

coulis de framboises [duh froNbwahz] raspberry sauce

coulis de langoustines [loNgoosteen] saltwater crayfish sauce

coulommiers [koolom-yay] rich medium-soft cheese

coupe [koop] ice cream dessert

coupe Danemark [danmark] vanilla ice cream with hot chocolate sauce

coupe des îles [day zeel] vanilla ice cream with syrup, fruit and whipped cream

courgette courgette, zucchini

court-bouillon [koor-booyoN] stock for poaching fish or meat

couscous [kooskooss] semolina (usually served with meat, vegetables and hot spicy sauce)

couscous royal [rwy-al] couscous with meat

couvert [koovair] cover charge

crabe [krab] crab

crème [krem] cream; creamy sauce or dessert

crème à la vanille [vanee] vanilla custard

crème anglaise [oNglez] custard

crème brûlée à la cassonade [brOOlay ala kassonad] custard covered with brown sugar and 'grilled'

crème Chantilly [shoNtee-yee] whipped cream

crème d'asperges [daspairj] cream of asparagus soup

crème de bolets [duh bolay] cream of mushroom soup

crème de marrons [maroN] chestnut purée

crème de volaille [vol-ī] cream of chicken soup

crème d'huîtres [weetr] cream of oyster soup

crème fouettée [foo-etay] whipped cream

crème pâtissière [pateessee-air] confectioner's custard

crème renversée [roNvairsay] custard dessert in a mould

crème vichyssoise [veeshee-swaz] cold potato and leek soup

crêpe [krep] pancake

crêpe à la béchamel [bayshamel] pancake with béchamel sauce

crêpe à la chantilly [shoNtee-yee] pancake with whipped cream

crêpe à la crème de marrons [krem de maroN] pancake with chestnut purée

crêpe à l'œuf [al-uhf] pancake with a fried egg

crêpe au chocolat [o shokola] pancake with chocolate sauce

crêpe au fromage [fromahj] cheese pancake

crêpe au jambon [jONbON] ham pancake

crêpe au sucre [sOOkr] pancake with sugar

crêpe au thon [tON] tuna pancake

crêpe de froment [duh fromON] wholemeal flour pancake

crêpes Suzette pancakes flambéd with orange sauce

crépinette [kraypeenet] sausage patty wrapped in fat

cresson [kressON] cress

crevette [kruhvet] prawn

crevette grise [greez] shrimp

crevette rose [roz] prawn

croque-madame [krok ma-dam] toasted cheese sandwich with ham and eggs

croque-monsieur [krok muhss-yuh] toasted cheese sandwich with ham

crottin de Chavignol [krotAN duh shaveen-yol] small goats' cheese

crottin de chèvre chaud [shevr sho] small goats' cheese served hot

croûte au fromage [kroot o fromahj] toasted cheese

croûte forestière [forest-yair] mushrooms on toast

crudités [krOOdeetay] selection of salads or chopped raw vegetables

crustacés [krOOstassay] shellfish

cuit cooked

cuisses de grenouille [kweess duh gruhnoo-yuh] frogs' legs

cuissot de chevreuil [kweeso duh shevruh-ee] haunch of venison

darne de saumon grillée [darn duh somON gree-yay] grilled salmon steak

dartois [dartwa] pastry with jam

datte [dat] date

daurade [dorad] gilthead (fish)

dinde [dANd] turkey

échalote [ayshalot] shallot

écrevisse [aykruhveess] freshwater crayfish

écrevisses à la nage [nahj] freshwater crayfish in wine and vegetable sauce

émincé de veau [aymANsay duh vo] finely cut veal in cream sauce

emporter: à emporter [ONportay] to take away; (US) to go

endive [ONdeev] chicory, endive

endives au jambon [o jONbON] chicory with ham baked in the oven

endives braisées [brezay] braised chicory

entrecôte [ONtr-koht] rib steak

entrecôte au poivre [o pwahvr] steak fried with black peppercorns

entrecôte maître d'hôtel [metr dotel] steak with butter

and parsley

entrée [ONtray] first course

entremets [ONtr-may] dessert

épaule d'agneau farcie [aypol dan-yo farsee] stuffed shoulder of lamb

éperlan [aypairlON] smelt (fish)

épice [aypeess] spice

épinards [aypeenar] spinach

épinards à la crème spinach with cream

épinards en branches [ON brONsh] leaf spinach

escalope à la crème escalope in cream sauce

escalope de dinde à la crème et aux champignons [duh dANd] turkey cutlet with cream and mushrooms

escalope de veau milanaise [duh vo meelanez] veal escalope with tomato sauce

escalope de veau normande [normONd] veal escalope in cream sauce

escalope panée [panay] breaded veal escalope

escargots [eskargo] snails

escargots de Bourgogne à la douzaine dozen Burgundy snails

espadon [espadON] swordfish

estouffade de bœuf [estoofad duh burf] beef casserole

estragon [estragON] tarragon

faisan [fezzON] pheasant

fait maison [fay mezzON] homemade

farci [farsee] stuffed

farine [fareen] flour

faux filet sauce béarnaise [fo feelay] fillet/sirloin steak with béarnaise sauce

fenouil [fenoo-yuh] fennel

fèves [fev] broad beans

ficelle [feessel] French stick thinner than a baguette

figue [feeg] fig

figue de barbarie prickly pear

filet [feelay] fillet

filet de bœuf Rossini [duh burf] fillet of beef with foie gras

filet de canard au poivre vert [duh kanar o pwahvr vair] duck breast with green pepper sauce

filet de perche [pairsh] perch fillet

financière [feenONss-yair] rich sauce (served with sweetbread, dumplings etc)

fines herbes [feen zairb] herbs

flageolets [flajolay] flageolets, small green beans

flambé [flONbay] flambé

flan [flON] custard tart; crème caramel; egg custard

flétan [flaytON] halibut

foie [fwa] liver

foie de veau [vo] calves' liver

foie gras [gra] duck or goose liver preserve

foies de volaille [vol-ī] chicken livers

fondant au chocolat [fONdON o shokola] chocolate fondant; kind of brownie

fonds d'artichaut [fON darteesho] artichoke hearts

fondue [fONd00] Swiss dish of cheese melted in white wine

fondue bourguignonne [boor-geen-yon] meat fondue (cooked in oil)

fondue savoyarde [savvy-ard] cheese fondue

forêt noire [foray nwahr] Black Forest gateau

fraise [frez] strawberry

fraise des bois [day bwa] wild strawberry

framboise [frONbwahz] raspberry

frangipane [frONjeepan] almond pastry

frisée [freezay] curly lettuce

frisée aux lardons [o lardON] curly lettuce with bacon

frit [free] deep fried

frites [freet] chips, French fries

fromage [fromahj] cheese

fromage blanc [blON] cream cheese

fromage de chèvre [duh shevr] goats' cheese

fruité [frweetay] fruity

fruits [frwee] fruit

fruits de mer [duh mair] seafood

fumé [f00may] smoked

galantine [galONteen] cold meat in aspic

galette [galet] round flat cake; buckwheat pancake

garni [garnee] with French fries or rice and/or vegetables

gâteau au fromage [o fromahj] cheesecake

gaufre [gohfr] wafer; waffle

gaufrette [gohfret] wafer

gelée [juhlay] jelly

en gelée [ON] in aspic

génisse [jayneess] heifer

génoise [jaynwahz] sponge cake

gésier [jayzee-ay] gizzard

gibelotte de lapin [jeeblot duh lapAN] rabbit stewed in white wine

gibier [jeeb-yay] game

gigot d'agneau [jeego dan-yo] leg of lamb

gigue de chevreuil [jeeg duh shuhvruh-ee] haunch of venison

girolle [jee-rol] chanterelle (mushroom)

glace [glass] ice cream; ice

goujon [goojON] gudgeon (fish)

grand veneur [grON vuhnurr] sauce for game

gras-double [gra-doobl] tripe

gratin [gratAN] baked cheese dish

au gratin [o] baked in a milk, cream and cheese sauce

gratin dauphinois [dofeen-wa] potato gratin with grated cheese

gratin de carottes [duh karot] carrots au gratin

gratin de langoustines

[lONgoosteen] saltwater crayfish au gratin

gratin de queues d'écrevisses [kuh daykruhveess] freshwater crayfish au gratin

gratinée [grateenay] onion soup with cheese topping

grenade [gruhnad] pomegranate

grillade [gree-yad] grilled meat

grillé [gree-yay] grilled

grive [greev] thrush

grondin [grONdAN] gurnard (fish)

groseille blanche [grossay blONsh] white currant

groseille rouge [rooj] red currant

gruyère [grwee-yair] hard Swiss cheese

hachis parmentier [ashee parmONtee-ay] shepherd's pie

hareng mariné [arON mareenay] marinated herring

haricot de mouton [areeko duh mootON] mutton stew with beans

haricots [areeko] green beans; beans

haricots blancs [blON] haricot beans

haricots verts [vair] green beans

herbes [airb] herbs

herbes de Provence [duh provONss] herbs from Provence

homard [omar] lobster

homard à l'américaine

[lamaireeken] lobster with tomato and white wine sauce

huile de soja [weel duh soja] soya oil

huile de tournesol [toornuhsol] sunflower oil

huile d'olive [doleev] olive oil

huître [weetr] oyster

îles flottantes [eel flotONt] floating islands (poached whisked egg whites on top of custard)

jambon [jONbON] ham

jambon au madère [o madair] ham in Madeira wine

jambon de Bayonne [duh ba-yon] smoked and cured ham

jardinière (de légumes) [jardeen-yair (duh laygOOm)] with mixed vegetables

jarret de veau [jarray duh vo] shin of veal

julienne (de légumes) [jOOlee-en (duh laygOOm)] soup with chopped vegetables

julienne type of white fish

kugelhof [kOOgelhohf] cake from Alsace

laitue [lettOO] lettuce

langouste [lONgoost] crayfish

langoustine [lONgoosteen] scampi

langue de bœuf [lON-g duh burf] ox tongue

langue de chat [sha] kind of finger biscuit (served with ice cream etc)

lapereau [lapero] young rabbit

lapin [lapAN] rabbit

lapin à la Lorraine rabbit in mushroom and cream sauce

lapin à la moutarde [mootard] rabbit in mustard sauce

lapin chasseur [shassurr] rabbit in white wine and herbs

lapin de garenne [garren] wild rabbit

lard [lar] bacon

lardons [lardON] small cubes of bacon

laurier [loree-ay] bay leaf

léger [layjay] light

légumes [laygoom] vegetables

lentilles [lONteel] lentils

lièvre [lee-evr] hare

limande [leemONd] dab, lemon sole

livarot [leevaro] strong, soft cheese from the north of France

longe [lONj] loin

lotte [lot] burbot

loup au fenouil [loo o fuhnoo-yuh] bass with fennel

macaron [makarON] macaroon

macaroni au gratin [o gratAN] macaroni cheese

macédoine de légumes [massaydwan duh laygoom] mixed vegetables with mayonnaise

mâche [mash] lamb's lettuce

magret de canard [magray duh kanar] duck breast

mangue [mON-g] mango

maquereau au vin blanc [makro o VAN blON] mackerel in white wine sauce

marcassin [marcassAN] young wild boar

marchand de vin [marshON duh van] in red wine sauce

mariné [mareenay] marinated

marrons [marrON] chestnuts

menthe [mONt] mint

menu [muhnoo] set menu

menu du jour [doo joor] today's menu

menu gastronomique [gastronomeek] gourmet menu

merlan au vin blanc [mairlON o VAN blON] whiting in white wine

mérou [mayroo] grouper

miel [mee-el] honey

millefeuille [meel-fuh-ee] custard slice

mont-blanc [mON-blON] chestnut sweet topped with whipped cream

morilles [moree] morels (mushroom)

morue [moroo] cod

mouclade [mooklad] mussels in creamy sauce with saffron, turmeric and white wine

moules [mool] mussels

moules à la poulette [poolet] mussels in rich white wine sauce

moules marinière [mareen-yair] mussels in white wine

mousse au chocolat [o shokola] chocolate mousse

mousse au jambon [jONbON] light ham pâté

mousse de foie [duh fwa] light liver pâté

moutarde [mootard] mustard

mouton [mootON] mutton

mulet [mOOlay] mullet

munster [mANstair] strong cheese from eastern France

mûre [mOOr] blackberry

muscade [mOOskad] nutmeg

myrtille [meertee] bilberry

nature [natOOr] plain

navarin [navaraN] mutton stew with vegetables

navet [navay] turnip

nèfle [nefl] medlar

noisettes [nwazet] hazelnuts

noisette d'agneau [dan-yo] small, round lamb steak

noix [nwa] walnuts; nuts

nouilles [noo-yuh] noodles

œuf [urf] egg

œuf à la coque [kok] soft-boiled egg

œuf cocotte à la tomate [kokot ala tomat] egg cooked with tomato in the oven

œuf dur [dOOr] hard-boiled egg

œuf en gelée [ON juhlay] egg in aspic

œuf mayonnaise egg mayonnaise

œuf mollet [molay] soft-boiled egg

œuf poché [poshay] poached egg

œufs à la neige [uh ala nej] floating islands (poached whisked egg whites on top of custard)

œufs au lait [o lay] egg custard

œufs au vin [VAN] eggs poached in red wine

œufs brouillés [broo-yay] scrambled eggs

œufs en meurette [ON murret] poached eggs in wine sauce

œuf sur le plat [urf sOOr luh pla] fried egg

oie [wa] goose

oignon [onyON] onion

olive [oleev] olive

omelette au fromage [fromahj] cheese omelette

omelette au jambon [jONbON] ham omelette

omelette au naturel [natOOrel] plain omelette

omelette aux champignons [o shONpeen-yON] mushroom omelette

omelette aux fines herbes [feen zairb] omelette with herbs

omelette nature [natOOr] plain omelette

omelette paysanne [pay-eezan] omelette with potatoes and bacon

opéra [opayra] plain chocolate and coffee gateau

orange givrée [geevray] orange
sorbet served in a scooped-
out orange

oseille [ohzay] sorrel

oursin [oorsAN] sea urchin

pain [pAN] bread; loaf

pain au chocolat [o shokola]
type of pastry with
chocolate filling

pain au lait [lay] kind of sweet
bun

pain aux noix [nwa] walnut
bread

pain aux raisins [o rezzAN] kind
of brioche with custard and
sultanas

pain bagnat [ban-ya] tuna salad
sandwich in wholemeal
bread roll (from the French
Riviera)

pain blanc [blON] white bread

pain complet [kONplay]
wholemeal bread

pain de campagne [kONpañ]
farmhouse bread/loaf

pain de mie [mee] sliced white
bread

pain de seigle [segl] rye bread

pain de son [sON] bran bread

pain viennois [vee-enwa]
Vienna loaf

palette de porc [palet duh por]
pork shoulder

palourde [paloord] clam

pamplemousse [pONpl-mooss]
grapefruit

panaché ... [panashay]
mixed ...

panade [panad] bread soup

pané [panay] breaded

papillote: en papillote [ON
papee-yot] baked in foil or
paper

parfait glacé [parfay glassay]
frozen sweet

pastèque [pastek] water melon

pâte d'amandes [paht damONd]
marzipan

pâté de canard [duh kanar]
duck pâté

pâté de foie de volaille [fwa duh
volī] chicken liver pâté

pâte feuilletée [paht fuh-ee-etay]
puff pastry

pâtes [paht] pasta

pâtisserie [pateesree] cake;
cake shop

pâtisserie maison [mezzON]
home made gateau

paupiettes de veau [pohp-yet
duh vo] rolled-up stuffed
slices of veal

pavé de rumsteak [pavay duh]
thick piece of steak

pêche [pesh] peach

pêche Melba peach melba

perdreau [pairdro] young
partridge

perdrix [pairdree] partridge

persil [pairsee] parsley

petit beurre [puhtee burr] biscuit/
cookie made with butter

petite friture [puhteet freetoor]
whitebait

petit gâteau biscuit

petit pain [pAN] roll

petits pois [puhtee pwa] peas

petits fours [foor] decorated small cakes and biscuits

petit suisse [sweess] light cream cheese

pieds de cochon/porc [p-yay duh koshON/por] pigs' trotters

pigeon [peejON] pigeon

pigeonneau [peejono] young pigeon

pignatelle [peen-yatel] small cheese fritter

pilaf rice dish with meat

pilaf de mouton [duh mootON] rice dish with mutton

pintade [pANtad] guinea fowl

piperade [peepuhrad] scrambled eggs with peppers and tomatoes

pissaladière [peessaladee-yair] Provençal dish similar to pizza

pissenlit [peess-ON-lee] dandelion

pistache [peestash] pistachio

pizza quatre saisons [katr sezzON] four seasons pizza

plat de résistance [pla duh rayseestONss] main course

plat du jour [pla doo joor] dish of the day

plateau de fromages [plato duh fromahj] cheese board

plateau de fruits de mer [duh frwee duh mair] seafood platter

plat principal [pla prANseepal] main course

pochouse [poshooz] fish casserole with white wine

point: à point [pwAN] medium

poire [pwahr] pear

poireau [pwahro] leek

poire belle-Hélène [bel aylen] pear in chocolate sauce

pois chiches [pwa sheesh] chickpeas

poisson [pwassON] fish

poivre [pwahvr] pepper (seasoning)

poivron [pwahvrON] pepper (vegetable)

poivron farci [farsee] stuffed pepper

pomme [pom] apple

pomme au four [o foor] jacket potato

pomme bonne femme [bon fam] baked apple

pomme de terre [duh tair] potato

pommes alumettes [pom alOOmet] French fries

pommes dauphine [dofeen] potato fritters

pommes de terre à l'anglaise [pom duh tair a lONglez] boiled potatoes

pommes (de terre) en robe de chambre [ON rob duh shONbr] jacket potatoes

pommes (de terre) en robe des champs [ON rob day shON] jacket potatoes

pommes (de terre) sautées [sotay] fried potatoes

pommes frites [freet] chips, French fries

pommes paille [pī] finely cut chips, French fries

pommes vapeur [vapurr] boiled potatoes

porc [por] pork

potage [potahj] soup

potage bilibi [beeleebee] fish and oyster soup

potage Crécy [kraysee] carrot and rice soup

potage cressonnière [kressonee-yair] watercress soup

potage parmentier [parmONt-yay] leek and potato soup

potage printanier [prANtan-yay] fine vegetable soup

potage Saint-Germain [SAN jairmAN] split pea soup

potage velouté [vuhlootay] creamy soup

pot-au-feu [potofuh] beef and vegetable stew

potée [potay] vegetable and meat hotpot

potiron [poteerON] pumpkin

poularde [poolard] fattened chicken

poule [pool] chicken

poule au pot [o po] chicken and vegetable stew

poule au riz [o ree] chicken with rice

poulet [poolay] chicken

poulet à l'estragon [lestragON] chicken in tarragon sauce

poulet basquaise [baskez] chicken with ham, tomatoes and peppers

poulet chasseur [shassurr] chicken with mushrooms

and white wine

poulet créole [kray-ol] chicken in white sauce served with rice

poulet grillé [gree-yay] grilled chicken

poulet rôti [ro-tee] roast chicken

poulpe [poolp] octopus

praire [prair] clam

provençale [provONsal] with tomatoes, garlic and herbs

prune [prOOn] plum

pruneau [prOOno] prune

pudding plum pudding

purée [pOOray] mashed potatoes

purée de marrons [duh marrON] chestnut purée

purée de pommes de terre [pom duh tair] mashed potatoes

quatre-quarts [katr-kar] similar to Madeira cake

quenelle [kuhnel] dumpling, generally made with chicken or pike

queue de bœuf [kuh duh burf] oxtail

quiche lorraine quiche with bacon

râble de chevreuil [rabl duh shuhvruh-ee] saddle of venison

râble de lièvre [duh lee-evr] saddle of hare

raclette [raklet] Swiss dish of

melted cheese with boiled
potatoes and cold meat

radis [radee] radish

ragoût [ragoo] stew

raie [ray] skate

raie au beurre noir [o burr
nwahr] skate fried in butter

raifort [rayfor] horseradish

raisin [rezzAN] grape(s)

râpé [rapay] grated

rascasse [raskass] scorpion
fish

ratatouille [ratatoo-yuh] dish of
stewed peppers, courgettes/
zucchinis, aubergines/
eggplants and tomatoes

ravigote [raveegot] dressing
with herbs and shallots

reblochon [ruhbloshON] strong
cheese from Savoie

reine-claude [ren-klohd]
greengage

religieuse au chocolat/au café
[ruhleejurz o shokola/o kafay]
cream puff with chocolate
or coffee icing/frosting

rémoulade [ray-moolad]
mayonnaise dressing with
mustard and herbs

rigotte [reegot] small goat
cheese from the Lyons area

rillettes [ree-yet] potted pork
and goose meat

**rillettes de saumon frais et
fumé** [duh somON fray ay fOOmay]
fresh and smoked salmon
paté

ris de veau [ree duh vo] veal
sweetbread

rissole [reessol] meat pie

riz [ree] rice

riz à l'impératrice [lANpayratrees]
sweet rice dish

riz pilaf spicy rice with meat
or seafood

rognon [rON-yON] kidney

rognons au madère [rON-yON zo
madair] kidneys in Madeira
wine

romarin [romarAN] rosemary

roquefort [rokfor] blue ewes'
milk cheese from the south
of France

rosette de Lyon [rozet duh lee-
ON] dry salami-type sausage

rôti de porc [rotee duh por] roast
pork

rouget [roo-jay] mullet

rouille [roo-yuh] spicy sauce to
go with bouillabaisse

sabayon [saba-yON] dessert
made from egg yolks and
Marsala wine

sablé [sablay] shortbread

saignant [sen-yON] rare

saint-honoré [sANt-onoray] cake
with cream and choux
pastry decoration

saint-marcellin [sAN-marsuh-lAN]
goats' cheese

salade [sa-lad] salad; lettuce

salade aux noix [o nwa] green
salad with walnuts

salade composée [kompozay]
mixed salad

salade de gésiers [jayzee-ay]
green salad with gizzards

221

salade de tomates [tomat] tomato salad

salade niçoise [neess-wahz] salad with olives, tomatoes, anchovies and hard boiled eggs

salade russe [rooss] diced vegetables in mayonnaise

salade verte [vairt] green salad

salmis [salmee] game stew

salsifis [salseefee] oyster plant, salsify

sandwich au fromage [sONdweech o fromahj] cheese sandwich

sandwich au jambon [jONbON] ham sandwich

sandwich au saucisson [soseesON] salami sandwich

sandwich aux rillettes [ree-yet] pâté sandwich

sandwich crudités salad sandwich

sandwich thon/mayonnaise [tON] tuna/mayonnaise sandwich

sanglier [sON-glee-yay] wild boar

sauce aurore [o-ror] white sauce with tomato purée

sauce aux câpres [o kapr] white sauce with capers

sauce béarnaise [bay-ar-nez] sauce made from egg yolks, lemon juice or vinegar, butter and herbs

sauce béchamel [bayshamel] white sauce

sauce blanche [blONsh] white sauce

sauce grand veneur [grON vuhnurr] sauce for game

sauce gribiche [greebeesh] dressing with hard boiled eggs, capers and herbs

sauce hollandaise [olONdez] rich sauce made with eggs, butter and vinegar, served with fish

sauce madère [madair] Madeira sauce

sauce matelote [matlot] wine sauce

sauce Mornay [mornay] béchamel sauce with cheese

sauce mousseline [moossleen] hollandaise sauce with cream

sauce poulette [poolet] sauce with mushrooms, egg yolks and wine

sauce ravigote [raveegot] dressing with shallots and herbs

sauce rémoulade [ray-moolad] dressing made from mayonnaise, mustard and herbs

sauce suprême [sooprem] creamy sauce

sauce tartare mayonnaise with herbs, gherkins and capers

sauce veloutée [vuhlootay] white sauce with egg yolks and cream

sauce vinot [veeno] wine sauce

saucisse [sosseess] sausage

saucisse de Francfort [duh froNkfor] frankfurter

saucisse de Strasbourg [strazboorg] beef sausage

saucisson [sosseessoN] salami

saumon [somoN] salmon

saumon à l'oseille [lozay] salmon with sorrel

saumon fumé [somoN foomay] smoked salmon

sauté de dindonneau [daNdonno] sauté of turkey poult

savarin [savaraN] crown-shaped rum baba

seiche [sesh] cuttlefish

sel salt

selle d'agneau [sel dan-yo] saddle of lamb

selon arrivage depending on availability

service (non) compris service (not) included

sole bonne femme [bon fam] sole in white wine and mushrooms

sole meunière [muhn-yair] sole dipped in flour and fried in butter

soufflé au chocolat [o shokola] chocolate soufflé

soufflé au fromage [fromahj] cheese soufflé

soufflé au jambon [joNboN] ham soufflé

soupe [soop] thick soup

soupe à l'ail [lī] garlic soup

soupe à la tomate [tomat] tomato soup

soupe à l'oignon [lonyoN] onion soup

soupe à l'oseille [lozay] sorrel soup

soupe au pistou [o peestoo] thick vegetable soup with basil

soupe aux choux [shoo] cabbage soup

soupe aux moules [o mool] mussel soup

soupe aux poireaux et pommes de terre [pwaro ay pom duh tair] leek and potato soup

soupe de légumes [laygoom] vegetable soup

soupe de poisson [pwassoN] fish soup

steak au poivre [o pwahvr] pepper steak

steak frites [freet] steak and chips/French fries

steak haché [ashay] minced meat

steak sauce au poivre [o pwahvr] steak with pepper sauce

steak sauce au roquefort [rokfor] steak with roquefort cheese sauce

steak tartare raw minced beef with a raw egg

sucre [sookr] sugar

suprême de volaille [sooprem duh volī] chicken in cream sauce

surgelés [soorjuhlay] frozen food

surprise du chef [sOOrpreez dOO shef] chef's surprise (gateau)

tajine [tajeen] North African stew of mutton or chicken, vegetables and prunes cooked in an earthenware dish

tanche [tONsh] tench (fish)

tartare tartar(e); raw

tarte [tart] tart; pie

tarte au citron meringuée [o seetrON muhrANgay] lemon meringue pie

tarte aux fraises [o frez] strawberry tart/pie

tarte aux myrtilles [meertee] bilberry tart

tarte aux poireaux [pwahro] leek flan

tarte aux pommes [pom] apple tart/pie

tarte frangipane [frONjeepan] almond cream tart/pie

tartelette [tartuh-let] small tart/pie

tarte Tatin [tatAN] baked apple dish

tartine [tarteen] buttered slice of bread

tendrons de veau [tONdrON duh vo] veal breast

terrine [terreen] rougher type of pâté

terrine du chef [dOO shef] pâté maison, chef's special pâté

tête de veau [tet duh vo] calf's head

thon [tON] tuna fish

thon Mirabeau [meerabo] tuna cooked in eggs and milk

thym [tAN] thyme

tomate [tomat] tomato

tomme de Savoie [tom duh savwa] white cheese from Savoie

tourte [toort] pie

tourteau [toorto] kind of crab

tous nos plats sont garnis all our dishes are served with vegetables

tripes [treep] tripe

tripes à la mode de Caen [duh kON] tripe in spicy vegetable sauce

truffe [trOOf] truffle

truite au bleu [trweet o bluh] poached trout

truite meunière [muhn-yair] trout coated in flour and fried in butter

vacherin [vashrAN] strong, soft cheese from the Jura area

vacherin glacé [glassay] ice cream meringue

veau [vo] veal

velouté d'asperges [vuhlootay daspairj] cream of asparagus soup

velouté de tomates [tomat] cream of tomato soup

velouté de volaille [volÏ] cream of chicken soup

velouté d'huîtres [dweetr] cream of oyster soup

vermicelle [vairmeesel] very fine pasta used in soups

viande [vee-ONd] meat
viande hachée [ashay] minced
 meat
vichyssoise [veesheeswahz] cold
 vegetable soup
vinaigre [veenegr] vinegar
volaille [volī] poultry

yaourt [ya-oort] yogurt

Menu Reader:
Drink

Essential Terms

beer la bière [bee-air]
bottle la bouteille [bootay]
brandy le cognac
coffee le café
cup la tasse [tass]
a cup of ... une tasse de ...
gin le gin [djeen]
gin and tonic un gin-tonic
glass le verre [vair]
a glass of ... un verre de ...
milk le lait [lay]
mineral water l'eau minérale **f** [o meenayral]
orange juice le jus d'orange [joo doronj]
port le porto
red wine le vin rouge [vaN rooj]
rosé le rosé [rozzay]
soda (water) le soda
soft drink la boisson non-alcoolisée [bwassoN noN-alkoleezay]
sugar le sucre [sookr]
tea le thé [tay]
tonic (water) le schweppes®
vodka la vodka
water l'eau **f** [o]
whisky le whisky
white wine le vin blanc [vaN bloN]
wine le vin [vaN]
wine list la carte des vins [kart day vaN]

another ..., please encore ..., s'il vous plaît [oNkor ..., seel voo play]

alcool [alkool] alcohol

AOC (Appellation d'Origine Contrôlée) guarantee of the quality of a wine

Banyuls® [banyoolss] a sweet apéritif wine

bière [bee-air] beer

bière (à la) pression [press-yON] draught beer

bière (blonde) lager

bière brune [brOOn] bitter; dark beer

bière rousse [rooss] relatively sweet, fairly dark beer

blanc [blON] white wine; white

blanc de blancs [duh blON] white wine from white grapes

blanquette de Limoux [blONket duh leemoo] sparkling white wine from Languedoc

boisson [bwassON] drink

Bourgogne [boor-goñ] wine from the Burgundy area

Brouilly [broo-yee] red wine from the Beaujolais area

brut [brOOt] very dry

café [kafay] espresso, very strong black coffee

café au lait [o lay] white coffee

café crème [krem] white coffee

café glacé [glassay] iced coffee

café soluble [solOObl] instant coffee

café viennois [vee-enwa] coffee with whipped cream

calvados apple brandy from Normandy

camomille [kamomee] camomile tea

capiteux [kapeetuh] heady

carte des vins [kart day vAN] wine list

Chablis [shablee] dry white wine from Burgundy

chambré [shONbray] at room temperature

champagne [shONpañ] champagne

champagnisé [shONpan-yeezay] sparkling

chartreuse [shartrurz] herb liqueur

Château-Margaux [shato margo] red wine from the Bordeaux area

Châteauneuf-du-Pape [shatonurf dOO pap] red wine from the Rhône valley

chocolat chaud [shokola sho] hot chocolate

chocolat glacé [glassay] iced chocolate drink

cidre [seedr] cider

cidre bouché [booshay] cider in bottle with a cork

cidre doux [doo] sweet cider

51® (cinquante-et-un) [sankONtay-AN] a brand of pastis

citron pressé [seetrON pressay] fresh lemon juice

cognac [kONyak] brandy

crème [krem] white coffee

crème de cassis [duh kasseess] blackcurrant liqueur

cru [kr00] vintage

cru classé high quality wine

décaféiné [daykafay-eenay] decaffeinated

délimité de qualité supérieure superior quality wine

demi [duhmee] small draught beer; quarter of a litre of beer

demi-sec [duhmee-sek] medium dry

diabolo menthe/fraise etc [d-yabolo mONt/frez] mint/strawberry etc cordial with lemonade

digestif [deejesteef] liqueur

eau [o] water

eau de vie [duh vee] spirit made from fruit

eau minérale [meenayral] mineral water

eau minérale gazeuse [gazurz] sparkling mineral water

Fendant [fONdON] Swiss dry white wine

fine [feen] fine brandy, liqueur brandy

Fleurie [flurree] red wine from Beaujolais

frappé [frapay] well chilled, on ice; iced

gazeux [gazurz] fizzy

Gewurztraminer [guh-w00rztrameenair] dry white wine from Alsace

gin-tonic gin and tonic

Gini® a kind of bitter lemon

glaçon [glassON] ice cube

grand crème [grON krem] large white coffee

grand cru [kr00] fine vintage

Graves [grahv] red wine from the Bordeaux area

infusion [anf00z-yON] herb tea

jus [j00] juice

jus de pommes [duh pom] apple juice

jus d'orange [dorONj] orange juice

kir white wine with blackcurrant liqueur

kir royal champagne with blackcurrant liqueur

kirsch cherry brandy

lait [lay] milk

lait fraise/grenadine [frez/gruhnadeen] milk with strawberry/grenadine cordial

limonade [leemonad] lemonade

Mâcon [makON] wine from Burgundy

marc [mar] clear spirit distilled from grape pulp

Médoc [maydok] red wine from the Bordeaux area

menthe à l'eau [mONt a lo] mint
  cordial
méthode champenoise
  made in the same way as
  champagne
Meursault [murrso] wine from
  Burgundy
millésime [meelay-zeem]
  vintage
mousseux [moossuh] sparkling
Muscadet [mooskaday] dry
  white wine from the
  Nantes area
muscat [mooska] sweet white
  wine

Noilly-Prat® [nwa-yee pra] an
  apéritif wine similar to Dry
  Martini
Nuits-Saint-Georges [nwee
  sAN jorj] red wine from
  Burgundy

orange pressée [orONj pressay]
  fresh orange juice

panaché [panashay] shandy
Passe-Tout-Grain [pass too grAN]
  red wine from Burgundy
pastis [pasteess] aniseed-
  flavoured alcoholic drink
Pernod® [pairno] a brand of
  pastis
pétillant [paytee-ON] sparkling
porto port
Pouilly-Fuissé [poo-yee-
  fweessay] dry white wine
  from Burgundy
premier cru [pruhm-yay croo]

vintage wine
pression [press-yON] draught
  beer, draught

rhum [rom] rum
Ricard® [reekar] a brand of
  pastis
Rivesaltes® [reevsalt] a sweet
  apéritif wine
rosé [rozzay] rosé wine
rouge [rooj] red

Saint-Amour [sANtamoor] red
  wine from Beaujolais
Saint-Emilion [sAN-taymeelee-
  yON] red wine from the
  Bordeaux area
Sauternes [sotairn] fruity
  white wine from the
  Bordeaux area
Schweppes® tonic water
scotch scotch whisky
sec [sek] dry; neat
servir frais serve cool
sirop [seero] cordial

thé [tay] tea
thé à la menthe [mONt] mint
  tea
thé au lait [o lay] tea with milk
thé citron [seetrON] lemon tea
thé nature [natoor] tea without
  milk
tilleul [tee-yurl] lime-flower tea

VDQS (Vin Délimité de Qualité
  Supérieure) a category of
  wine between vin de table
  and AOC

verveine [vairven] verbena tea
vin [VAN] wine
vin blanc [blON] white wine
vin de pays [duh payee]
  regional wine
vin de table [duh tahbl] table
  wine
vin rosé [rozzay] rosé wine
vin rouge [rooj] red wine

Yvorne [eevorn] Swiss dry
  white wine

How the
Language
Works

How the
Language
Works

Pronunciation

In this phrasebook, the French has been written in a system of imitated pronunciation so that it can be read as though it were English. Bear in mind the notes on pronunciation given below:

AN	a French nasal sound; say the English word 'tan' clipping off the final 'n' and you are close
ay	as in m**ay**
e	as in g**e**t
g	always hard as in **g**oat
ī	as the 'i' sound in m**i**ght
j	like the 's' sound in plea**s**ure
ñ	like the final sound in 'lasa**gne**'
ON	a French nasal sound; say the English word 'on' through your nose and cutting off the final 'n'
∞	like the 'ew' in f**ew** but without any 'y' sound
r	comes from the back of the throat
uh	like the 'e' in butt**e**r but a little longer
y	as in **y**es

The French often run together or elide a word ending with a consonant and a following word that starts with a vowel. This has been shown in the pronunciation as, for example:
'do you have ...?' **est-ce que vous avez ...?** [eskuh voo zavay].
The 'z' at the beginning of 'zavay' has been run on from the preceding word.

Abbreviations

adj	adjective	**m**	masculine
f	feminine	**mpl**	masculine plural
fpl	feminine plural	**sing**	singular

Notes

In the English-French section, when two forms of the verb are given in phrases such as 'can you ...?' **est-ce que tu peux/vous pouvez ... ?**, the first is the familiar form and the second the polite form (see entry for **you**).

An asterisk (★) next to a word means that you should refer to the **How the Language Works** section for further information.

Nouns

All French nouns have one of two genders – masculine (**un / le**) or feminine (**une / la**).

Plural Nouns

The most common way of forming the plural of a noun – of saying, for example, 'the passports' instead of 'the passport' – is by adding an **-s** to the singular:

le passeport	**les passeports**
luh pass-por	lay pass-por
the passport	the passports
le magasin	**les magasins**
luh magazAN	lay magazAN
the shop	the shops

This **-s** is not normally pronounced in French.

To make the plural of words ending in **-au** or **-eu** you add an **-x**:

un bureau	**leurs bureaux**
AN bOOro	lurr bOOro
an office	their offices
le lieu	**les lieux**
luh l-yuh	lay l-yuh
the place	the places

This **-x** is not normally pronounced in French.

To make the plural of words ending in **-al** change **-al** to **-aux**:

un cheval	**deux chevaux**
AN shuhval	duh shuhvo
a horse	two horses

One important irregular plural:

mon oeil	mes yeux
mON uh-ee	may z-yuh
my eye	my eyes

Articles

The words for articles ('the' and 'a') in French vary according to three elements:

> the gender of the noun
> the first letter of the noun
> whether the noun is singular or plural

Singular Articles

The equivalents for saying 'the' are:

le luh   for masculine singular nouns
la   for feminine singular nouns

In front of a noun beginning with a vowel (or an 'h' that is not pronounced) **le** and **la** change to **l'**.

le marché	la gare
luh marshay	la gar
the market	the station

l'homme	l'actrice
lom	laktreess
the man	the actress

The equivalents for saying 'a' are:

un AN   for all masculine nouns
une OOn   for all feminine nouns

un marché	une gare
AN marshay	OOn gar
a market	a station

Plural Articles

les lay   for both masculine and feminine nouns

les marchés	**les gares**
lay marshay	lay gar
the markets	the stations

les hommes	**les actrices**
lay zom	lay zaktreess
the men	the actresses

The plural form of the indefinite article, translated in English as 'some', or often omitted, is **des** day:

des marchés	**des gares**
day marshay	day gar
(some) markets	(some) stations

Prepositions

When used with the prepositions **de** and **à**, the definite article may change its form:

If you are using **le / les** with **de** (of; from) make the following changes:

de + le	= du	doo
de + les	= des	day

With **à** (to; at) make these changes:

à + le	= au	o
à + les	= aux	o

le nom du supermarché
luh nON doo soopairmarshay
the name of the supermarket

il vient des Etats-Unis
eel v-yAN day zaytazoonee
he comes from the United States

au supermarché
o sOOpairmarshay
at the supermarket

aux Etats-Unis
o zaytazOOnee
to the United States

If you are using **la** or **l'** the preposition does not change.

à la plage
a la plahj
at the beach

à l'hôtel
a lotel
at the hotel

Adjectives and Adverbs

In French, adjectives have to 'agree' with the noun they are used with. This means that if a noun is feminine, then an adjective used with it must be in the feminine form too. If a noun is plural, then an adjective used with it must be in the plural form too, masculine or feminine. In the English into French section of this book, all adjectives are translated by the masculine form – the form used with nouns preceded by **un** or **le**.

For most adjectives, the feminine form is made by adding **-e**. The plural is formed in two ways: for those with masculine nouns, by adding **-s**; and for those with feminine nouns, by adding **-es**. Plurals for adjectives ending in **-au** are usually formed by adding **-x**, although the **-s** or **-x** is not pronounced.

Important exceptions are shown in the English into French section.

un journal allemand
AN joornal almON
a German newspaper

une famille allemande
OOn famee almONd
a German family

des journaux américains
day joorno zamaayreekAN
American newspapers

deux familles écossaises
duh famee zaykossez
two Scottish families

Most adjectives in French, as in these examples, are placed after the noun, not in front of it as in English.

Some common adjectives, however, are put in front of nouns:

beau	bo	beautiful	nouveau	noovo	new
long	lON	long	grand	grON	big
bon	bON	good	petit	puhtee	little
joli	jolee	pretty	jeune	jurn	young
mauvais	movay	bad	vieux	vyuh	old
gentil	jONtee	nice			

Comparatives

To say that something is, for example, more expensive or faster than something else, you use the comparative form of the adjective (or adverb). In French these are all formed by using the word plus in front of the adjective or adverb:

grand	plus grand
grON	plOO grON
big	bigger

intéressant	plus intéressant
ANtayressON	plOO zANtayressON
interesting	more interesting

je voudrais une plus grande chambre
juh voodray zOOn plOO grONd shONbr
I'd like a bigger room

c'est plus intéressant que le château
say plOO zANtayressON kuh luh shato
it's more interesting than the castle

cette plage est plus calme que l'autre
set plahj ay plOO kalm kuh lohtr
this beach is quieter than the other one

pouvez-vous parler plus clairement, s'il vous plaît?
poovay-voo parlay ploo klairmON seel voo play
could you speak more clearly please?

'As ... as' is translated as follows:

ce restaurant est aussi cher que l'autre
suh restorON ay tohsee shair kuh lohtr
this restaurant is as expensive as the other one

ce n'était pas aussi cher que je croyais
suh naytay pa zohsee shair kuh juh krwy-ay
it wasn't as expensive as I thought

aussi lentement que possible
ohsee lONtuhmON kuh posseebl
as slowly as possible

Superlatives

To say that something is, for example, the most expensive or the fastest, you use the superlative form of the adjective (or adverb). This is formed by using the words **le plus** in front of the adjective for a masculine singular noun; **la plus** for a feminine singular noun; and **les plus** for a plural noun (see Adjectives):

grand	**le plus grand**
grON	luh ploo grON
big	biggest
intéressant	**le plus intéressant**
ANtayressON	luh ploo zANtayressON
interesting	most interesting

le plus grand hôtel de la ville
luh ploo grON otel duh la veel
the biggest hotel in town

où est la poste la plus proche?
oo ay la posst la ploo prosh
where is the nearest post office?

le barman parle le plus clairement
luh barman parl luh plOO klairmON
the barman speaks the most clearly

Some forms are irregular:

bon	bON	good
meilleur	may-yurr	better
le meilleur	luh may-yurr	best
mauvais	mo-vay	bad
pire	peer	worse
le pire	luh peer	worst

Adverbs

Adverbs are formed by adding **-ment** to the feminine form of the adjective if it ends in a consonant, and to the masc-uline form if it ends in a vowel:

vrai / vraie	vraiment	final / finale	finalement
vray	vraymON	feenal	feenalmON
real	really	final	finally

Adjectives which end in **-ent** and **-ant** change to **-emment** and **-amment**:

évident	évidemment	constant	constamment
ayveedON	ayveedamON	kONstON	kONstamON
obvious	obviously	constant	constantly

But not:

lent	lentement
lON	lONtuhmON
slow	slowly

Some forms are irregular:

bon	bien	mauvais	mal	meilleur	mieux
bON	b-yAN	movay	mal	may-yurr	m-yuh
good	well	bad	badly	better	better

Possessive Adjectives

If you want to say that something is 'your car' or 'his car' or 'her car' etc, then you use the following words in French. Notice that there are three forms: one for masculine words (given with **le** in the phrase book); one for feminine words (given with **la**); and one for plural words.

	masculine		feminine		plural	
my	**mon**	mON	**ma**	ma	**mes**	may
your	**ton**	tON	**ta**	ta	**tes**	tay
his / its	**son**	sON	**sa**	sa	**ses**	say
her / its	**son**	sON	**sa**	sa	**ses**	say
our	**notre**	notr	**notre**	notr	**nos**	no
your	**votre**	votr	**votre**	votr	**vos**	vo
their	**leur**	lurr	**leur**	lurr	**leurs**	lurr

Some points to note:

The forms **ton / ta / tes** are used for people you are speaking to as **tu**. The forms **votre / vos** are used for people you are speaking to as **vous** (see **Pronouns**).

Whether you use **son / sa** or **mon / ma** depends on the gender of the thing / person 'possessed'. So for example:

> **ma chambre**
> > ma shONbr
> > my room

can be said by both a man and a woman. Likewise:

> **sa chambre**
> > sa shONbr

can mean either 'his room' or 'her room'.

If this is confusing you can say:

sa chambre à lui	sa chambre à elle
sa shONbr a lwee	sa shONbr a el
his room	her room

Ma / ta / sa change to **mon / ton / son** in front of a vowel:

> **mon épouse**
>
> mON aypooz
>
> my wife

Pronouns

Subject Pronouns

If you are using a pronoun as the subject of a verb, saying 'he is' or 'we are' or 'can you?' etc, the words are:

je	juh	I	nous	noo	we
tu	too	you	vous	voo	you
il	eel	he / it	ils	eel	they
elle	el	she / it	elles	el	they

Points to note:

YOU: **tu** is used when speaking to someone who is a friend, or to someone of your own general age group with whom you want to establish a friendly atmosphere. **Vous** is used when speaking to several friends (ie it is the plural of **tu**) or when speaking to someone you don't know. In the vast majority of cases, as a foreigner in France you will use the **vous** form. Certainly, if you are in any doubt as to which form to use, choose the **vous** form.

IT: if you are using 'it' to refer to something like 'the car', 'the train' etc (as opposed to saying 'it is cold today' etc), you should use either **il** or **elle** depending on the gender of the thing you are talking about (see **Articles**). For example, **la voi-ture** (the car) is **elle** (it) and **le train** (the train) is **il** (it).

Direct Object Pronouns

If you are using the pronoun as an object, saying 'Peter knows him' or 'Mary saw them' etc, you must use the following object pronouns, which will normally precede the verb:

me	muh	me	**nous**	noo	us
te	tuh	you	**vous**	voo	you
le	luh	him / it	**les**	lay	them
la	la	her / it			

je le vois	il les a achetés
juh luh vwa	eel lay za ashtay
I see him	he bought them

vous me comprenez?
voo muh KONpruhnay
do you understand me?

Indirect Object Pronouns

If you are using a pronoun to say, for example, you sent something to her or that you spoke to him, then you must use the following indirect object pronouns:

me	muh	to me	**nous**	noo	to us
te	tuh	to you	**vous**	voo	to you
lui	lwee	to him / her / it	**leur**	lurr	to them

je lui ai écrit	je le lui ai expliqué
juh lwee ay aykree	juh luh lwee ay expleekay
I wrote to him	I explained it to him

Emphatic Pronouns

If you are using a pronoun to say 'it's me', 'with her', 'for them' etc, then you must use the following emphatic pronouns:

moi	mwa	me	nous	noo	us
toi	twa	you	vous	voo	you
lui	lwee	him	eux	uh	them
elle	el	her	elles	el	them

c'est eux
set uh
it's them

venez avec moi
vuhnay avek mwa
come with me

ces cafés sont pour nous
say kafay SON poor noo
those coffees are for us

A useful word for 'it' or 'that' to refer to a specific thing, or a more general situation, is **ça** sa:

donne-moi ça!
don mwa sa
give it / that to me!

tu as vu ça?
too a voo sa
did you see that?

Reflexive Pronouns

These are used with reflexive verbs like **se laver** (to get washed, to wash oneself), where the subject and the object are the same.

me	muh	myself
te	tuh	yourself
se	suh	himself / herself / itself
nous	noo	ourselves
vous	voo	yourself / yourselves
se	suh	themselves

There are many more verbs used reflexively in French than in English. Some examples are:

je m'appelle Anna
juh mapel anna
I am called Anna

247

nous nous levons toujours de bonne heure

noo noo luhvON toojoor duh bon urr

we always get up early

ils se sont bien amusés

eel suh SON b-yAN amOOzay

they enjoyed themselves very much

Possessive Pronouns

If you want to say that something is yours or his or hers etc, then you use the following possessive pronouns. Notice that there are four forms: masculine singular and plural, and feminine singular and plural:

	m sing	mpl	
mine	**le mien**	**les miens**	luh / lay m-yAN
yours	**le tien**	**les tiens**	luh / lay t-yAN
his / its	**le sien**	**les siens**	luh / lay s-yAN
hers / its	**le sien**	**les siens**	luh / lay s-yAN
ours	**le nôtre**	**les nôtres**	luh / lay nohtr
yours	**le vôtre**	**les vôtres**	luh / lay vohtr
theirs	**le leur**	**les leurs**	luh / lay lurr

	f sing	fpl	
mine	**la mienne**	**les miennes**	luh / lay m-yen
yours	**la tienne**	**les tiennes**	luh / lay t-yen
his / its	**la sienne**	**les siennes**	luh / lay s-yen
hers / its	**la sienne**	**les siennes**	luh / lay s-yen
ours	**la nôtre**	**les nôtres**	luh / lay nohtr
yours	**la vôtre**	**les vôtres**	luh / lay vohtr
theirs	**la leur**	**les leurs**	luh / lay lurr

Again, the use of 'le sien / la sienne' and 'le mien / la mienne' etc will depend on the gender of the thing(s) possessed:

cette voiture n'est pas la nôtre

set vwatOOr nay pa la nohtr

this car isn't ours

cette valise est la mienne, la tienne est là-bas
set valeez ay la m-yen, la t-yen ay la-ba
this suitcase is mine, yours is over there

After the verb **être** (to be), the possessive pronouns can be replaced by **à** + the appropriate emphatic pronoun (see **Pronouns**).

ce sac est à moi
suh sak ay ta mwa
this bag is mine

est-ce que cet appareil photo est à vous?
eskuh set aparay foto ay ta voo
is this camera yours?

Verbs

There are three main verb types, recognizable by their endings: **-er**, **-ir**, and **-re**.

Present Tense

The present tense of a verb corresponds to 'you are doing' or 'you do' or 'something happens' etc. To form the present tense for the three main types of verb, remove the endings and conjugate as follows:

donner (to give)

je donne [juh don]	I give	
tu donnes [too don]	you give	
il / elle donne [eel / el don]	he / she gives	
nous donnons [noo donON]	we give	
vous donnez [voo donay]	you give	
ils / elles donnent [eel / el don]	they give	

finir (to finish)

je finis [juh feenee]	I finish
tu finis [too feenee]	you finish
il / elle finit [eel / el feenee]	he / she finishes
nous finissons [noo feeneessON]	we finish
vous finissez [voo feeneessay]	you finish
ils / elles finissent [eel / el feeneess]	they finish

attendre (to wait)

j'attends [jatON]	I wait
tu attends [too atON]	you wait
il / elle attend [eel / el atON]	he / she waits
nous attendons [noo zatONdON]	we wait
vous attendez [voo zatONday]	you wait
ils / elles attendent [eel / el zatONd]	they wait

Remember that this tense also covers English forms like 'I am doing':

je lui parle
juh lwee parl
I talk to him OR I'm talking to him

Some common verbs have irregular forms in the present tense:

aller (to go)		**boire** (to drink)	
je vais	juh vay	**je bois**	bwa
tu vas	too va	**tu bois**	bwa
il / elle va	eel / el va	**il / elle boit**	bwa
nous allons	noo zalON	**nous buvons**	boovON
vous allez	voo zalay	**vous buvez**	boovay
ils / elles vont	eel / el vON	**ils / elles boivent**	bwav

devoir (to have to, must)

je dois	dwa
tu dois	dwa
il / elle doit	dwa
nous devons	duhvON
vous devez	duhvay
ils / elles doivent	dwav

dire (to say)

je dis	dee
tu dis	dee
il / elle dit	dee
nous disons	deezON
vous dites	deet
ils / elles disent	deez

faire (to do, to make)

je fais	fay
tu fais	fay
il / elle fait	fay
nous faisons	fuhzON
vous faites	fet
ils / elles font	fON

partir (to leave, to go away)

je pars	par
tu pars	par
il / elle part	par
nous partons	partON
vous partez	partay
ils / elles partent	part

pouvoir (to be able to)

je peux	juh puh
tu peux	tOO puh
il / elle peut	eel / el puh
nous pouvons	noo poovON
vous pouvez	voo poovay
ils / elles peuvent	eel / el puhv

savoir (to know)

je sais	say
tu sais	say
il / elle sait	say
nous savons	savON
vous savez	savay
ils / elles savent	sav

sortir (to go out)

je sors	sor
tu sors	sor
il / elle sort	sor
nous sortons	sortON
vous sortez	sortay
ils / elles sortent	sort

venir (to come)

je viens	juh v-yAN
tu viens	tOO v-yAN
il / elle vient	eel / el v-yAN
nous venons	noo vuhnON
vous venez	voo vuhnay
ils / elles viennent	eel / el v-yen

vouloir (to want)

je veux	juh vuh
tu veux	too vuh
il / elle veut	eel / el vuh
nous voulons	noo voolON
vous voulez	voo voolay
ils / elles veulent	eel / el vurl

See also **Past Tenses** for **avoir** (to have) and **être** (to be).

Past Tenses:
Perfect Tense

To put something into the perfect tense – to say that 'you have done' or 'did do' something – you use the present tense of the verb avoir plus the past participle of the verb:

avoir (to have)

j'ai	jay
tu as	too a
il / elle a	eel / el a
nous avons	noo zavON
vous avez	voo zavay
ils / elles ont	eel / el zON

A basic rule for forming the past participle is: for verbs ending in -er, change -er to -é (pronunciation the same: ay); for verbs ending in -ir, change -ir to -i; for verbs ending in -re, change -re to -u.

où est-ce que vous avez mangé hier soir?
oo eskuh voo zavay mONjay yair swahr
where did you eat last night?

nous avons visité la cathédrale cet après-midi
noo zavON veezeetay la kataydral set apray-meedee
we visited the cathedral this afternoon

vous avez fini de manger?	**je l'ai attendu toute la journée**
voo zavay feenee duh mONjay	juh lay atONdOO toot la joornay
have you finished eating?	I waited for him all day

For some verbs the perfect tense is formed using **être** instead of **avoir**.

être (literal sense: to be)

je suis	juh swee
tu es	tOO ay
il / elle est	eel / el ay
nous sommes	noo som
vous êtes	voo zet
ils / elles sont	eel / el sON

The most common and useful of these are:

aller	to go	**je suis allé**	juh swee alay
arriver	to arrive	**arrivé**	areevay
descendre	to go / come down	**descendu**	duhsONdOO
entrer	to go / come in	**entré**	ONtray
monter	to go / come up	**monté**	mONtay
naître	to be born	**né**	nay
partir	to leave / go away	**parti**	partee
passer	to pass	**passé**	passay
rentrer	to go / come back	**rentré**	rONtray
rester	to stay	**resté**	restay
retourner	to return	**retourné**	ruhtoornay
revenir	to come back	**revenu**	ruhvuhnOO
sortir	to go / come out	**sorti**	sortee
tomber	to fall	**tombé**	tONbay
venir	to come	**venu**	vuhnOO

il est parti	**nous sommes revenus samedi dernier**
eel ay partee	noo som ruhvuhnOO samdee dairn-yay
he has left	we came back last Saturday

elle est restée deux semaines
el ay restay duh suhmen
she stayed for two weeks

je suis rentré très tard hier soir
juh swee rONtray tray tar yair swahr
I got home very late last night

The following verbs have irregular past participles:

avoir	to have	eu	00
comprendre	to understand	compris	kONpree
connaître	to know (person, place)	connu	kon00
croire	to believe	cru	kr00
devoir	to have to	dû	d00
dire	to say	dit	dee
disparaître	to disappear	disparu	deespar00
être	to be	été	aytay
mourir*	to die	mort	mor
naître*	to be born	né	nay
offrir	to offer	offert	ofair
ouvrir	to open	ouvert	oovair
permettre	to allow	permis	pairmee
plaire	to please	plu	pl00
pouvoir	to be able to	pu	p00
prendre	to take	pris	pree
recevoir	to receive	reçu	ruhs00
s'asseoir*	to sit down	assis	assee
savoir	to know	su	s00
venir*	to come	venu	vuhn00
voir	to see	vu	v00
vouloir	to want	voulu	vool00

* conjugated with **être**

Imperfect Tense

This is used to describe an action in the past which was repeated, habitual, or often taking place over a period of time. To put something into the imperfect tense – to say that you 'were doing', 'used to do', or 'did do' something – change the verb endings as follows:

donner (to give)

I was giving, I used to give, I gave etc

je donnais	juh donay
tu donnais	too donay
il / elle donnait	eel / el donay
nous donnions	noo donee-ON
vous donniez	voo donee-ay
ils / elles donnaient	eel / el donay

finir (to finish)

I was finishing, I used to finish, I finished etc

je finissais	juh feeneessay
tu finissais	too feeneessay
il / elle finissait	eel / el feeneessay
nous finissions	noo feeneessee-ON
vous finissiez	voo feeneessee-ay
ils / elles finnissaient	eel / el feeneessay

attendre (to wait)

I was waiting, I used to wait, I waited etc

j'attendais	jatONday
tu attendais	too atONday
il / elle attendait	eel / el atONday
nous attendions	noo zatONdee-ON
vous attendiez	voo zatONdee-ay
ils / elles attendaient	eel / el zatONday

Three common verbs have irregular imperfect tenses:

être (to be)

j'étais	jaytay	I was
tu étais	too aytay	you were
il / elle était	eel / el aytay	he / she / it was
nous étions	noo zaytee-ON	we were
vous étiez	voo zaytee-ay	you were
ils / elles étaient	eel / el zaytay	they were

avoir (to have)

j'avais	javay	I had
tu avais	too avay	you had
il / elle avait	eel / el avay	he / she / it had
nous avions	noo zavee-ON	we had
vous aviez	voo zavee-ay	you had
ils / elles avaient	eel / el zavay	they had

faire (to do, to make)

je faisais	juh fuhzay	I did
tu faisais	too fuhzay	you did
il / elle faisait	eel / el fuhzay	he / she / it / did
nous faisions	noo fuhzee-ON	we did
vous faisiez	voo fuhzee-ay	you did
ils / elles faisaient	eel / el fuhzay	they did

Future Tense

To talk about what is going to happen in the future both French and English very often use the present tense (see **Present**), for example:

nous allons à la plage demain
noo zalON a la plahj duhmAN
we're going to the beach tomorrow

il rentre bientôt à Londres
eel rONtr b-yANto a lONdr
he's going back to London soon

French often uses the present tense where English uses the future:

j'arrive dans une minute
jareev dON zOOn meenOOt
I'll be there in a minute

The actual future tense in French, used to say 'I will, you will' etc, is formed by making the following changes:

donner (to give) - I etc will give

je donnerai	donuhray	**nous donnerons**	donuhrON
tu donneras	donuhra	**vous donnerez**	donuhray
il / elle donnera	donuhra	**ils / elles donneront**	donuhrON

finir (to finish) - I etc will finish

je finirai	feeneeray	**nous finirons**	feeneerON
tu finiras	feeneera	**vous finirez**	feeneeray
il / elle finira	feeneera	**ils / elles finiront**	feeneerON

attendre (to wait) - I etc will wait

j'attendrai	atONdray	**nous attendrons**	atONdrON
tu attendras	atONdra	**vous attendrez**	atONdray
il / elle attendra	atONdra	**ils / elles attendront**	atONdrON

Some common irregular verbs:

être (to be) - I etc will be

je serai	suhray	**nous serons**	suhrON
tu seras	suhra	**vous serez**	suhray
il / elle sera	suhra	**ils / elles seront**	suhrON

avoir (to have) - I etc will have

j'aurai	joray	**nous aurons**	orON
tu auras	ora	**vous aurez**	oray
il / elle aura	ora	**ils / elles auront**	orON

aller (to go) - I etc will go

j'irai	jeeray	nous irons	eerON
tu iras	eera	vous irez	eeray
il / elle ira	eera	ils / elles iront	eerON

venir (to come) - I etc will come

je viendrai	v-yANdray	nous viendrons	v-yANdrON
tu viendras	v-yANdra	vous viendrez	v-yANdray
il / elle viendra	v-yANdra	ils / elles viendront	v-yANdrON

Some examples:

mes enfants arriveront demain
may zONfON areevuhrON duhmAN
my children will be arriving tomorrow

j'espère qu'il fera beau demain
jespair keel fuhra bo duhmAN
I hope it'll be fine tomorrow

Negatives

To express a negative in French – to say 'I don't know', 'it's not here' etc – you use the words ne ... pas placed around the verb:

j'ai faim	**je n'ai pas faim**
jay fAN	juh nay pa fAN
I'm hungry	I'm not hungry

il aime la glace	**il n'aime pas la glace**
eel em la glass	eel nem pa la glass
he likes ice cream	he doesn't like ice cream

elle a une voiture	**elle n'a pas de voiture**
el a OOn vwatOOr	el na pa duh vwatOOr
she has a car	she doesn't have a car

If the verb is in the past tense (see Perfect Tense) the ne ... pas is used as follows:

je l'ai vu
juh lay v00
I saw him

je ne l'ai pas vu
juh nuh lay pa v00
I didn't see him

The following negatives work in the same way as ne ... pas:

ne ... jamais
nuh ... jamay
never

ne ... plus
nuh ... pl00
no more

ne ... rien
nuh ... ree-AN
nothing

je n'y suis jamais allé
juh nee swee jamay alay
I've never been there

il ne boit plus de bière
eel nuh bwa pl00 duh bee-air
he doesn't drink beer any more

nous n'avons rien acheté
noo navON ree-AN ashtay
we didn't buy anything

If there is no verb, just use pas:

pas toi!
pa twa
not you!

comment vas-tu? – pas mal
komON va-t00 – pa mal
how are you? – not bad

In spoken French, the **ne** is often left out:

c'est pas possible!
say pa posseebl
impossible!

To say 'no' with nouns (no sugar, no cigarettes) use **pas de**:

pas de vin pour moi, merci
pa duh vAN poor mwa mairsee
no wine for me thanks

il n'y a pas d'eau chaude
eel nya pa do shohd
there is no (isn't any) hot water

259

Imperative

To express commands in French, remove the endings **-er**, **-ir** or **-re** and then add the following endings.

	tu	vous
donner (to give)	**donne** don give	**donnez** donay
finir (to finish)	**finis** feenee finish	**finissez** feeneessay
attendre (to wait)	**attends** atON wait	**attendez** atONday

Some examples:

regardez! ruhgarday look!	**allez-vous-en!** alay-voo zON go away!
dites-moi! deet-mwa tell me!	**apporte-moi ça!** aport-mwa sa bring me that!

To tell someone not to do something, to give a negative command, put the words **ne ... pas** around the forms as given above, for example:

n'attends pas natON pa don't wait	**n'attendez pas** natONday pa
ne parlez pas si vite! nuh parlay pa see veet don't speak so quickly!	**ne me regarde pas comme ça!** nuh muh ruhgard pa kom sa don't look at me like that!

Some irregular forms:

ne sois / soyez pas en colère
nuh swa / swy-yay pa ON kolair
don't be angry

viens / venez avec moi!
v-yAN / vuhnay avek mwa
come with me!

On signs you might see the form:

ne pas toucher
nuh pa tooshay
do not touch

Questions

Often word order remains the same in a question, but the intonation changes – the voice should be raised at the end of the question.

vous parlez anglais?
voo parlay ONglay
do you speak English?

The word order can also be inverted to form a question. If the subject is a pronoun, subject and verb are inverted, and linked with a hyphen:

parlez-vous anglais?
parlay-voo ONglay
do you speak English?

If the subject is a noun, the verb is placed with the relevant pronoun after the subject, inserting **-t-** between verb and pronoun where the verb ends in a vowel:

le directeur parle-t-il anglais?
luh deerekturr parlteel ONglay
does the manager speak English?

Both the above types of question may be introduced by **est-ce que?** The word order then remains the same as that of a statement:

est-ce que vous parlez anglais?
eskuh voo parlay ONglay
do you speak English?

Dates

Use the numbers on pages 264-265 to express the date, except for the first, when **le premier** should be used:

le premier septembre
luh pruhm-yay septONbr
the first of September

le deux décembre
luh duh daysONbr
the second of December

le trois mars
luh trwa marss
the third of March

le vingt mai
luh vAN may
the twentieth of May

le vingt-et-un juin
luh vANtay-AN jwAN
the twenty-first of June

Days

Monday	lundi	[lANdee]
Tuesday	mardi	[mardee]
Wednesday	mercredi	[mairkruhdee]
Thursday	jeudi	[juhdee]
Friday	vendredi	[vONdruhdee]
Saturday	samedi	[samdee]
Sunday	dimanche	[deemONsh]

Months

January	janvier [joNvee-ay]
February	février [fayvree-ay]
March	mars [marss]
April	april [apreel]
May	mai [may]
June	juin [jwAN]
July	juillet [jwee-yay]
August	août [oo]
September	septembre [septoNbr]
October	octobre [oktobr]
November	novembre [novoNbr]
December	décembre [daysoNbr]

Time

a.m.		du matin	doo matAN
p.m.	(afternoon)	de l'après-midi	duh lapray-meedee
	(evening)	du soir	doo swahr

what time is it? quelle heure est-il? [kel urr eteel]
one o'clock une heure [oon urr]
two o'clock deux heures [duh zur]
it's one o'clock il est une heure [eel ay oon urr]
it's two o'clock il est deux heures [eel ay duh zurr]
it's ten o'clock il est dix heures [eel ay dee zurr]
five past one une heure cinq [oon urr sANk]
ten past two deux heures dix [duh zurr deess]
quarter past one une heure et quart [oon urr ay kar]
quarter past two deux heures et quart [duh zurr ay kar]
half past ten dix heures et demie [dee zurr ay duhmee]
twenty to ten dix heures moins vingt [dee zurr mwAN VAN]
quarter to two deux heures moins le quart [duh zurr mwAN luh kar]
at half past four à quatre heures et demie [a katr urr ay duhmee]

at eight o'clock à huit heures [a weet urr]

14.00 quatorze heures [katorz urr]

17.30 dix-sept heures trente [deesset urr trONt]

2 a.m. deux heures du matin [duh zurr dOO matAN]

2 p.m. deux heures de l'après-midi [duh zurr duh lapray-meedee]

6 a.m. six heures du matin [seez urr dOO matAN]

6 p.m. six heures du soir [seez urr dOO swahr]

noon midi [meedee]

midnight minuit [meenwee]

an hour une heure [OOn urr]

a minute une minute [OOn meenOOt]

two minutes deux minutes [duh meenOOt]

a second une seconde [OOn suhgONd]

a quarter of an hour un quart d'heure [AN kar durr]

half an hour une demi-heure [OOn duhmee urr]

three quarters of an hour trois quarts d'heure [trwa kar durr]

Numbers

0	zéro	[zayro]
1	un	[AN]
2	deux	[duh]
3	trois	[trwa]
4	quatre	[katr]
5	cinq	[SANk]
6	six	[seess]
7	sept	[set]
8	huit	[weet]
9	neuf	[nuhf]
10	dix	[deess]
11	onze	[ONz]
12	douze	[dooz]
13	treize	[trez]
14	quartorze	[katorz]

15	quinze [kANz]
16	seize [sez]
17	dix-sept [deesset]
18	dix-huit [deez-weet]
19	dix-neuf [deez-nuhf]
20	vingt [vAN]
21	vingt-et-un [vANtay-AN]
22	vingt-deux [vAN-duh]
23	vingt-trois [vAN-trwa]
30	trente [trONt]
31	trente-et-un [trONtay-an]
40	quarante [karONt]
50	cinquante [sANkONt]
60	soixante [swassONt]
70	soixante-dix [swassONt-deess]
80	quatre-vingts [katr-vAN]
90	quatre-vingt-dix [katr-vAN-deess]
100	cent [sON]
110	cent dix [sON deess]
200	deux cents [duh sON]
1,000	mille [meel]
2,000	deux mille [duh meel]
5,000	cinq mille [sANk meel]
1,000,000	un million [AN meel-yON]

In French, millions are written with spaces instead of commas, e.g. 1 500 000. Thousands are written without spaces or commas, e.g. 2700. Decimals are written with a comma, e.g. 3.5 would be 3,5 in French.

Ordinals

1st	premier	[pruhm-yay]
2nd	deuxième	[duhz-yem]
3rd	troisième	[trwaz-yem]
4th	quatrième	[katree-yem]
5th	cinquième	[sANk-yem]
6th	sixième	[seez-yem]
7th	septième	[set-yem]
8th	huitième	[weet-yem]
9th	neuvième	[nuhv-yem]
10th	dixième	[deez-yem]

Conversion Tables

1 centimetre = 0.39 inches   1 inch = 2.54 cm

1 metre = 39.37 inches = 1.09 yards   1 foot = 30.48 cm

1 kilometre = 0.62 miles = 5/8 mile   1 yard = 0.91 m

1 mile = 1.61 km

km	1	2	3	4	5	10	20	30	40	50	100
miles	0.6	1.2	1.9	2.5	3.1	6.2	12.4	18.6	24.8	31.0	62.1

miles	1	2	3	4	5	10	20	30	40	50	100
km	1.6	3.2	4.8	6.4	8.0	16.1	32.2	48.3	64.4	80.5	161

1 gram = 0.035 ounces   1 kilo = 1000 g = 2.2 pounds

g	100	250	500
oz	3.5	8.75	17.5

1 oz = 28.35 g

1 lb = 0.45 kg

kg	0.5	1	2	3	4	5	6	7	8	9	10
lb	1.1	2.2	4.4	6.6	8.8	11.0	13.2	15.4	17.6	19.8	22.0

kg	20	30	40	50	60	70	80	90	100
lb	44	66	88	110	132	154	176	198	220

lb	0.5	1	2	3	4	5	6	7	8	9	10	20
kg	0.2	0.5	0.9	1.4	1.8	2.3	2.7	3.2	3.6	4.1	4.5	9.0

1 litre = 1.75 UK pints / 2.13 US pints

1 UK pint = 0.57 l   1 UK gallon = 4.55 l
1 US pint = 0.47 l   1 US gallon = 3.79 l

centigrade / Celsius   °C = (°F - 32) x 5/9

°C	-5	0	5	10	15	18	20	25	30	36.8	38
°F	23	32	41	50	59	64	68	77	86	98.4	100.4

Fahrenheit   °F = (°C x 9/5) + 32

°F	23	32	40	50	60	65	70	80	85	98.4	101
°C	-5	0	4	10	16	18	21	27	29	36.8	38.3